HANNIBAL

Hannibal's Expedition into Italy
(INCLUDING HIS PROBABLE ROUTE FROM THE RHÔNE TO THE ALPS)

COL DE LA TRAVERSETTE
Chateauqueyras
RHÔNE → Embrun
La Batie Montsaleon
COL DE GRIMONE
Valence
Loriol
Donzère
St.Paul
Trois-
Chateaux
"THE ISLAND
Avignon
Maillane
Aigues-
Mortes
Arles
Oulx
Turin
PC
Gap
Saluzzo
COL DE
L'ARCHE
Nice
Antibes
VOCONTII
GA
DRUENTIA
CAVARI
Narbo Martius
Massilia
Illiberis
Emporion
PYRENEES
ILLERGETES
ILERGETES
Iberus
Ilerda
LACETANIA
Barcelona
Tarraco
CELTIBERI
Etovissa
Saguntum
Valencia
SUCRO
BALEARES
HISPANIA
Corrus
Neapolis
MARE INTERNUM
Cartagena
Narragara
A F R I

LEONARD COTTRELL

HANNIBAL ENEMY OF ROME

DA CAPO PRESS • NEW YORK

To Captain B. H. LIDDELL HART
in appreciation of his
kindness to an unmilitary historian

Library of Congress Cataloging in Publication Data

Cottrell, Leonard.
  [Enemy of Rome]
  Hannibal: enemy of Rome / Leonard Cottrell. — 1st Da Capo Press
ed.
    p.   cm.
  Originally published: Enemy of Rome. London: Evans Bros., 1960.
  Includes index.
  ISBN 0-306-80498-0
  1. Hannibal, 247-182 B.C. 2. Punic wars. 3. Generals — Tunisia —
Carthage (Ancient) — Biography. I. Title.
DG249.C63   1992
937′.04′092 — dc20   92-14948
[B]   CIP

First Da Capo Press edition 1992

This Da Capo Press paperback edition of *Hannibal* is an unabridged republication
of the edition published in New York in 1961. It is reprinted by arrangement
with Henry Holt and Company, and with Joyce Martin.

Published by Da Capo Press, Inc.
A Subsidiary of Plenum Publishing Corporation
233 Spring Street, New York, N.Y. 10013

INTRODUCTION

"Of making many books there is no end," wrote Ecclesiastes, *"and much study is a weariness of the flesh."* Books on Hannibal run into hundreds, from Polybius, who talked to men who knew him, to authors writing more than two thousand years after he was born. Doubtless in another thousand years men will be still attracted to his personality and achievements; attracted, or repelled, according to their temperaments. Most writers on Hannibal have idolized their hero, and there is admittedly much to admire. The man who challenged the growing might of Rome, who led a great army across the Alps, who for sixteen long years harried the enemy on his own territory, winning battle after battle, and holding together, by military genius and force of personality, an army composed of many disparate elements, has every right to heroic status. Yet the genius—like Hitler's—may have been an evil one.

When one analyzes these numerous books, one finds that many were written by scholars who never experienced the realities of war or attempted to explore the ground over which their hero marched and fought. There are notable exceptions, of course, from Polybius, Hannibal's first biographer, who was himself a cavalry general and served in the household of the Scipios, to soldiers and military historians such as Clausewitz, von Schlieffen, and Wavell.

vii

The present writer is neither a soldier nor a professional historian, but one whose interest in Hannibal goes back to his schooldays, and who recently realized a lifetime's ambition—to travel in the footsteps of the general from Cartagena to Rome. There was nothing spectacular in this journey—no elephants took part, and it was not "covered" by newspapermen and film cameras. It was in fact a personal Odyssey, undertaken mainly for pleasure.

I hope something of this pleasure will be shared by the reader, for the journey took me through parts of Europe which are not only scenically magnificent but of which "the stones cry out" the history of our race. If any reader can stand, say, in the Pass of Ronçevalles and not think of Charlemagne, or at Thermopylae without recalling Leonidas, this book is not for him. But for those for whom a landscape, however beautiful, is lifeless without its ghosts, there may be some pleasure, and perhaps a little profit, in endeavoring to follow the problematical path of the great Carthaginian along the southern coast of Spain, across the reedy Camargue, up the Rhône Valley and eastwards through the Alpes du Dauphiné to the Po Valley and the rich heartland of Italy.

I say "problematical" because one must admit that, though the major part of Hannibal's route can be followed with some accuracy, his path across the Alps is still subject to much speculation, and pending archaeological confirmation, must remain so. The route I followed was that suggested by Sir Gavin de Beer in his absorbing little book, *Alps and Elephants*. For reasons which I shall try to explain in the following pages, I believe, with Sir Gavin, that Hannibal used this route; but we may both be wrong. To me this was unimportant: it was impossible, in six short weeks, to cover the entire route *and* explore every pass which Hannibal may have taken. Even if I could have done this my opinions would still be as speculative as the rest, for the fact is that no one will know which route Hannibal used to cross the Alps until firm archaeological evidence—discarded weapons and equipment, perhaps, or human and animal remains—is found in one of the high passes.

My main purpose was enjoyment, first by attempting to re-

create one of the greatest dramas in the early history of Europe in
the actual theater where it was enacted. There were ancillary
pleasures, too: in landscape, wine, food, and people. Hannibal's
achievement, as described in the pages of Polybius, can be stimu-
lating or dull, depending on the degree of imagination brought
to it; but there is a world of difference between reading those
pages in an armchair and reading them among the hills and valleys, rivers, mountains, and plains which Hannibal and Polybius
saw.

In a small village beside the River Drôme I came upon a café
with a sun awning bearing the words, "Le Relais d'Annibal."
When I asked why it was called "Hannibal's Inn," Madame la
Patronne looked at me with the indulgent smile of one addressing
a child. Setting down my Pernod and waving her hand towards
the mountains she exclaimed, *"Voilà la route, monsieur, la route
d'Annibal."*

Under such conditions, and among such people, history ceases
to be a record of the dead past, and becomes an extension and en-
richment of the present.

For those who are interested, the journey which my wife and
I undertook in the track of Hannibal was accomplished in a
1½-ton Austin bus converted into a trailer, and called "Vairee
Luvlee." The name was given to her by an enthusiastic French
peasant whom we met in the valley of the Loire; and it stuck.
"Vairee Luvlee" carried us some four thousand miles in six weeks,
a journey which involved two crossings of the Pyrenees, the Alps
and the Apennines. Our purpose in using this form of transport
was (*a*) to save cost; (*b*) to enable us to camp where we liked,
independently of hotels and (*c*) because it would take us over
roads and tracks which might balk a car. This proved a great
advantage in the Alpes du Dauphiné, when severe flooding had
washed away the roads, and for many miles we were lurching
and bumping over river boulders.

Though arduous at times, the trip was not an exercise of
endurance. I drove and kept notes; my wife cooked and kept
house. Most of the journey could, in fact, have been accomplished
by car, but traveling in this fashion, starting and stopping where

we pleased, walking with the dawn, cooking by the roadside, and sometimes venturing along unfrequented routes, seemed to bring us nearer, in spirit, to the long-dead armies whose route we endeavored to follow. I can certainly recommend this method of transport to any readers who may be inspired to make similar quests.

LEONARD COTTRELL

High House,
Stainton,
nr. Kendal,
Westmorland.

ACKNOWLEDGMENTS

THE author and publishers are indebted to the Loeb Classical Library and Harvard University Press for permission to quote from *The Histories of Polybius*, translated by W. R. Paton; to E. P. Dutton & Co., Inc., for quotations from *Alps and Elephants*, by Sir Gavin de Beer; to Oxford University Press for quotations from *The Odyssey of Homer*, translated by T. E. Lawrence; to Captain B. H. Liddell Hart for quotations from *A Greater Than Napoleon—Scipio Africanus;* and to G. Bell & Sons, Ltd., for passages from Livy, *The History of Rome*, Bohn's Library.

CONTENTS

HANNIBAL

1

INSPIRATION

The consul had encamped in the evening on the side of the lake just within the present Roman frontier, and on the Tuscan side of Passignano; he had made a forced march, and had arrived at his position so late that he could not examine the ground before him. Early next morning he set forward again; the morning mist hung thickly over the lake and the low ground, leaving the heights, as is often the case, quite clear. Flaminius, anxious to overtake his enemy, rejoiced in the friendly veil which thus concealed his advance, and hoping to fall upon Hannibal's army while it was still in marching order and its columns encumbered with the plunder of the valley of the Arno. He passed through the defile of Passignano and found no enemy; this confirmed him in his belief that Hannibal did not mean to fight. Already Hannibal's Numidian cavalry were on the edge of the basin of the Tiber; unless he could overtake them speedily they would have reached the plain, and Africans, Spaniards and Gauls would be rioting in the devastation of the garden of Italy.

I N an R.A.F. hospital near Naples, in 1944, it is almost time for Lights Out. The night nurse, making her inspection, consults her watch. Through the open windows, which face north, distant flashes of gunfire suddenly silhouette the hills. Kesselring's army is retreating towards the Gustav Line, pressed hard by the advancing Allies, but not one of the figures under the mosquito nets looks up. Some are reading, some with hands clasped behind their heads, lie just thinking. A few are asleep.

Among the readers one man has a very old book propped on his pillow. It is *The Second Punic War* by Dr. Thomas Arnold—the great Arnold of Rugby. I was that man, and I was reading his description of the Battle of Lake Trasimene. Hannibal, having crossed the Alps and defeated the Romans in the Po Valley, has marched south, crossed the Arno and is now moving irresistibly towards Rome. Flaminius, the Consul, commands the Roman army which is in pursuit of Hannibal. Near the shores of Lake Trasimene the Carthaginian army has successfully passed through the narrow defile of Passignano, between the cliffs and the water, and their rear guard has already been seen crossing the lip of the hills beyond. Flaminius, eager to catch Hannibal in column of route and encouraged by the sight of the enemy's rear guard, presses on confidently through the wall of mist which prevents his seeing on either side. Then, writes Arnold:

> At this moment the stillness of the mist was broken by barbarian war-cries on every side, and both flanks of the Roman column were assailed at once. Their right was overwhelmed by a storm of javelins and arrows shot as if from the midst of darkness and striking into the soldier's unguarded side where he had no shield to cover him; while ponderous stones, against which no shield or helmet could avail, came crashing down upon their heads. On the left were heard the trampling of horse, and the well-known war-cries of the Gauls; and presently Hannibal's cavalry emerged from the mist, and were in an instant in the midst of their ranks; and the huge forms of the Gauls and their vast broadswords broke in upon them at the same time. . . . [1]

[1] All quotations attributed to Arnold in this book are from Arnold, T., *The Second Punic War*, Macmillan, London, 1886.

Meanwhile the advanced Roman force, which had climbed the valley ahead of their companions, came to the top of the ridge

> . . . and to their astonishment no enemy was there; but the mist drew up, and as they looked behind they saw too plainly where Hannibal was; the whole valley was a scene of carnage, while on the sides of the hills above were the masses of the Spanish and African foot witnessing the destruction of the Roman army which had scarcely cost them a single stroke.

"Lights out!" came the cry, and the ward was in darkness. Laying the heavy volume on my locker I settled back, listening to the far-off thudding of the guns and, then and there, resolved that one day I would visit not only Lake Trasimene but the sites of other Hannibalic battlefields. For reasons which are not important, I was not able to realize this ambition while serving as a war correspondent in Italy. The opportunity did not come until fifteen years later, when my youthful interest in warfare had mellowed into the pacific skepticism of middle age. But the character and achievements of the young Carthaginian retained their hold, though I could appreciate that cynical jibe of Juvenal: "Forward, you madman, and hurry across those horrid Alps, so that you may become the delight of schoolboys."

During those fifteen years I had the opportunity to visit the site of Carthage itself, and to spend some time in the Lebanon, home of Hannibal's ancestors, the Phoenicians. I also read, sporadically, a great deal about him. When the opportunity came to make the journey, I knew—or thought I knew—rather more than when I read Arnold's account of the Battle of Lake Trasimene within earshot of another great combat.

Yet, when all those books on Hannibal are sifted and analyzed, what remains of hard fact? There are only two main sources of information, and of these one is slightly suspect. There is Polybius, generally regarded as the most reliable; and there is Livy, born over 150 years after the events he describes. He had, as Sir Gavin de Beer aptly says, "a fly-paper mind but without much critical faculty. He collected and strung together whatever he could find in the works of his predecessors to illustrate the glorious pageant of the Eternal City."

Both Polybius and Livy had access to earlier sources, including books written by Greek "war correspondents" who marched with Hannibal. One of these, Sosilos, taught him Greek and wrote his biography. Another, Silenos, likewise accompanied the Carthaginian army. There was also a Roman, Lucius Cincius Alimentus, who fought against Hannibal, was captured in the fighting, and learned from the Carthaginian himself how many men were lost in the crossing of the Alps. No doubt there were other sources too, but all, including those just mentioned, have since been lost. We know about them only because later historians, such as Polybius, Livy, Coelius, Cicero and others quoted from them. Another writer who described the march, though he was born long after Hannibal, was Timagenes of Alexandria, a skillful historian. His work has also perished, though a much later writer, Ammianus Marcellinus, quotes a fragment of his book. There are other useful scraps of information preserved in later works such as those of Cornelius Nepos (first century A.D.) who, with his windy rhetoric and passion for overcondensation, tells us little we do not already know from Polybius and Livy.

What was the inspiration for Hannibal's great march on Italy? The answer, surely, is hate; and if we are to comprehend the diamond-hard determination, the fanatical, dedicated will which drove him to sacrifice the lives of some 30,000 men—half his total force—in that terrible crossing of the Alps, it is necessary to understand the reasons for that hate.

The first fact to bear in mind is that, at the time of Hannibal's birth, Rome was not the great power that she subsequently became. To the Carthaginians, Hannibal's people, she was an upstart nation which had begun to challenge the authority they had wielded in the western Mediterranean for hundreds of years. Carthage, which stood near modern Tunis in North Africa, was a colony founded by the Phoenicians —a Semitic race who formerly inhabited the coast of the eastern Mediterranean, between the mountains of the Lebanon and the sea. Their most famous ports, Tyre and Sidon, are mentioned in the Bible. Another port, Byblos, gave its name to the Bible itself, since it was the principal mart from which Egyptian papyrus was exported. The earliest books were made from papyrus, hence the name of the port, Byblos or *Biblos*, became the Greek name for book.

From about 1200 B.C. onwards these industrious people, merchants and traders, dominated the maritime traffic of the eastern Mediterranean. Their numerous ships traded between the Lebanon, Asia Minor, Greece, Italy, Africa, Spain and the Mediterranean islands. The prophet Ezekiel writes of them in the Old Testament:

> O thou that are situate at the entry of the sea, which art a merchant of the people for many isles. Thus saith the Lord God; O Tyrus (Tyre) thou hast said, I am of perfect beauty.
> Thy borders are in the midst of the seas, thy builders have perfected thy beauty. . . .
> Of the oaks of Bashan have they made thine oars; the company of the Ashurites have made thy benches of ivory, brought out of the isles of Chittim. . . .
> The inhabitants of Zidon and Arvad were thy mariners: thy wise men, O Tyrus, that were in thee, were thy pilots.
> The ancients of Gebal [Byblos] and the wise men thereof were in thee thy calkers; all the ships of the sea with their mariners were in thee to occupy thy merchandise.

The Phoenicians were hardheaded merchants but not warriors. One can still see their faces carved on a row of coffins in the museum at Beirut; faces of men who knew money, markets, interest rates, when to buy and sell. There is nothing noble or heroic in any of them: yet Hannibal was one of their descendants. They were great colonists, particularly after the Assyrians attacked their country in the ninth century B.C., and eventually subdued it. Phoenicia itself, a narrow coastal strip between the two great empires of Assyria and Egypt, was always vulnerable to attack, and it was natural that the more adventurous and independent of the Phoenicians decided to settle in what had formerly been their trading posts along the shores of the Mediterranean. There were many of these —in Cyprus, Sicily, Sardinia, Spain, Malta, and along the coast of North Africa. But the colonists soon came into conflict with another maritime power, Greece, whose mariners and merchants were also founding trading colonies. Under this pressure the formerly peaceful traders became doughty fighters, able and willing to challenge the Greeks in naval warfare.

For four centuries there was a bitter struggle for control of the coasts and islands of the west Mediterranean, and battle after battle was fought in the seas around Sicily, between the Phoenicians, who wanted to preserve their monopoly of trade in these regions, and the Greeks, who were equally determined to secure their share. It was one of the bitterest of trade wars in which the descendants of the Phoenicians more than held their own, under the leadership of their most powerful colony, Carthage. In fact, by 500 B.C.—more than three hundred years before Hannibal—Carthage, with its splendid harbor near modern Tunis, had emerged as a major power. Its navigators were not only supreme in the west Mediterranean but had even begun to penetrate into the Atlantic and explore the coasts of West Africa.

Just when an uneasy balance had been established between Greek and Carthaginian power, a new threat arose in the north. Rome. The very name, nowadays, spells empire and dominion, but not to the Carthaginians of the fifth and fourth centuries B.C. To them, Rome was a Latin State which, beginning as a small community of farmers beside the Tiber, had

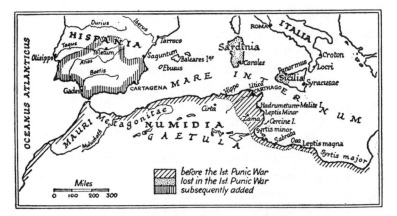

CARTHAGINIAN DOMINIONS

increased its power by warfare and territorial annexation until it controlled the whole of southern Italy. Rome had also, by a system of alliances, secured the allegiance of a number of independent states in the northern part of the peninsula. Then she had begun to infiltrate into Sicily, across the straits of Messina.

At first the Carthaginian government tried to come to terms with the newcomers. A treaty was signed with Rome in 508 B.C., and again in 348 B.C., under which Carthaginian commercial interests in Sicily were recognized, but relations were complicated by the presence of Greek colonies in southern Italy, some of whom sought Roman help against the Carthaginians. And Sicily, so much nearer to Italy than Africa, was a continuing source of friction. Eventually tension broke into open war.

For twenty-four years the Romans fought the Carthaginians among the capes and bays, mountains and valleys of Sicily, winning victories at Mylae and Cape Econmus but suffering defeat when, in 255 B.C., their general, Regulus, landed in North Africa. The Carthaginian military leaders were handi-

capped by an "appeasing" home government, which procras-
tinated, delayed making decisions, and hindered the active
prosecution of the war. Bitterness arose between the civilian
and military leaders, of whom the greatest was Hamilcar Barca.

Hamilcar took command in Sicily in 247 B.C., and in that
same year his wife bore him a son who was named Hannibal.
For a time Hamilcar, a brilliant and brave general, was successful in land operations against the Romans who also suffered
defeat at sea. By this time the Romans had learned that against
the Carthaginians the naval arm would be decisive. Regaining
superiority they defeated their enemies in a great naval battle
at Aegates Insulae. One by one the Carthaginian garrisons in
Sicily were reduced—Agrigentum, Drepanum, Panormus, Lilybaeum, and others. For a long time Hamilcar made a stubborn and heroic stand from his stronghold at Eryx, but at last
this too fell to the triumphant enemy. The Carthaginian government sued for peace, which was granted in return for the
virtual surrender of Sicily.

Shortly afterwards some of the Carthaginian mercenaries
mutinied. Rome made this a pretext for renewing hostilities
and annexing the neighboring islands of Sardinia and Corsica.
Thus Carthage was excluded from all waters west of Italy,
and Sicily and Sardinia were organized as Roman provinces.
The First Punic War was over, leaving a sour legacy of hate
among the military leaders of Carthage, and especially in the
heart of Hamilcar Barca.

Sicily had been taken; Corsica and Sardinia were lost; but
there remained Spain, where Carthage had established a powerful colony; and Spain was on the European mainland, providing a base from which land armies might—though with
difficulty— invade Italy. After the abortive Roman attempt to
invade Africa, Hamilcar was charged with the task of transporting troops and equipment to Spain. His son Hannibal was
then about nine years of age. In the words of Livy:

Hannibal . . . while he boyishly coaxed his father that he might
be taken to Spain . . . was conducted to an altar; and, having
laid his hand on the offerings, was bound by an oath to prove
himself, as soon as he could, an enemy of the Roman people.
The loss of Sicily and Sardinia grieved the high spirit of Hamilcar; for he deemed that Sicily had been given up through a
premature despair of their affairs; and that Sardinia, during the
disturbances in Africa, had been treacherously taken by the
Romans, while, in addition, the payment of a tribute had been
imposed.[2]

Marxist historians attribute all great historic events to eco-
nomic causes. They might, with justice, cite the trade rivalry
between Rome and Carthage as an illustration of this thesis,
yet human emotions remain the dominant factor. Was the boy
Hannibal thinking of a trade war as he laid his trembling
hand on the altar of Baal, and, with all the anger and pity of
a hero-worshiping child, watched the grief of his beloved
father? Obviously not; and if the child had been an ordinary
boy his rage would have spent itself in futile tears, and history
would have taken a different course. But there lay dormant
in that child's mind qualities of which neither he nor the world
were yet aware: a terrible capacity for sustained hate, an irresistible will, ability to inspire unquestioning loyalty of men,
and military genius. The ultimate result of that oath-taking
was the death of hundreds of thousands, the sacking of many
cities, and the destruction of an empire.

[2] All quoted material attributed to Livy in this book is from Titus Livius,
The History of Rome, translated by Spillan and Edmunds, G. Bell and
Sons Ltd., London, 1919.

2

PREPARATION

THERE is little doubt, says Livy, that had Hamilcar lived long enough, he would have invaded Italy. "Through the nine years employed in augmenting the Carthaginian empire in Spain . . . it was obvious that he was revolving in his mind a greater war than he was then engaged in. . . . The timely death of Hamilcar and the youth of Hannibal occasioned the delay." But during those nine years, as Hannibal grew to manhood, his father must often have discussed with him his plans and how they might be implemented. Meanwhile, on Hamilcar's death in 228 B.C., his son-in-law Hasdrubal took over command in Spain.

Hasdrubal must have been a man of great charm and diplomatic skill. He was first endeared to Hamilcar, Livy tells us, "by reason of his youthful beauty, and then adopted by him, when advanced in age, as his son-in-law, on account of his eminent abilities." Regrettably, classical historians have left us little through which we can form a picture of these Carthaginian nobles and their families. Even the character of Hannibal himself, though described by both Polybius and Livy, is embellished with few of the human details which a modern biographer would think necessary. We know nothing of Hamilcar's wife, Hannibal's mother, and Hamilcar himself remains a powerful but shadowy figure. As for Hannibal's brother, also named Hasdrubal; Maharbal, the great cavalry leader and tactician; Gisgo, another general; and Synhus, the army surgeon—we know them only through their deeds, so that when the time comes for them to play their parts in the great drama, it is always Hannibal who holds the stage.

Imagination, disciplined by known facts, must here come into play. It is fair to assume that these aristocrats would have shared the same background and education as those which Hannibal enjoyed. Their religion was that of their Phoenician ancestors. Their principal deity was Baal, the Semitic sun-god, but their culture was deeply penetrated by that of the Greeks with whom they had been in contact for centuries. Hannibal had a Greek tutor, who taught him the language. He knew his Homer, and Greek poetry and philosophy would have been familiar to him. Besides Greek and his mother tongue, he had command of several languages. He and his brother officers were, in fact, highly civilized men.

During the period of Hasdrubal's command in Spain, Hamilcar's gifted son-in-law made a series of useful alliances. Says Livy:

> Prosecuting his designs rather by stratagem than force, by entertaining the princes, and by means of the friendship of their leaders, gaining the favour of unknown nations, he aggrandized the Carthaginian power, more than by arms and battles.

Hasdrubal's diplomatic skill was successful in obtaining an agreement with Rome. The Romans, watchful of Carthaginian penetration into Spain, were also trying to establish a "sphere of influence" within the northern part of the peninsula. They were in alliance with the flourishing Greek colony of Massilia

—modern Marseilles—and were concerned lest their ally should be threatened by Carthaginian expansion northward. Massilia was in close relations with the city of Saguntum (modern Sagunto) on the northern coast of Spain, and Rome also took this town under her protection. Under the terms of the treaty which they made with Hasdrubal it was agreed that the southern limit of Roman penetration should be the river Ebro. The territory south of that river was recognized as coming under Carthaginian control, *with the exception of Saguntum.*

Meanwhile, under Hasdrubal's leadership, more and more of the Celtic and Iberian tribes were brought under Carthaginian control. There were battles and sieges in which the young Hannibal, now grown to manhood, distinguished himself both by his personal courage and his tactical skill. In the ancient world men matured and took great responsibility earlier in life than they do today. Hannibal, who had served under his father in his boyhood and subsequently under his brother-in-law, Hasdrubal, was an experienced commander by the time he reached his middle twenties. Livy describes him:

> The veteran soldiers imagined that Hamilcar, in his youth, was restored to them; they remarked the same vigour in his looks and animation in his eye, the same features and expression of countenance; and then, in a short time, he took care that his father should be of the least powerful consideration in conciliating their esteem. There never was a genius more fitted for the two most opposite duties of obeying and commanding, so that you could not easily decide whether he was dearer to the general or the army; and neither did Hasdrubal prefer giving the command to any other, when anything was to be done with courage and activity; nor did the soldiers feel more confidence and boldness under any other leader.

His popularity with the troops was such that, on Hasdrubal's early death, they unanimously chose Hannibal as their commander. The Carthaginian government, hastily summoning an assembly, ratified the soldiers' choice. So, at the age of twenty-nine, the young commander, seasoned in war and possessing the unbounded loyalty of the army, prepared to fulfill the oath which he had sworn at his father's side.

No portrait, no sculptured head, not even a coin, has preserved his appearance. From his known character, in which charm, authority, and high intelligence were blended, he must have had a memorable face. He would be dark, and probably not tall, but agile and well-built. His physical powers were formidable. "His body could not be exhausted, nor his mind subdued, by any toil. He could alike endure either heat or cold. The quantity of his food and drink were determined by the wants of nature, and not by pleasure." And like Napoleon, he could sleep whenever he wished.

> The time that remained after the transaction of business was given to repose; but that repose was neither invited by a soft bed nor by quiet. Many have seen him wrapped in a military cloak, lying on the ground amid the watches and outposts of his soldiers. His dress was not at all superior to that of his equals; his arms and his horses were conspicuous. He was at once by far the first of the cavalry and infantry; and, foremost to advance to the charge, was last to leave the engagement.

His relations with women have been much disputed. One Roman writer, Justin, remarks that his chivalrous behavior towards his female captives was such that one would not think that he was born in Africa." On the other hand, it is recorded by Appianus, on whose authority we know not, that while wintering in Lucania he "abandoned himself to unaccustomed luxury and the delights of love." Even if this is true it is hardly surprising in a soldier who spent seventeen years campaigning away from home. Probably he was as abstemious sexually as he was in other sensual delights, but relaxed on occasion. He was married to a lady named Imilce, who came from Castulo which was founded by one of her ancestors, a native of Delphi. She was probably of Greek descent. They were married round about 220 B.C., two years before Hannibal invaded Italy, and had a son. There is a tradition, related in a poem by Silius Italicus, that she pleaded with him to allow her to accompany him across the Alps, but that he refused. Whether she survived to greet him again after his long absence is not known. They must have corresponded, however, and if only one of those letters had remained it would probably have told us more about Hannibal's character than anything which Livy and Polybius have recorded.

On the negative side, classical authors speak of his "cruelty" and "more than Punic perfidy." The difficulty here is that the authors who have left us the only surviving accounts of Hannibal's life were concerned to glorify his enemies, the Romans. His cruelty, even if the accounts of it are true, did not exceed that of our own age. Moreover, there are no instances of cruelty for its own sake; the purpose behind them was always political or military: to impose discipline or to break the spirit of an enemy. "Saturation bombing" of cities in the last war provides a useful parallel. As for his "Punic perfidy," Hannibal had more than his share of the cunning which the Romans always attributed to their Phoenician enemies. This was naturally a sore point with them, since Hannibal never did what was expected of him, and the tricks and subterfuges he used cost them battle after battle.

Nevertheless, when all these allowances are made, there remains an element of iron ruthlessness in some of Hannibal's actions which suggests, to this writer at least, that he had little compassion for his fellow men, though he knew how to manage them—and make them love him. I do not include in these actions his sack of Saguntum which he attacked in open contempt of the treaty which Carthage had signed with Rome. Hannibal having decided on war, the treaty was bound to be violated. He could not begin his march with an ally of the enemy on his flank; moreover, Saguntum was a rich and fertile colony whose spoils would help to provision and equip his army. And he may well have had another, more subtle reason for openly attacking an ally of Rome in Spain. He probably hoped by so doing to delude the Romans into thinking that he intended to wage war in Spain itself. This, as we shall see, is exactly what the Romans did think—to their cost.

The siege of Saguntum took eight months. There is a story that when the city finally fell, after heroic resistance, many of the inhabitants made a funeral pyre of their possessions, and then flung themselves upon it, preferring to perish in the flames rather than surrender to the enemy. Hannibal divided some of the spoil among his troops and sent much to Carthage, which disposed the government favorably towards him.. This was important to him, because the old hostility between the military and civil powers, which had so hampered his father, still remained. Now, however, when the indignant Romans sent an embassy to Carthage demanding the surrender of Hannibal, the *Suffete* (senate) plucked up sufficient courage to refuse. One of the Roman ambassadors, with a taste for histrionics, pointed to the bosom of his toga and, according to Polybius said:

"I have here both peace and war. I will let fall from it which ever of the two you choose."

The Carthaginian Suffete bade him let fall whichever the Romans chose, and when the envoy said he would let fall war, many of the Senators cried out at once, "We accept it!" The ambassadors and the Senate parted on these terms.[1]

Thus Hannibal was able to begin his war not only with the enthusiastic support of his troops, but with the backing of the civil power. The more one scrutinizes his actions the more clear it becomes that every step he took was carefully thought out in advance. Courage and military skill, which he

[1] All quoted material attributed to Polybius in this book is from Polybius, *The Histories*, translated by W. R. Paton, William Heinemann, London, 1922.

possessed in abundance, would have made him a good company officer or even a divisional commander. But it was his political forethought, his capacity for over-all planning and preparation—plus the ability to change his plans quickly when need arose—that made him one of the greatest generals of all time.

These powers are evident in the steps he took on hearing that the Suffete had accepted war with Rome. When the news arrived he was wintering at New Carthage, a city which Hasdrubal had created on the site of modern Cartagena. First he dismissed to their cities the Iberians who had fought against him, believing that this clemency would make them more ready to help in the future. Next he had to secure the communications between Spain and Africa, and see that both were adequately protected. He used the method which the Romans were later to adopt in garrisoning their Empire —that of sending recruits from newly conquered territory to garrison provinces far from their homes. Thus he sent Iberian and Celtiberian troops from Spain—13,850 foot soldiers, 1,200 cavalry, and 870 slingers from the Balearics—to Africa, stationing some at Megatonia in Libya and some in Carthage. From Africa he brought troops to Spain and put them under the command of his brother—another Hasdrubal—together with a navy to secure communications with the home base. There were "fifty quinqueremes" (ships with five banks of oars) "two tetraremes" (four banks) "five triremes" (three banks) and others. But many of the African troops, including the crack Numidian cavalry, were intended to accompany Hannibal into Italy.

The two brothers made their plans. "Hannibal," writes Polybius "instructed Hasdrubal how to manage the government of Spain and prepare to resist the Romans if he himself happened to be absent." Their strategy was based on the fact that Rome had virtual command of the sea. The Carthaginians had only the small naval force with which they hoped to keep open their communications with Africa, and protect their Spanish possessions. Well aware of this, the Romans would never suspect that Hannibal planned to carry war into their homeland. He could not come by sea, and to reach Italy by land would involve a journey of fifteen hundred miles through strange and often hostile territory, besides crossing the Pyrenees and the Alps, the greatest mountain barrier in Europe. It was an obvious impossibility. So the Romans prepared to fight the war in Spain, and began fitting out a fleet for the purpose. Meanwhile, Hasdrubal prepared to meet them while his brother made ready to attempt the impossible.

3

ARMS AND THE MEN

B EFORE we attempt to follow Hannibal's journey, it is
worth while considering the military resources available
to him, and the geographical and political situation of
the countries over which he planned to march and fight. This
seems to me important, because a modern general and a modern army, faced with the same task, would have tackled it in
a different manner, aided by facilities which Hannibal did not
possess. It is essential, if we are to appreciate his achievement,
to understand the world in which he lived; the kind of men
who fought for and against him; and the arms they used. It
requires a considerable exercise of the imagination to achieve
this, our world having changed so much in two thousand
years, but it is worth the effort.

The first fact to remember is that the European nations
which we know had not come into existence. There was no
France, no Spain, no Italy, in the sense of homogeneous units.
From the Tagus to the Tiber, Europe was divided among a
number of independent tribes. In Spain, which the Romans
called Iberia, there were Iberians (the aboriginal inhabitants),
the Celts who had infiltrated into many parts of Europe, and
an admixture of the two races called the "Celtiberians."

Most of the country now called France was occupied by the Gauls, again divided into numerous tribal divisions, from the Rhône to the Rhine, and from the Pyrenees to the Alps. The Gauls, too, were of Celtic stock, and their many languages had a common root. Even today the language of the modern Welsh, who are Celtic, has strong links with the ancient languages of Brittany, Eire, and northern Scotland. They were of lighter color than the Mediterranean peoples (such as the Iberians) in whose countries they settled. They were also taller and more strongly built. Desperately courageous in battle—especially in attack—they also had a reputation for unreliability amounting at times to treachery. They wore little or no armor, and their principal weapon was the broad "leaf-bladed" iron sword, of which many examples survive.

Their civilization probably corresponded roughly to that of the Iron Age peoples described in the poems of Homer. Each tribe was ruled by a hereditary aristocracy under a warrior-king. They were not, as a rule, organized in professional armies. In times of peace the mass of the people lived off the land, cultivating wheat, the olive, and the vine, and raising cattle. Only in times of war were they expected to leave the plough and take up the sword. They had no cities in the sense that we understand the word, but usually their fields and pastures were grouped around a military citadel near which stood the homes of the nobles, and which formed the nucleus of defense and a place of retreat when attacked.

The Greeks, whose numerous colonies studded the coasts of the Mediterranean and its islands, may be ignored since they took little part in the struggle. In any case, by this time, the end of the third century B.C., their fighting days were over. Though their literature kept alive memories of the Trojan War, their epic struggle with the Persians, and the war between Athens and Sparta, they were now peaceful merchants and traders, relying for protection, when needed, on the two dominant powers, Rome and Carthage.

Rome was unlike any other state then existing in the world. It was not a commercial oligarchy, like Carthage, nor did it resemble any of the Celtic monarchies with their warrior castes and servile peasantry. Long ago it had been ruled by kings, but had got rid of them and was now a republic. Though it had an aristocracy—the Patricians—its working population, the Plebeians, had secured an increasing control of the government, and its rulers, the Senate, were elected. The phrase *Senatus Populusque Romanus*—the Senate and the *People* of Roman—which was proudly borne on their military standards, indicates the essentially popular basis of Roman government.

In Republican Rome it would have been impossible for a professional soldier such as Hannibal, however gifted, to have become permanent commander in chief of the Army. Like other senior government officials, Roman generals were elected by the Senate and usually served only for a short time. At this period there was no such creature as a Roman professional soldier. When enemies threatened the State, two Consuls were deputed to command the army. But though each may have carried a sword and shield as a legionary soldier and had some knowledge of parade-ground drill and elementary tactics, he was essentially a civilian, probably a judge or magistrate, more accustomed to civil administration than military command.

Roman military organization and discipline was in advance of the Celts. The Romans had learned much from the Greeks, and the backbone of their army was the heavily armed infantryman, the legionary. In times of peace he was a farmer, but when war threatened he put on his heavy body armor, took up his semicylindrical shield and iron helmet, buckled on his *gladius* (short sword), grasped his *pilum* (throwing spear) and joined his legion. The nominal strength of this unit was 6,000 men. It was rather like a modern infantry brigade. Like a modern regiment, each legion had its own name, number, history, and traditions. Each legion consisted of nine ordinary cohorts, 500 strong. It had a double-sized Number One Cohort which included the best fighting troops and the H.Q. personnel. In each cohort there were six "centuries" or companies, each with eighty (nominally one hundred) men under a centurion (company commander). Although the Roman army used cavalry as an auxiliary arm, this played a minor part and was usually recruited from among the subject or allied tribes. The backbone of the army at this period, and for centuries afterwards was the legion, made up of Roman farmer-citizens, who left the plough to bear arms for the State. It was one of the most highly disciplined military units the world has ever seen; solid slow-moving, heavily armed, irresistible. Unlike the wild Celtic tribes to which it was often opposed, it was strictly drilled, moving as one man at the word of command.

At the time when Hannibal was planning his march, Rome was in firm control of southern Italy, Sicily, Sardinia, and Corsica. The Italian tribes occupying the country north of Rome, though not subject to her, were bound by a system of alliances. But farther north, though still south of the mighty Alpine barrier, lay Cisalpine Gaul, and beyond it Transalpine Gaul, both occupied by related peoples with a long tradition of hostility to Rome. Less than two hundred years earlier the Gauls had stormed down into Italy and sacked Rome itself. Two generations back, Rome had conquered the *Ager Gallicus* (gallic land) and established an outpost at Ariminium (Rimini on the Adriatic). Seven years before the Hannibalic war a large force of Gaulish invaders was defeated by the Romans at the Battle of Telamon (225 B.C.), but the Gauls were still unsubdued, and less than a year before the Carthaginians began their march Rome had to establish two colonies at Cremona and Placentia (modern Piacenza) to keep watch on the Po Valley.

Now we will move from the Po Valley, with its recalcitrant Gallic tribesmen, to New Carthage over one thousand miles away. It is a winter's day in the two hundred and nineteenth year before the birth of Christ. The army is in its winter quarters; the Carthaginian warships and merchantmen lie at anchor, save for a stately quinquereme which moves through the entrance of the harbor to the rhythmical threshing of many oars. On the rocky heights above the blue water of the bay the temples and palaces of New Carthage reflect the westering sun.

On a balcony overlooking the scene a young man stands with folded arms, smiling as he watches the ship berth at the quayside. Then, with a sudden movement, he turns and, bounding up the steps, goes indoors to give news to his family and household. The young man is Hasdrubal, and on board the arriving vessel is Hannibal, his brother, returning from Gades (modern Cadiz) where he has been to sacrifice at the temple of Hercules.

Hasdrubal has much to discuss. Some months earlier Hannibal had sent "messengers" (we would call them agents) into Gaul to study the terrain, talk with the tribal leaders, and find what their attitude would be if a Carthaginian army attempted to pass through their territory. Some of the messengers have already returned, and that night, Hannibal, relaxing with his family and friends, listens intently while Hasdrubal pours out the news they have brought—most of it good.

Later, in the presence of his brothers, Hasdrubal, Hanno and Mago—the "lion's brood," as their father Hamilcar used to call them—he interviews the messengers personally, while clerks take notes. Maharbal and Gisgo, two of Hannibal's most trusted officers, are also present. The swarthy, sunburned faces are cheerful and confident, and spirits rise as the intelligence reports build up an increasingly satisfactory picture. The Vocontii and the Tricorii, who live between the Rhône and the Durance, will welcome the Carthaginians, says one agent. Another, questioned concerning the Allobroges who live farther up the Rhône, says that this tribe would not commit themselves but are unlikely to give trouble. The messengers who have crossed the Alps and talked with the tribes living in Cisalpine Gaul are confident that the Boii and other Gallic peoples living near the Po will co-operate, once they see that Hannibal has come to destroy their Roman enemies. They have promised food, supplies, and men.

This detailed preparation was characteristic of Hannibal's methods. Like any competent modern general he first studied the geographical and political situation of the terrain through which he proposed to march, but unlike a modern general he could not have a long line of communication back to base. Nor could his army carry its own supplies, but would have to live off the land. As Polybius, himself a former soldier, truly states:

> He knew that the only means of carrying the war against the Romans into Italy was, after surmounting if possible, the diffi-culties of the route, to reach the above country and employ the Celts as co-operators and confederates in his enterprise.

Having looked at the Roman military formations, let us now try to form a picture of the forces which Hannibal was assembling at Cartagena. They were quite unlike the Romans. They were not of one race or one speech, but recruited from many tribes, some from North Africa, others from Spain. Unlike the citizen-soldiers of Rome, who were bound by a common loyalty to a State—in fact they *were* the State—the vast majority of his soldiers owed no such allegiance. They were soldiers; their trade was war; and the only interest which could bind them together, apart from the promise of plunder, was personal loyalty to their commander.

Such loyalties have existed in modern armies, but usually they are incidental and local. Soldiers may admire and respect a Patton, a Montgomery, or a Rommel, but their underlying loyalty is to their country. It is important to remember this, because it makes Hannibal's achievements all the more extraordinary. His army was composed at various times of Africans, Spaniards, Ligurians, Phoenicians, Gauls, Italians, Greeks. Apart from their comradeship in arms, they had nothing in common with each other or with their commander, who would have to convey his orders to them through a dozen or more interpreters. Yet, in the entire seventeen years during which Hannibal commanded this heterogeneous force, most of its members serving far from their homes, there was never a murmur of dissension among them or against their leader.

Hannibal's army changed its composition and character over the years, as new allies joined it or withdrew. Here we are concerned only with the force which he gathered at Cartagena in the spring of 218 B.C.; its arms, equipment, and organization.

The army with which he started numbered over 100,000 men, made up of 90,000 foot and 12,000 cavalry. Large numbers of the foot soldiers came from the Iberian and Celtiberian tribes of Spain, many of whom had recently been fighting the Carthaginians. Precise details of their arms are lacking, but they were probably lightly armed troops, carrying short sword, spear, and shield, and wearing little body armor. Other soldiers, both horse and foot, came from Africa, ancestors of the modern Berber tribes who live in Algeria, Tunisia, and Libya, between the sea and the Atlas Mountains. Of these the most formidable were the Numidian cavalrymen, commanded by Maharbal, one of the greatest cavalry commanders of his or any other time.

He must have been an able officer to handle the Numidians, tough desert horsemen from a race of nomad warriors who had settled on the African coast and were gradually becoming pastoralists and farmers. Probably, as in the case of other warrior peoples in the process of becoming civilized, there was an excess of spirited young men who knew no trade but war, and the Carthaginians, their neighbors, were glad to employ them as mercenaries. Their principal weapon was the javelin.

Then there were the elephants, thirty-seven of them under their native *mahouts*. They were the "heavy tanks" of the Carthaginian army. Except at very close range, their tough hides were almost impervious to spears, and their earth-shaking charge was often sufficient to break the enemy ranks, trampling down infantry, while their hugeness and their smell terrified the horses. And if their use seems slightly grotesque in the light of modern methods of war, imagine being armed with a short sword and a little spear, and faced by a line of thirty-seven charging elephants.

Historians still dispute whether Hannibal's elephants were African, Indian, or both types. African elephants would have been easily accessible to the Carthaginians, but are notoriously difficult to train. Indian elephants, smaller and more amenable, would have had to be brought from a long distance, but the Carthaginians could have obtained them via the trade routes linking north Africa with Egypt, Syria, and India.

Sir Gavin de Beer, President of the Royal Geographical Society, has made a close study of the subject. In his book, *Alps and Elephants*, he states his belief that most of Hannibal's animals were African. He bases his theory mainly on the fact that a Carthaginian coin, struck in the time of Hannibal (220 B.C.), bears an unmistakable picture of an African elephant, distinguishable from the Indian type by several physical characteristics.

Nevertheless, there is the curious and romantic story that the one elephant which survived the war, and which Hannibal is said to have ridden himself, was called *Surus* meaning "the Syrian." Syria was the country from which Ptolemy, king of Egypt, obtained his elephants, which would be Indian. "It is therefore almost certain," writes Sir Gavin "that Hannibal's elephants included at least one Indian. It is also possible that

Hannibal's surviving elephant *Surus*, is depicted on Etrurian coins."

Besides horses and elephants there were numerous pack animals, and the heavy, unwieldly siege engines, battering rams and storming-towers which were needed for reducing fortified cities. These clumsy engines may have been dragged by mules or oxen.

Winter brightens into spring. Men and women throw off their cloaks, and servants no longer light braziers in the palace chambers at night. There is a sound of singing from the women's quarters, and barefoot children run laughing and screaming over the sun-warmed terraces of New Carthage. Hannibal's wife, Imilce, with her two-year-old boy, sees from her high window the peasants tending the young vines, and in the brown fields beyond the silver olive groves, other men ploughing the land in preparation for the spring sowing. And she sees other things: a new brightness in her husband's eyes, an energy in his eager step, and perhaps a new tenderness. And every day, along the dusty roads which lead into the distant mountains, more and more columns of soldiers are arriving: hardy Numidians with their splendid horses; and small, dark, well-knit Iberian infantry; slingers from the Balearic Islands; cursing mule drivers; swarthy warriors from Africa. And sometimes, from a distant quarter of the city, comes the trumpeting of elephants.

It is 218 B.C., and Hannibal is almost ready for his great enterprise. One day the town is astir with more than usual movement. Imilce hears the murmur of many men, the tramp of marching feet, shouted orders, and the blast of trumpets. Thousands are assembling to hear her husband speak. When at last he mounts the podium, his armor glittering in the sun, his eyes are confident, his mouth set and determined. When he raises his hand for silence all sounds die away, and the inter-

preters—Greeks, Iberians, Numidians, and others—stand ready
to translate each phrase.

Then the general begins his speech. He tells them that the
Romans have demanded that he and all their old commanders
(with a wave of the hand to Mago, Hanno, Hasdrubal, Maharbal) must be given up to them unconditionally because
they have dared to attack Saguntum. There is a snarl from
the crowd, which fades into silence as Hannibal speaks again.

"The Romans sent their ambassadors to Carthage," he says,
"and these were their terms; either I and my brothers are
sent to them in chains, or else it is war."

"Then war it is," shout the soldiers.

No doubt Hannibal, who was noted for his wit, seasoned
his remarks with some dry comments comparing Roman and
Carthaginian valor, but these have not been recorded. He recalls to the listeners' minds Hamilcar, his great father, under
whom many of them have served. He goes on to describe
the countries across which they must march. The journey will
be long, and not easy, but they will not always be fighting
across enemy territory. The Gauls also hate the Romans.
They will help with food, supplies, and men.

There will be mountains to cross, but all of those listening
to him, Africans or Iberians, have seen mountains before. Finally he paints a picture of the richness of Italy: the wealth-filled
towns ripe for plunder; women for their pleasure; fat cattle,
corn and wine for their bellies. There is nothing that a stout
heart and a strong sword arm cannot take if they will follow
and trust him. When he finishes his peroration the stamping
of feet, clashing of spears on shields, and hoarse cheering goes
on for minutes. At last, when the noise begins to die down,
Hannibal speaks again. He thanks the troops for their loyalty,
recalls the former victories he has shared with them, and re-
suming the voice of command, dismisses them to their homes,
ordering them to be ready on the day fixed for departure.
But it is hours before the heavy tramping of feet, the clitter-

clatter of hoofs, and the officers' cries of command, die on the wind.

Hannibal, who has been watching his departing army, reluctantly turns and goes to his chamber. Imilce is waiting for him. He kisses her, tries to console her, and for a time manages to divert her mind from the imminent parting by playing with their baby son. But soon a messenger comes with the news that Hasdrubal has summoned a conference of the senior officers. Imilce is left with her child and her thoughts as the sun sets and pale lights begin to glow from the windows of New Carthage.

4

MARCH ON THE RHÔNE

I MAGINE that almost the entire population of Paterson, New Jersey,—men, women and children—had decided to leave their homes and march on midtown Manhattan, most of them on foot, but with 12,000 mounted. Marching four abreast, by the time the tail end of the procession had left the center of Paterson, the front end would be entering New York. That was the size of the army which Hannibal led out of New Carthage in May of 218 B.C.

Over open country, of course, they would not have moved in such a narrow formation, but even if they marched ten abreast, with the horsemen guarding the flanks on either side, still the column would have been between five and seven miles long, allowing for the pack animals, the siege train, and the elephants.

It is doubtful if any one man since Alexander the Great had controlled such a concentration for force as Hannibal commanded on that day.

Joy is in his heart, power in his hand, as he rides near the head of the endless column of men and animals which snakes out of New Carthage and moves slowly across the Murcian

31

plain towards the northern mountains. Hasdrubal remains behind to guard Spain, but at Hannibal's side ride his brothers, Mago and Hanno, and officers such as Maharbal and Gisgo, men tried and tested in war, dependable instruments of his will. Turning in his saddle, he sees behind him the long, trudging line of foot soldiers—the "P.B.I.," [1] as the British infantry was known in the First World War—sometimes jocular, sometimes morose, and usually grumbling, but the backbone of any great army, past or present. Ahead and on either side rides the Numidian cavalry, screening the flanks; spirited young warriors who at times are apt to relieve the boredom of the march by wild demonstrations of horsemanship, until called to order by their officers. But as this is the start of the adventure, no one checks them, and Hannibal smiles as he watches them wheeling in formation, their bright spear points catching the sunlight. Miles back, and out of his sight, comes the line of plodding elephants, trunks swinging, great feet thudding the ground. And behind them come the pack animals and the wagons.

The first object had been achieved. Hannibal had his army, and, with the backing of the civil power, was leading it towards Rome. But he knew—none better—that personal charm, stirring speeches, flattery, and the promise of plunder would not hold together a mixed, polyglot force of raw levies and mercenaries on a journey of more than one thousand miles through some of the most difficult country in the known world.

It demands too much of human credulity to believe—as some authors appear to—that Hannibal achieved this feat by sheer power of personality.

In the writer's view, a quality of mind difficult to define, but more important than leadership, power of personality, or military genius, enabled Hannibal to achieve his ambition. He possessed—as Napoleon did—a ruthless ability to exploit

[1] "Poor Bloody Infantry."

the strength and weakness, courage and cowardice, self-sacrifice and self-interest of other human beings. Let us call it, for want of a better phrase, "psychological strategy." I shall try to illustrate it as the story proceeds.

Cartagena today is a busy but unattractive city—large, noisy, modern, and industrial. The setting, however, is still splendid. The town stands on a steep hill overlooking a magnificent harbor; huge yellow-funnelled steamers and gray destroyers ride where the triremes and quinqueremes once berthed. But nothing remains of the old walls which Hannibal knew; they were pulled down at the beginning of the present century.

To the north the road runs across the dull plain, then climbs a mountain ridge and crosses another plain to Murcia where there are Roman remains which did not exist in Hannibal's time. North of Alicante it divides, one branch hugging the coast, the other going due north, winding through the foothills past Albaida to rejoin the coast at Valencia. This is most likely to have been the route which Hannibal took. About twelve miles north of Valencia lies Sagunto (ancient Saguntum) which has retained far more of its past than Cartagena. There is a Roman amphitheater scooped out of the hillside, and, crowning the hilltop where the old city stood, a maze of ancient walls where old women peer from doorways and the young dark-eyed Saguntines, lithe and swarthy like their Iberian ancestors, still look at the stranger with a casual insolence. Many peoples and cultures have set their mark on Saguntum since Hannibal left it a blackened, smoking wreck.

Two hundred miles of twisting road join Cartagena with Sagunto. Another hundred link Sagunto with Tortosa, and a further two hundred lie between Tortosa and the present French frontier. It is not always realized that more than one-third of Hannibal's total journey was within the borders of Spain itself, and many of those five hundred miles ran through unfriendly territory. The Carthaginians did not dominate the whole of Spain; south of Saguntum their hold was firm, but north of the river Ebro, the frontier which the Carthaginians had agreed not to cross, lived suspicious Celtic tribes, and on the coast lay the wealthy and still unsubdued colony of Emporion, closely connected with Massilia (modern Marseilles), both Greek colonies being closely allied with Rome.

It was necessary to subdue or win over the Celtic tribes living south of the Pyrenees, and to gain control of Emporion which otherwise could become a base for a Roman offensive against Spain. At or near Tortosa, Hannibal crossed the Ebro, that tremendous river, the mightiest in Spain, which rises in the Pyrenees, sweeps southeastwards down its broad valley, past Logrono, Zaragoza, and Tortosa, and then loses its identity, first in wide marshes and reedy lagoons and finally in the Great Sea itself. The Romans had hoped by treaty to hold the Carthaginians at this natural frontier, but they had failed. One hundred thousand men had crossed it and were moving northward towards the Pyrenees.

Hannibal now had to deal with the Celtic tribes living between the Ebro and the Pyrenean passes. Of this operation Livy briefly states:

> He led ninety thousand infantry and twelve thousand cavalry across the Iberus (Ebro). He then subdued the Ilergetes, the Bargusii, the Austoni, and that part of Lacetania which lies at the foot of the Pyrenees mountains; and he placed Hanno in command over all the district, that the narrow gorges which connect Spain with Gaul might be under his power. Ten thousand infantry and a thousand cavalry were given to Hanno for the defence of the country he was to occupy.

Though the campaign was short it must have been bitter. Polybius mentions "many severe engagements and great loss." Just how great is difficult to estimate, but a simple sum of arithmetic shows that, after deducting from the original 102,-000 men Hanno's 11,000, plus a further 10,000 who were sent home before Hannibal advanced into Gaul, there are still 81,000 left. Yet Polybius expressly states that Hannibal marched through the Pyrenees with only "fifty thousand foot and about nine thousand horse." If Polybius's figures are only roughly correct, there are still some 22,000 unaccounted for. This suggests a very high casualty rate in the Spanish campaign, and probably more men deserted or were sent home than either Livy or Polybius admits.

Now, with Hanno established south of the Pyrenees with his 11,000 troops, Hannibal moved on along the coast road which can still be followed, through Tarragona and Barcelona, between the mountains and the sea. But many influences have changed the scene since he passed this way. The wild red mountain landscape remains much as he must have known it, but Tarragona, with its Roman remains and superbly poised medieval cathedral, speaks of a later age. And Barcelona, sweeping up the hillside from its great harbor, its packed streets surging with irresistible Catalan life and noise, would drown even the tramp of Hannibal's army. Farther north still, the dreary industrial suburbs which straggle along the coast towards Arenys de Mar are a dirty smear across the clean landscape which Hannibal knew. In fact, at this stage one begins to wonder if the journey was worth attempting.

And then, suddenly, the railway sidings, decrepit-looking factories, and mean streets are left behind, as one enters the Costa Brava. Away to the left the high, rocky sierras pile up, fold on fold. Lower down the red earth is terraced with vines descending, like a green staircase, to the rocky capes enclosing blue bays and clusters of whitewashed houses. The "Brave Coast" which knew Phoenician traders, Roman galleys, Barbary pirates, and Norman adventurers, remains unchanged— from a distance. Closer inspection reveals that the little white-wall fishing ports, such as Tossa and Cadaques, have developed a rash of smart hotels, beauty parlors, sun plages, and souvenir shops.

But if you can escape from the crowds—it is not difficult, since they tend to congregate near the beaches—and climb one of the numerous medieval towers left by the Norman invaders, you look out over a landscape which can have changed little since Hannibal's time. There is the same clear, hard brightness, shadowing the clefts in the ancient hills; the same cobalt-blue sea with its white fringe of waves, creaming around the rocks; umbrella pines still sweep down the ocherous hillsides to the capes and bays which Odysseus knew.

There are few places in Spain at which one can truthfully say, "Hannibal passed this way," since his precise route is not known. There is, however, one city which he is known to have visited, and which modern archaeology has revealed and preserved for us. This is the city of Ampurias, anciently called Emporion, the Greek colony to which Rome was allied. It lies on the coast between Gerona and Figueras, and even today is not easy to find, the roads to the coast being badly signposted. But it is worth finding.

Ampurias was a distant colony out on the fringes of the known world. As Señor Almagro, who excavated the site, writes in his excellent little guide:

> Greek Emporion was always in danger; the gigantic stones that form its ramparts still bear witness to the perils and hardships its founders must have undergone. But though it may never have attained the power enjoyed by other Greek cultural centres, its importance to western civilization was enormous. . . . Through Ampurias, as though through a magnificent window looking out across the Mediterranean, the fresh breeze of culture blew, bringing us the breath of history.[1]

You approach Ampurias along a dusty road which wanders through the pines beside the restless sea; on the right are sand, sun-baked rocks, blue water, and white wave crests. On the

[1] "*Ampurias*. History of the City and Guide to the Excavations," by Martin Almagro, Barcelona, 1959.

left, beside the road, stands the sea wall of the city, broken at one point by a gateway, through which one enters and begins to climb the gentle slope towards the main square. Turning to face the sea one finds, to the right, a long promontory shaped like the snout of a basking crocodile, and to the left another cape which looks like the upper jawbone of a human skull. Between lies a crescent of beach and groves of umbrella pines which sweep down almost to the water. And all around, under the clear sky, stretches the flat, fertile plain where Hannibal's army must have camped.

Apart from one large hotel and the museum there are no modern buildings, and it is quite easy to visualize the sprawl of tents, the Numidians grazing their horses, and hosts of lithe Iberians stripping off their arms and rushing into the sea to wash from their bodies the sweat of the long march. Hannibal was probably among them. We know he was a powerful swimmer. On one occasion recorded by Livy he swam across a swollen river to bring relief to part of his threatened army, urging the rest to follow him.[2]

Now, refreshed by his swim and wearing his most splendid robes, he is received by the city elders of Emporion. Hannibal did not conquer the city; he had no need to. It was sufficient that Hanno, with his 11,000 troops, would remain behind to watch over the tribes and also to keep an eye on the Greek colony which was known to be friendly to Rome. Passing through the sea gate Hannibal would mount the same paved road which we can tread today, thanks to the excavations of Dr. Almagro and other Spanish archaeologists. The square, with its empty plinths where statues once stood, and the pillared foundations of the public buildings, are still there. In one of these buildings Hannibal and his brothers talked

[2] It may be argued that Hannibal would not swim for pleasure, but only when he had to. With this I disagree. He had had a Greek education and to the Greeks the exercise of the body was almost as important as that of the mind. L.C.

with the Greek civic leaders in their own language, and later, perhaps, visited the little temple of Æsculapius, where the statue of the god of medicine and healing still looks down over the tumbled ruins to the pine-fringed bay. And from the great walls, built of massive blocks, he would see his army camped among the vineyards and cornfields of the colony. I imagine that the conversation was courteous but restrained. Emporion was a mart, an exchange, a commercial center, and its citizens were merchants, not soldiers. They had enjoyed Roman protection, but the Carthaginians were a powerful people, and the presence of Hanno's army would be more than sufficient to ensure an appearance at least of neutrality. Hannibal probably enjoyed the irony of the situation.

One imagines him, with his followers, wandering through the sunlit streets, admiring the temples of Zeus and Serapis, the villas, warehouses and docks, and occasionally quoting from Homer or Plato to show that he was no Asiatic barbarian. When he came to Ampurias the city was already more than two hundred and fifty years old. Planted in a barbarian land it provided a window through which the light of Hellas shone, illuminating the darkness of western Europe. I had expected a few pathetic fragments of stone walls scattered among thistles, a few scrubby mounds and a lot of potsherds. Instead I found a maze of carefully excavated walls, the foundations of streets, houses, warehouses, shops, and temples, bright with blue cornflowers and warmed by the same beneficent sunshine, scented by the same wild thyme, which the young Carthaginians enjoyed over two thousand years ago.

One morning the watchmen on the walls of Ampurias see unusual activity in the Carthaginian camp. The first pinkness of dawn has hardly begun to color the horizon, and the cocks are still crowing, when the bray of trumpets, the whinnying of horses, and the stir and tumult of voices roll across the plain. As the sun lifts above the sea's rim, it catches the gleam of spears and armor as the marching ranks begin to file past the city and along the northern road. For hours their heavy tramping shakes the walls, as Hannibal leads his army out towards the Pyrenees.

From Ampurias he could possibly have entered Gaul by following the coast, but the road winds through precipitous forested gorges and the pass leading through the mountains to Port Bou is high and difficult. I suggest that he is more likely to have struck inland through Figueras and followed the course of the modern highway which crosses the frontier between Junqueras and le Perthus, where the pass is wide and comparatively low.

From the frontier the road descends gradually in a series of long, sweeping curves as far as Le Boulou, and then runs straight to Perpignan. In the evening light, when we drove along it, the golden wheatfields, the pale green of the vines, and the red earth of Rousillon seemed to smile in welcome. It was the old, immemorial Mediterranean landscape, and can have changed little in two thousand years, though in Hannibal's time there would probably have been more uncultivated land. But there would also have been cornfields and olive groves, as there are now. From the foot of the Pyrenees the modern highway, which follows close to the course of the old Roman road into Spain, runs along the flat coastline, skirting the Gulf of Lions. It is open, easy marching country, through Narbonne and Beziers, to Montpellier and the Rhône.

Between Perpignan and Narbonne, as the Pyrenees recede farther and farther behind one, the road passes through a country of vineyards. For mile after mile, on each side of the straight, plane-bordered tarmac road, one sees nothing but blue sky and endless ranks of young vines. This is the Aude Department which, with its neighbor the Department of Herault, produces more wine than any other district in France. It is good wine, too, though not ranking with the best products of Burgundy and Bordeaux.

After Narbonne—which takes its name from the ancient Roman province of Gallia Narbonensis—and Béziers, the white limestone spurs of the Alpilles begin to rise ahead, and then accompany the traveler on his left as far as Montpellier. East of this town Hannibal's road skirts the great brackish lagoon known as the Bassin de Thau as one approaches the *Bouches du Rhône*.

As Hannibal's 59,000 thousand moved across the marshy Camargue towards the western mouth of the great river, he must have felt fairly confident about his communications. The "lion's brood" was working in concert. Hasdrubal commanded at New Carthage. Hanno guarded the Pyrenean passes and Ampurias, and Hannibal himself, on reaching Gaul, had taken precautions to propitiate the tribes living on the western side of the mountains. "The princes of the Gauls," writes Livy ". . . came without reluctance to the Carthaginian, being won by his presents, and suffered his army to pass through their territories . . . without any molestation."

His main anxiety must have been to discover the intentions of the Romans. They could not, by this time, have failed to learn about his movements. And, in fact, as the Carthaginians were moving up the western branch of the Rhône, seeking a crossing, a Roman fleet of sixty warships, carrying a legion commanded by Publius Cornelius Scipio, had arrived already at nearby Marseilles.

5

ELEPHANTS AFLOAT

From Aigues-Mortes almost to Arles the western arm of the Rhône flows through the most desolate country in France —the Camargue. As flat as the Nile Delta (which, in shape, it resembles), it is a land of marshes, reeds, and scrub, broken up by sluggish streams which sometimes spill over into broad brown lagoons. Though the northern part is now chiefly given over to rice-growing, the southern area near the coast is still as wild as it was in Hannibal's time, though then, of course, the marshes covered a much wider area. Near the coastal village of Les Saintes-Maries, however, it remains very much as it was when the Carthaginians came this way, splashing through the mud, sending up clouds of flamingos in startled flight, and occasionally stampeding a herd of wild white horses or black bulls pursued by the whooping Numidian horsemen.

The flamingos, horses, and bulls can still be seen occasionally. Some are protected in nature reserves, and the bulls are caught and bred for the arenas of Arles and Nîmes.

Some fifty miles eastwards, beyond the other main branch of the Rhône stood the Greek colony of Massilia which, like

Ampurias, was in alliance with Rome. There, as Hannibal's army was marching up the river towards Arles, the Roman legionaries which Publius Cornelius Scipio had brought to Massilia were recovering from seasickness. According to Livy, the Roman commander

> . . . scarcely as yet believing that Hannibal had crossed the Pyrenean mountains; whom, when he ascertained to be also meditating the passage of the Rhône, uncertain in what place he might meet him, his soldiers not yet being sufficiently recovered from the tossing of the sea, he sends forward, in the meantime, three hundred chosen horses, with Massilian guides and Gallic auxiliaries, to explore all the country, and observe the enemy from a safe distance.

In these days of air reconnaissance, radar, and radio communication, military movements on the other side of the globe may be detected and reported within a matter of minutes or even seconds. In 218 B.C., fifty miles of marshland were sufficient to allow 59,000 men to pass almost under Publius Cornelius Scipio's Roman nose without that worthy officer knowing anything about it. By the time his scouts had caught up with Hannibal's rear guard and were mauled for their pains, the bulk of the Carthaginian army—men, horses, mules, and elephants—were across the Rhône and moving north.

The point at which the crossing was made is much disputed by historians. De Beer thinks it was at or near Arles, and I think his argument has much to commend it. Polybius states that Hannibal crossed the Rhône "where it is a single stream . . . at a distance of four day's march from the sea." Says Sir Gavin:

> He had come from Spain along the coast and must have left the sea near Aigues-Mortes where the western mouth of the Rhône runs into it. The distance from the sea below Aigues-Mortes to Fourques opposite Arles is about sixty kilometres [about forty miles], for the length of Hannibal's route from

Ampurias to the point where he crossed the Rhône, Polybius gave a distance of 1,600 *stadia* or 284 kilometres (approximately 200 miles). From Ampurias to Fourques by the shortest route the distance is 289 kilometres. There is therefore no doubt that the crossing of the Rhône was made from Fourques to Arles.[1]

Hannibal would probably have disliked modern Arles, for it is full of monuments left by the people he tried and failed to conquer. There is a huge Roman theater, a Roman arena, a Roman cemetery (the Aylescamps), and a ponderous Roman arch is built into the wall of one of the principal hotels. But if De Beer is right, the general would have recognized the spot where the river sweeps in a broad, shallow curve near Fourques as the place where he made the crossing. It was not an easy passage. Apart from the difficulty of transporting his troops, horses, and elephants across a wide stretch of swift-flowing water, he was faced with the fierce Volcae, a Gallic tribe who were determined to oppose his crossing.

Fortunately Polybius, whose account is often terse and lacking in detail, has left us a description of Hannibal's Rhône crossing which is so vivid that it might have been written by an eyewitness. In fact it was probably lifted almost intact from one of the lost books of Sosilos or one of the other Greek "war correspondents" who accompanied the Carthaginian army. I make no apology, therefore, for quoting it at some length:

Hannibal, on reaching the neighbourhood of the river at once set about attempting to cross it where the stream is single at a distance of about four day's march from the sea. Doing his best to make friends with the inhabitants of the bank, he bought up all their canoes and boats, amounting to a considerable number, since many of the people on the banks of the Rhône engage in maritime traffic. He also got from them the logs suitable for making the canoes, so that in two days he had an innumerable

[1] All quotations attributed to de Beer in this book are from de Beer, Sir Gavin, *Alps and Elephants*, Dutton, N. Y. 1959.

quantity of ferry-boats, every one doing his best to dispense with any assistance and relying on himself for his chance of getting across.

Livy, describing the same event, tells how "the soldiers themselves, at once induced by the plenty of materials and the easiness of the work, hastily formed shapeless hulks, in which they could transport themselves and their baggage, caring nothing else, provided they could float and contain their burden." One imagines that some very strange craft were seen crossing the Rhône on that day.

Hannibal's next problem was to deal with the Volcae, who were assembling in great force on the opposite bank, shouting and brandishing their spears. It was to be an opposed landing.

The general's sharp order is rapidly passed down the long line of men, crouched in their boats along several miles of riverbank. A great cheering and shouting rises as paddles and oars strike the water and thousands of craft, large and small, begin to swarm across the wide, strongly flowing river. From the opposite bank comes an answering roar as the Gauls grasp their spears, waiting for the Carthaginians to come within range. Higher up the river the bigger boats and rafts are crossing, each packed with Numidian cavalrymen, some with their mounts on board, saddled and bridled, ready to leap ashore, while other horses swim behind, tethered to the boats. Hannibal has wisely ordered these large craft to cross upstream, in order to break the force of the current and make the water smoother for the thousands of tiny cockleshells—coracles, canoes, even hollowed-out tree trunks—which are struggling to cross farther down.

This is how Polybius describes the scene which followed:

... now, with the men in the boats shouting as they vied with one another in their efforts and struggled to stem the current, with the two armies standing on either bank at the very brink of the river, the Carthaginians following the progress of the boats with loud cheers and sharing in the fearful suspense, and the barbarians yelling their war-cry and challenging to combat, the scene was in the highest degree striking and thrilling.

Suddenly, just as the Gauls are about to meet the first wave of incoming boats, a shock of sound bursts on their right; wild war cries mixed with the thunder of hoofs. Before their right flank has time to turn about, Hanno's terrifying Numidian horsemen are among them, and flames and smoke burst from the Gallic tents, which other Numidians have fired.

The barbarians, taken quite by surprise, rushed, some of them to save their tents, while others defended themselves against their assailants. Hannibal, all falling out favourably as he had purposed, at once marshalled those of his men who were the first to land, and after addressing some words of exhortation to them, led them to meet the barbarians, upon which the Celts, owing to their disordered condition and to their being taken by surprise, soon turned to flight.

Once having established a beachhead on the east bank, it is relatively easy to get the rest of the army across. But there remain the elephants, for the transport of which Hannibal has made careful and ingenious preparations. After camping for the night he recrosses the river to superintend the operation. Rafts are made, fifty feet wide and two hundred feet long, moored to the banks by strong cables and jutting out into the river. Another raft of the same breadth and one hundred feet long is joined to the end of the first, but so constructed that it can be quickly detached from its moorings. The whole structure is piled with earth, so that the elephants will tread on it without fear, thinking they are on solid ground.

Two cow elephants are led on first, and the males, each weighing between five and seven tons, interestedly follow. The beasts once aboard, the moorings joining the raft to the anchored pier are cut, and the pachyderms find themselves afloat. At first there is pandemonium; stamping and trumpeting, the elephants threaten to upset the raft. But eventually, Livy tells us, "mere terror, when they saw water all around, produced quiet. Some indeed becoming infuriated, fell into the river; but, steadied by their own weight, having thrown their riders, and seeking step by step the shallows, they escaped to the shore."

After discharging its cargo, the raft returned to the west bank to repeat the operation, until at last all thirty-seven elephants had been safely ferried across with the loss of some of their *mahouts*, who were drowned. This loss must have caused Hannibal some staff problems, since the *mahouts* must have been highly trained men and not easily replaceable.

Meanwhile, Hannibal, having heard that Publius Cornelius was near, sent five hundred Numidian horsemen downstream to observe the Roman forces and, if possible, find out their strength and intentions. Somewhere between Arles and Aigues-Mortes they met the 300 Roman cavalry which had been sent to spy on the Carthaginian camp. In the fierce fight which ensued, the Romans lost 160, and the Numidians rather more. When the survivors reported to their respective commanders, Publius immediately gave orders for his main force to strike camp and march up the Rhône, hoping to make contact with the enemy near the point at which they had crossed the river.

Livy states that Hannibal was "uncertain whether he should pursue the march he had commenced into Italy, or fight with the Romans," but in this I am sure Livy was wrong. The general must have guessed, if he did not know, that his own army would far outnumber any force which the Romans could have assembled in the time and in any case it was in his interest to avoid contact, and keep the enemy guessing at his intended movements. However, before striking camp he employed a vivid example of that "psychological strategy" mentioned earlier. A number of envoys from the Boii tribe who lived beyond the Alps, arrived at his camp. They had recently been at war with the Romans, being incensed by the establishment of two colonies, at Placentia and Cremona, within their territory. Now they offered to guide the Carthaginian Army across the Alps and into Italy. Hannibal saw, in the ambassadors' presence, the opportunity to raise the spirits of his troops, some of whom had begun to murmur against the long hazardous journey. Livy puts into his mouth an oration which may well be based on an actual report. The speech is entirely in character and worth quoting. I have shortened and paraphrased it slightly, putting it in the first person, but have not altered the sense.

"Why are you afraid? You, who for so many years have won victory after victory? Did we leave Spain with one nation which lives between the Two Seas unsubdued? . . . The greater part of our journey is accomplished. We have surmounted the Pyrenees; we have crossed the Rhône, that mighty river, in spite of the opposition of thousands of Gauls and the fury of the river itself. Now we have the Alps in sight. On the other side of those mountains lies Italy. Is this the time to grow weary, when we are at the very gates of the enemy? Does anyone imagine the Alps to be anything but what they are—lofty mountains? Suppose them to be higher even than the Pyrenees, what of it? No part of the earth reaches the sky, or is insurmountable to mankind! The Alps are inhabited and cultivated. They produce and support living things. Do you think that, if they are passable by a few men, they are impassable to armies?"

Then he introduced the Boiian envoys who stood behind him.

"These very ambassadors whom you see before you," he said, "have crossed the Alps. They didn't fly over them on wings! And remember, the ancestors of these noblemen who have come to help us, were not natives of Italy. They came from foreign countries, as we do. They crossed the Alps in immense bodies, with their wives and children. You are soldiers, carrying nothing but your weapons.

"What, in reality, is impervious or insurmountable? Saguntum fell in eight months. Now, when our aim is Rome, the capital of the world, can anything appear so difficult or dangerous as to delay us? Are you going to let it be said that the Gauls gained possession of a country which the Carthaginians were afraid even to approach? Take your choice. Either admit that the Gauls are better men than you, or else follow me; and look forward at the end of your journey, to that rich plain which spreads between the Tiber and the walls of Rome."

There is no more certain way of making men attempt a task than by hinting that perhaps they may not be equal to it. When Hannibal finished his peroration the cheers could be heard far out across the marshy plains of the Rhône. A few days later, when Publius and his army arrived, they found the burned-out fires of the camp, and a few of the Volcae picking about for anything useful the Carthaginians might have left behind. On being questioned, the tribesmen told the Roman commander that Hannibal had left three days ago. Polybius says:

> . . . finding the enemy gone, he was in the highest degree astonished, as he had been convinced that they would never venture to march on Italy by this route owing to the number and unruly character of the native inhabitants. On seeing that they had done he returned with all speed to his ships and began to embark his forces. Sending his brother to conduct the campaign in Spain he himself turned back and made sail for Italy with the design of marching rapidly through Etruria and reaching the foot of the pass over the Alps before the enemy.

6

TO THE ALPS

W<small>E</small> are now about to enter a field which is as much fought over by scholars as it was by Hannibal and his enemies. From Cartagena to the Rhône his route is hardly disputed, but northwards of Avignon there is a division of opinion. The main point at issue is the place at which Hannibal turned eastwards from the Rhône and began the last stage of his march towards Italy. Some authorities believe that the turning point was at the place where the river Drôme flows into the Rhône, between Montelimar and Valence. Others believe that he turned off much farther north than this, along the valley of the Isère which enters the Rhône north of Valence. For reasons which appear to me very strong, I believe, with De Beer, that it was the Drôme he followed.

From Arles our route passed through Avignon along the east bank of the river. Before reaching Avignon, however, we turned off a side road to the right leading to the village of Maillane. It is an extremely ordinary little Provençal village, just a couple of streets, a little *Place* with three cafés, a church, a school, and—its one pride—the house in which lived the great Provençal poet, Mistral, when he was writing *Mireille*.

None of the inhabitants to whom I spoke knew anything about Maillane's other claim to fame. It is a strange and fascinating story. About the year 1777 a gentleman named M. Barthelemy Daillan was digging in his cellar (why, one wonders?), when he found the skeleton of an elephant, twelve feet long. With it was a copper medallion, which Monsieur Daillan then fixed to his pick handle as an ornament. The bones were broken up in getting them out, but as late as 1824 a French scholar, the Comte de Villeneuve, recorded that a M. Toulousan had seen a piece of the femur in a farm near St. Etienne du Gres, and had confirmed that the bone was that of an elephant. At the same time the widowed Madame Daillan still possessed one of the molar teeth of the animal.

The elephant found by M. Daillan may well have been one of Hannibal's beasts; or it may not have been. Putting aside the unlikely possibility that it came with a traveling circus, it could have been one of the animals which the Roman generals, Domitius and Fabius, brought when they conquered Provence in 121 B.C. But it was found near Hannibal's route, and it could not have been the remains of an extinct meridional elephant or a mammoth, because the copper medallion was buried with it. If that medallion would turn up somewhere, and happened to be inscribed, we might discover that the animal was one which crossed the Rhône with Hannibal, and subsequently became a casualty.

But Maillane today remembers little; not even much about Mistral and his fellow artists of the Félibrige—Bizet, Daudet and the rest. I sat outside a café as the local gendarme bicycled solemnly across the *Place*, watched by two old ladies in black, a basking dog, and the pretty waitress, whose dark eyes might have been those of *l'Arlésienne* herself. She neither knew nor cared that Hannibal's elephants may once have shaken the ground on which she stood. . . . And neither, at the moment, did I.

From Maillane we rejoined the main road, crossed the Durance, passed through Avignon, and joined the familiar Route Nationale Sept, the main highway from Paris to the Midi. As it was June, N7 was crowded with southbound traffic hotfooting it for the Riviera. The monotonous, tree-lined strip of tarmac streamed on over a landscape defaced by strident advertising signs. It has no poetry, nothing which recalls the superb Provençal countryside through which it passes. It is just an extension of the Big City. The fact that Hannibal passed this way over two thousand years ago really meant nothing. One could imagine him in the Camargue and in the Craux. One could visualize him, on the Costa Brava, particularly at Ampurias. But not on the N7.

So at Orange, after one glance at the traffic-crowded streets, I decided to turn eastwards for twenty miles to one of the loveliest Provençal towns, Vaison-la-Romaine. Set in a valley surrounded by gentle hills, vineyards, and olive groves, with a twelfth-century keep crowning the hilltop, Vaison is much nearer to the age which Hannibal knew. The columned streets of its Roman city drowse in the sunshine among cypresses and pink oleanders. There is much color: orange, pink, scarlet. In places acres of lavender drench the air with heady perfume. There are a Roman bridge, golden-gray limestone houses with roofs of the familiar semicylindrical Provençal tiles, ranging from deep pink, when new, to a bleached sand-color when old; all under a hyacinth-blue sky by day, and a scintillation of stars by night.

Against that sky, to the east, rises the superb peak of Mont Ventoux, startlingly, dramatically high in this country of gentle hills, like a giant which has lost his way, or an Alp which has strayed from its brothers. To the northeast rises the tumbled, irregular, serrated blue outline of the Barronies mountains. And within these natural boundaries lies a complete, enchanted little world, almost a separate kingdom, a magical stage set for some pageant in which it is always golden afternoon.

There was a Gaulish stronghold here before the Romans built their city, and it is possible that Hannibal knew the site. In any case it provided me with an ideal spot from which to survey the triangular area of land which Polybius calls "The Island."

> Hannibal, marching steadily from the crossing-place for four days, reached a place called the "Island", a populous district deriving its name from its situation; for the Rhône and the *Skaras* meet at its point. It is similar in size and shape to the Egyptian Delta, only in that case the sea forms the base-line uniting the two branches of the Nile, while here the base-line is formed by a range of mountains difficult to climb or to penetrate, and one may say, almost inaccessible.

Some scholars have tried to identify the Skaras with the Isère, which flows into the Rhône much farther north. Others are convinced that the Skaras was, in fact the Aygues, which enters the main river just north of Orange. There seems to me strong reasons for taking the latter view. There is no other triangular area of land bordering the Rhône which answers so exactly Polybius's careful description. A glance at the map will show this. One side of the triangle is the Rhône; another is formed by the Aygues, and the third by the Barronies mountains. Within that area the land is fairly flat and richly fertile, growing mainly corn and vines. On the contrary, the land enclosed between the Rhône, the Isère and the Mont du Chat, is not flat, not triangular, and not especially fertile. Also, apart from these topographical reasons, there are others, connected with place names and their derivation, which make the Skaras far more likely to have been the Aygues than the Isère.

Polybius says that two brothers were disputing for control of this rich territory, and that the Carthaginians united with one, named Brancus, to attack and repel the other. Brancus, in gratitude, furnished Hannibal with "plenty of corn and other provisions" and "replaced all their old and worn weapons by new, thus freshing up the whole force very opportunely. He also supplied most of them with warm clothing and footwear, things of the greatest possible service to them in crossing the mountains." But perhaps the Gaulish chieftain's most helpful act was to provide guides and an armed rear guard to help the Carthaginians pass through the land of the Allobroges. This was another Gaulish tribe which Hannibal had less reason to trust; they lived north of the "Island" between the Rhône and the Isère.

Refreshed, rested, and partly re-equipped, the army struck camp and moved on up the river. The accounts given by Livy and Polybius of the approach to the alps differ somewhat, but Livy gives the names of the tribal areas through which the army passed. These provide a valuable clue because it has been proved by a French scholar, M. Auguste Longnon, that these areas corresponded very clearly with the limits of the dioceses of the early Christian church in Gaul. The borders of these dioceses have remained little changed down to the present day, so it is possible to trace the ancient tribal territories on a modern map. Another French scholar, the late M. Etienne Clouzot, gives the boundaries in his book *Pouilles de la France*.

Now we will see how this throws light on Hannibal's much-disputed route. Livy states that, after leaving the "Island," Hannibal did not march directly towards the Alps but "turned left into the country of the Tricastini, thence by the extreme boundary of the Vocontii he proceeded to the Tricorii." Another ancient author, Silius Italicus, gives the same names in describing Hannibal's route. And according to de Beer, Timagenes of Alexandria adds a few precious details —that Hannibal, having passed through the land of the Tricastini "skirted the edge of the territory of the Vocontii on his way to the gorges of the Tricorii."

Without going into too much detail, this suggests that

Hannibal passed through the diocese of St. Paul-Trois-Chateaux, northwestward of the Aygues, and bounded on the west by the Rhône; thence his route lay to the east, through part of the dioceses of Die and Vaison-la-Romaine, the ancient territory of the Vocontii. In this country lies the Pass known as the Col de Grimone in the Alpes du Dauphiné. The "gorges of the Tricorii" are to be found in the modern diocese of Gap through which runs the magnificent Route Nationale 94, part of the "Route des Alpes." Of course these dioceses cover enormous areas and provide only the vaguest of clues, but at least they limit the area of search. Nor are they the only clues, but to give more would only clog the story with confusing detail.

From the "Island" Hannibal continued to follow the Rhône northward, over country which is now completely transformed by the great hydroelectric works near Mondragon. At Donzère the river has carved a narrow cleft through the Barronies known as the Défilé de Donzère, though French hydraulic engineers, with the curt irreverence of their kind, give it a more practical name, *le robinet*—"the tap." Through this gigantic faucet, in the flood season, billions of gallons used to pour in waste. But now the mighty Rhône has been tamed, dammed, controlled, and made to flow through sluices and along broad canals. The river comes up to the cliff edge, and if Hannibal's army tried to pass through the defile today, it would have to swim part of the way.

Why, one might ask, did Hannibal pursue this northerly course so far, instead of turning eastward and making for Italy earlier? The answer is that he wanted to deceive the Romans as to his intentions, and above all, avoid fighting them on foreign soil. If he could beat them on their own territory the moral effect would be much greater. So he deliberately avoided Scipio and, as Polybius says, marched "towards the heart of Europe" with "the river on his left." It is important to remember that Polybius does not specify which river; it must have been the Rhône at this stage of the journey, but if he turned up one of its tributaries it would still be "the river."

As the Carthaginians marched about ten miles a day, along the marshy banks, halting each night to camp, they must often have gazed at the blue outline of the mountains on the eastern horizon, and wondered. Beyond those peaks lay their general's objective, Italy. Then why did he not turn? Surely he would soon. But when next day came the northward march continued.

One evening the vanguard reached a point where another river, the Drôme, pours into the Rhône just north of Loriol. Today a modern bridge carries the N7 across the shallow, gravelly Drôme. When I stood on that bridge and looked eastward the cornfields lay golden in the afternoon light. There were vineyards, purple splashes of lavender, and many market gardens running down to the murmuring river. In this part of the Côte du Rhône they grow excellent tomatoes and potatoes, and the whole land has a rich, fat, prosperous look, but some ten miles to the east, breaking the gentle skyline, the mountains begin. There stands, away to the right, an enormous upthrusting blue mass, shaped like the knuckles of a clenched fist; and beyond this defiant symbol, echeloned in range upon purple range, rise the Alpes du Dauphiné.

Here, I am sure, Hannibal gave the command to turn eastward. In spite of the roar of holiday traffic, the streams of Renaults and Citröens hurrying southward on the annual July trek to the Côte d'Azur, a sense of that great moment came to me. It was not difficult to imagine the huge army bivouacked along the banks of the river for several miles; the men resting, or grooming their horses, or foraging for food among the fields and orchards. I imagined the group of tents belonging to the general's staff and senior officers. Hannibal, in conference, told them his decision, giving at long last the order for which they had waited. Then came the swelling roar of excitement as the news spread through the ranks, and men laughed, slapped each other's backs, and no doubt the Numidians indulged in wild gallops and leaps to release their high spirits.

Somewhere, near the water, the elephants were tethered, or splashing in the river. Did they, too, sense the excitment of their masters and trumpet their defiance at Rome? Early next morning, at first light, the army fell into ranks, and nearly 60,000 men, footsloggers from Spain, horsemen from Africa, slingers from the Balearic islands, swordsmen from Gaul, wheeled in a long column and began moving eastward, along the pebbly banks of the frothing river, towards the Alps.

7

BATTLE FOR THE GORGE

To those who are unacquainted with Provence, Dauphiné, and Savoy [says de Beer], it might seem that from the Rhône the route to Italy was uphill all the way to the watershed on the frontier ridge of the Alps, and then down again. But unless the route lay along the banks of the river Isère or Durance all the way, this is not so. The Alps form a wide belt of over two hundred kilometres deep between the Rhône and the frontier ridge, and from the region of the "island" it is necessary to cross first a pass out of the Rhône valley and to descend again into the secondary valleys and plains in the midst of the Alps before climbing a second pass to the frontier ridge. From the distances given by Polybius it is clear that the place described as "the ascent towards the Alps" must be the first pass, leading out of the Rhône valley.

I F the boundaries of the modern dioceses do, in fact, represent roughly those of the old Gaulish tribal territories, as seems most probable, Hannibal could not have followed either the Isère or the Durance (in its lower reaches). His journey must have taken him over country answering to the above description, *i.e.*, he climbed one pass, descended into lower land, then climbed a second, more difficult pass which led him into the valley of the Po, in northern Italy. Such geographical conditions exactly fit the account given by Polybius, though not that of Livy. I prefer to follow the Greek historian, who lived closer to Hannibal's time. He writes:

> On these points, I speak with some confidence, as I have inquired about the circumstances from men present on the occasion and have personally inspected the country and made the passage of the Alps to learn for myself and see.

The first part of the route passes through the rich lowlands beside the Drôme, a green landscape, more lush than Provence. Gradually the pines and dark cypresses give way to deciduous trees—evidence of heavier rainfall. The Drôme, much clearer and faster-running than the Rhône, foams over its clean gravel bed, fed by the mountains which loom nearer and nearer as the road winds along the valley. To the right, beyond the river, lies the Fôret de Marsanne and the Fôret de Saou, backed by limestone hills bearing such names as "La Pierre Sanglante" (the Bloody Stone), "Le Piège" (the Trap) and "Le Pertuis" (the Sluice). There are pleasant little riverside villages, such as Crest and Saillans, each with ancient stone bridges and a promenade bordered by planes or chestnuts. (It was at Saillans that I found the café called "Hannibal's Inn.")

Beyond Saillans the road, still clinging to the river, takes a wide northward sweep, then swings eastwards again towards the enchanting little mountain hamlet of Die, which produces a delicious (and cheap) champagne-type wine called "Clairette de Die." But from Die onwards vineyards are rare, for now begins the northern range of the Alpes du Dauphiné. Die itself is surrounded by mountains, not very high but impressive. They are of limestone, partly forested, and worn into eccentric shapes, some like the heads of men and animals, giants and devils.

Everywhere there is the sound of water rushing over stone, and the moist, cool air hints at rain not far away. White clouds drift around the high crags then suddenly disappear, revealing blue sky, and there are sudden unpredictable winds which buffet one's car and set boughs bending. The nearby mountains are relatively low, but every now and then one of the white cloud puffs, drifting away from a gap in the hills, reveals beyond it a monstrous peak which for a moment changes the whole scale of the landscape. Then the cloud curtain is drawn again and the smaller, more comforting world returns. So these peaks must have appeared to Hannibal.

In musical terms, this part of the route was the pianissimo beginning of a slowly swelling crescendo or, to change the simile, the first act of a great tragic drama. Whereas before one had needed to exercise some imagination to visualize Hannibal's march, now impressions crowd in willy-nilly, and the tremendous story leaps from the terse pages of Polybius like the genie released from Aladdin's lamp. One could think of nothing else, and as the landscape expanded in greater and greater splendor, so the march of Hannibal's men sounded louder and clearer in the mind.

A little to the east of Die I turned off the main road along a much narrower, steeper highway which plunges into the mountains. At every turn of the climbing, twisting road the limestone cliffs and crags became higher and more ominous. Between the villages of Chatillon and Glandage we came upon the Gorge des Gas, which De Beer believes was the site of Hannibal's first battle in the Alps. It is frighteningly narrow, a mere corridor with the river running close beside the road, flanked by sheer walls of rock ascending vertically for some eight hundred to one thousand feet. At one point the road climbs a ledge cut out of the cliff, and there is a precipitous drop on the right.

Certainly this corridor fits Polybius's description very closely, and is the only gorge answering to his description which lies at the correct distance from the crossing of the Rhône near Arles. Polybius was very careful in recording mileages, and the distance he gives from the crossing of the Rhône to the "ascent towards the Alps," *anabole pros tas Alpeis*, is about 1,400 *stadia* or approximately 250 kilometers. De Beer states that there are only two passes which are suitable as regards distance, the Col de Cabre and the Col de Grimone. The route to the Col de Grimone passes through a little gorge such as Polybius describes. The Col de Cabre does not. Moreover the Col de Grimone route "passed through the far edge of the territory of the Vocontii," as Livy said. "When he had crossed the pass he had entered the territory of the Tricorii." It all seems to fit.

Even if one assumes that the modern road through the gorge does not follow the track which Hannibal used, the configuration of the Gorge des Gas is such that it would have been impossible throughout much of its length for more than six or eight ranks of men to have marched abreast. This means that the column must have been at least six miles long, and would take nearly a day to pass through the gorge, even if unimpeded. One cannot help asking why, if Hannibal was as brilliant a general as the historians believe, he allowed his army to march through such an obvious deathtrap? He may have been overconfident. He may have been betrayed by the promise of Gaulish friendship. Or he may have taken a "calculated risk." But if this was indeed the site, it is not difficult to see why the battle was both bloody and costly.

Summer is turning to autumn as the Carthaginians begin the long climb towards the Col de Grimone. The Gaulish escort provided by Brancus has returned home, but as long as Hannibal's force remained in flat country, the hostile Allobroges kept at a respectful distance. Now, however, as Hannibal rides near the head of the slow-moving column his eyes rarely leave the rocky crags which tower on either side of the narrow way. Frequently his scouts, riding ahead of the main army, return with disquieting news. Again and again they have seen men watching them from the heights, and at one point a considerable body of Gauls were seen crossing a ridge. When the Carthaginians camp for the night, strung out along the tortuous valley, sentinels and scouts are watching anxiously from the slopes above. Sometimes there is a night alarm, and the sentry's cries echo and re-echo from the rocks. Next morning the army moves on again, deeper and deeper into the mountains.

One day the Gaulish guides, who have escorted Hannibal from the Rhône crossing come to his tent with vital intelligence and the general summons a council of war to hear them. Riding ahead with the scouts, they have come upon the Gorge des Gas, so narrow and tortuous that in places there is barely room for four men to march abreast, and dominated for most of the way by steep cliffs. The local tribesmen are holding this pass, and have occupied strategic positions on the heights above it. There is no suitable alternative route, and unless the enemy is dislodged the Carthaginians are bound to be attacked when they are most vulnerable, strung out in column of route with no room for a cavalry screen. There is, however, one hope. The Gaulish interpreters have talked to prisoners, and learned from them that the enemy patrols only occupy their positions during the day. At night they retire to their town, some miles away.

Hannibal makes his decision, and dismisses the council. Next day he strikes camp as usual, advances openly with his whole army, and then camps within sight of the enemy. As soon as night falls he orders all the campfires to be lit, to make as big a show as possible. The enemy patrols, seeing the whole of the valley floor a mass of twinkling lights, conclude that the Carthaginians will not attack that night, and even if they did they could not possibly advance far into the pass before daybreak. So they retire as usual, to their town.

Meanwhile, in the Carthaginian camp there is secret activity. Hannibal has selected a small force of picked men "most fitted for this enterprise." Discarding their heavy accouterments and carrying only light arms, they are mounting their fast horses. Hannibal swings into the saddle, the firelight glinting on his helmet, and there is a subdued cheer as he leads the cavalcade away from the friendly glow of the camp fires and into the darkness beyond.

Early next morning messengers from the advance party ride jubilantly back into the camp. All is well. Hannibal and his men have secured all the vital positions previously occupied by the Allobroges and are standing guard to protect the main army as it marches through. Again the trumpets sound shrilly on the morning air as the men fall into ranks. The mules kick and struggle as their packs are loaded, and the elephants lumber clumsily into line. So the march begins.

The dawn light is rosy on the mountaintops when the Allobroges, hurrying over their secret trackways high above the pass, look down and see, at the places they had formerly occupied, masses of Carthaginian troops, while far below, along the narrow gorge, 50,000 armed men, pack animals, and elephants, are ponderously moving.

At first the Allobroges hang back, frustrated, watching in helpless anger the endless column snaking through the gorge. But when they see the long line of sumpter animals loaded with potential loot stumbling along the narrowest part of the defile, lust for plunder overcomes every other consideration. Rapidly splitting their forces into several compact bodies, they select their targets, and then, sword in hand and yelling their war cries, storm down the hillsides onto the advancing column.

At one part of the Gorge des Gas, on the northern side, where the cliffs break away in fairly steep slopes, there is just room for a small force to deploy. High above that slope Hannibal is watching, astride his horse, surrounded by his picked Numidian cavalry, with a small body of his veteran

Spanish infantry. Only his hands, nervously twisting the idle reins, betray his feelings as he watches the Gauls attack. He had suspected that this might happen, but had hoped desperately that it would not. He knows well that, in that narrow gorge, with a precipice on one side, the least disturbance can pitch the pack animals and their precious loads onto the rocks below. To counterattack might make matters even worse by adding to the confusion, so for a time he holds his hand, hoping that the casualties will not be too high.

Crammed in the narrow space, the Carthaginians can do little to hold back the Allobroges who, attacking at several points, hew down the mule drivers while others roll boulders from the heights. Terrible sounds rise from the struggling mass in the defile below: the terrified screaming of the wounded horses which, in their agony, run amok, throwing their riders and creating further havoc among the hemmed-in column; the wild war shouts of the Gauls, the cries of wounded and dying, and the ghastly sound made by the helpless pack animals as they crash to death on the rocks below the precipice.

The men around Hannibal keep turning their eyes first to the carnage below them and then to their leader's face. Still he makes no sign, as more and more men, horses, and mules pitch like toys over the lip of the precipice while their companions, further along the column, struggle helplessly to come to their aid. Polybius says:

> The wounded horses, terrified by the pain, turned and met the pack animals and others rushing on ahead and pushing aside everything that came in their way, created a general confusion. Hannibal . . . reflected that there would be no chance of safety even for those who escaped from the battle if the pack train was destroyed. . . .

Suddenly Hannibal's sword is out; he shouts an order, and with the war shouts of the Numidians echoing from the crags, the relief force plunges down the steep slope to the struggling, fighting mass below. For a time there is only confusion, with the swinging broadswords of the Gauls cutting arcs in the air, the spears of the Numidians sending blood splashing on the white rocks, the gasps of men struggling in the press, hardly able to distinguish friend from foe. Then suddenly it is over. The Gauls are scattering up the slopes, pursued by the Carthaginians, and the angry sounds of battle gradually die away, leaving only the moans of dying men and animals mingled with the roar of the rushing river.

Hannibal, sheathing his sword, takes off his helmet, and sitting on a rock, wipes his forehead. Below him on the blood-stained boulders, lie scores of his pack animals, dead or dying, and hundreds of his followers whom he had promised to lead "to the fertile plain which spreads between the Tiber and the walls of Rome." Other wounded lie propped against the rocks for miles along the gorge, as companions try to tend their injuries. A dying man is groaning on the grass nearby, and far along the line Hannibal hears the hoarse shouts of his officers trying to restore order, while other men are struggling to re-trieve the packs from the dead animals, for without these precious supplies the army must perish in the mountains.

The oath which he had sworn on the altar of Baal, twenty years before, had required a blood sacrifice. Much blood was to flow in fulfillment of that vow, but so far it had been mainly that of his own followers.

8

AMBUSH

Leaving the death gorge and its ghosts, we continued climbing steadily over a well-engineered mountain road to the small red-roofed yellow limestone village of Grimone, and so to the great Col de Grimone itself, the pass which led the Carthaginians through the first mountain chain beyond the Rhône and so into the upper valley of the Durance, which Livy calls the *Druentia*.[1] It is a superb pass, flanked by towering limestone crags which stand at the knees of even higher peaks. Jagged at the tops, the steep slopes are green near the bottom, with many oaks, sycamores, birches and ash trees. Though there are pockets of cultivated soil in the lower valleys, there are few vineyards and those very small. In Hannibal's time food supplies, apart from mountain goats and scraggy cattle, would have been extremely scanty.

Gradually the landscape and the villages changed their character, becoming still more ruggedly alpine. The semicircular tiles gave way entirely to flat slates, and the flat-fronted, wooden-shuttered houses, instead of being whitewashed as in the Côte du Rhône, were usually gray, with deep eaves as a

[1] Though he puts it in the wrong place, *before* the battle for the gorge.

protection against the winter snows. Now we were never out of sight of the mountains, usually looking at them from the valley floor, but occasionally keeping their company in the high passes, where the fierce winds clawed at our trailer, though at times even their noise was drowned by the thresh and thunder of waterfalls.

After descending the far side of the Col we struck the main road to Gap. From there we cruised contentedly down the long, long slope towards the valley of the Durance. It had been windy and wet in the Col, but now the sun reappeared, and one felt the relief which Hannibal's troops must have experienced when, after fighting through ambushes in the mountains, they came upon this broad, fertile valley. They had the satisfaction, too, of taking the Gaulish town from which their assailants had come.

Polybius says:

> He (Hannibal) found it nearly deserted, as all the inhabitants had been tempted out by the hope of pillage, and seized it. This proved of great service to him for the future as well as the present; for not only did he recover a number of pack animals and horses and the men who had been captured together with them, but he got a supply of corn and cattle amply sufficient for two or three days. . . .

The distance is about forty miles, which in easy country such as this, could easily be covered in a four-day march. Livy says that "during these days, as the soldiers were neither obstructed by the mountaineers, who had been daunted by the first engagement, nor yet much by the ground, he made considerable way."

Near Mont Dauphin the main trunk road (N94) swings northward through l'Argentière, Briançon, and the Col de Montgenèvre, a low and easy pass which would have afforded Hannibal a much easier passage than the one he took. Yet he cannot have used the Montgenèvre for several reasons, the most important of which is that in October when he made the ascent, the road through the Col de Montgenèvre does not reach the snow line, whereas the pass which Hannibal used lay over last winter's snow. And authorities have demonstrated that climatic conditions in the Alps were substantially the same as at present. The same reasoning rules out the Mont Cenis Pass, further north, as well as the Little St. Bernard and the Col de Larche. (For a detailed exposition of this story see De Beer.)

However, eastward of Mont Dauphin there is a narrow secondary road which passes through Guillestre, Chateau-queyras, and Aiguilles, traversing narrow and difficult gorges closely resembling those described by Polybius and Livy, and leading to one of the highest passes in the Alps, the Col de la Traversette. This pass, which is little used today—the upper reaches of the road hardly exist—rises to a height of nearly 10,000 feet, roughly level with the present snow line. Moreover it is one of the few passes from which an army could look down directly on to the plains of the Po, as—according to the ancient authors—Hannibal's army did. The road on the Italian side, which has a steep and dangerous descent, takes one down directly into the ancient territory of the Taurini through which Hannibal entered Italy.

This, therefore, was the route which we decided to follow, as far as our vehicle—and failing that, our feet—would carry us.

After Mont Dauphin the mountains closed in on either side. The road began to climb, at first in long sweeping curves which quickly tightened into snakelike convolutions as the ascent grew steeper. Now the real mountains began; the whole of the eastern sky was piled with them, gloriously blue and purple and crimson in the declining sun. One wondered what Hannibal's men felt as they saw this terrifying barrier mounting before them, tier upon tier of snow-capped peaks, like an assembly of gods looking down on an army of ants. The Pyrenees had been formidable, the Alps du Dauphiné dangerous, yet compared with these titans the former obstacles now seemed puny.

Yet why, if Hannibal approached the Hautes Alpes along the Durance Valley, did he use this difficult and dangerous approach over a high, snow-covered pass when he could have entered Italy via the easier Col de Montgenèvre? The answer is almost certainly treachery. He was unfamiliar with the country. He had to rely on Gaulish guides, who were not dependable. He may have lost his way, but treachery seems the more likely explanation.

He had already lost a considerable number of men as his army wound its way along the narrow approaches to the Comb de Chateauqueyras. Before leaving the valley of the Durance he had been approached by Gaulish chieftains bearing olive branches as a sign of peace. These men, having heard of the defeat inflicted on their fellow Gauls in the Col de Grimone, were anxious to propitiate the Carthaginian, and offered hostages as tokens of their good faith. They also promised to guide him through the mountains. Hannibal was not so naïve as to accept these protestations at their face value, but reflecting that their offer of friendship, even if feigned, was preferable to open hostility, decided to accept it.

When we followed this route, heavy winter flooding had reduced it nearly to the condition which must have prevailed when Hannibal made the passage of the Hautes Alpes. For several miles the tarmac surface had been washed away completely, and our vehicle bumped and staggered over river boulders and deep gullies which threatened to break the springs. Driving was an ordeal, and several times our $1\frac{1}{2}$-ton bus nearly capsized. Teams of bulldozers were clearing away vast landslides, and in several places we were warned that we proceeded at our own risk. This, naturally, only added savor to the adventure.

Our first obstacle was the Gorge de Guil, which some

authorities believe was the site of Hannibal's second Alpine battle with the Gauls. The fast-running river, not more than twenty to thirty feet wide at this point, rushes over boulders through a rocky canyon with sheer sides rising hundreds of feet above the river. At places the cliffs arch over the torrent, and the road, very narrow and pitted with holes, hugs the cliff wall. Other streams join it frequently, tumbling down the hillsides and either cutting channels through the road or diving under it. A more obvious place for an ambush would be difficult to find, unless it is the Valley of the Queyras, farther on.

Along the latter, for part of the way, the road is a good five hundred feet above the valley side, built on a narrow ledge from which one can look down on the white-flecked river, and up towards the snow-covered peaks more than three thousand feet higher. The Combe is a superb V-shaped valley, with pine-covered slopes climbing for a thousand feet towards the peaks, which gleam in the sun. At the foot the sea-green river, whipped into white froth like sea breakers, sends up a constant, rushing roar like a mighty wind tearing through a forest.

Hannibal's depleted force, a seven-mile column of weary foot soldiers, horsemen, elephants, and pack animals, is painfully threading its way towards the gorge. Riding with them, but watched suspiciously by Hannibal and his officers, are the Gauls who have offered to lead them into Italy. And some way behind, perhaps unknown to Hannibal, a large force of the guides' fellow Gauls are following the army at a distance, waiting for a chance to pounce. Some of them have already taken up their positions on the heights above the gorge, collecting the boulders which, rolled down into the canyon, will, they hope, help them to destroy the Carthaginian army.

As he leads his men into that ominous ravine, Hannibal suspects treachery, but it is now too late to retreat. So the column moves on, splashing through the river, and looking up warily at the cliffs which tower on either side.

Suddenly, from behind, an explosion of terror reverberates along the narrow corridor, as if through a funnel: the crash and thunder of falling rocks, the scream of men and animals in agony, the terrified shouts of men. A few moments later a rain of heavy boulders, each weighing several tons, crashes into the column ahead, killing and maiming men and beasts. The troops break ranks and seek desperately for cover, but there is none. Hannibal spurs his horse, struggling through the press of confused and terrified men, leaping over the dead and dying, and shouting hoarsely above the roar of the river, "Keep moving!" Farther along the gorge he comes upon a tight mass of struggling men, and recognizes, at grips with his own soldiers, the wild towheaded Gallic warriors with their round shields and short swords, hacking and thrusting, killing and dying. He dismounts, draws his sword, and with his bodyguard, hews out a passage. From behind him comes a continuous, desperate, defiant sound: the war cries of his Africans and Spaniards mingled with those of the exultant Gauls.

For hours the fight goes on, with the heavy, burdened Carthaginian column stumbling on over the bodies of fallen comrades and animals, sometimes halted by their opponents, sometimes clearing a way for a brief space, only to find more enemies round the next bend in the gorge. Blood stains the river; its banks are littered with men and animals, some lying inert, others struggling. Hannibal looks desperately around for space in which to maneuver, but the rocks close him in. He cannot go back to assist his army; the only hope is to fight his way through to more open ground. There is no opportunity for tactical maneuver. It is a question of men against men, sword against sword, with the Carthaginians fighting for sheer survival, and the Gauls for plunder. The general's one consolation is that this time he has sent his elephants ahead to clear the way, and placed his infantry at the rear of the column to act as a covering force.

When at last the vanguard struggles out of the gorge's mouth, it finds little relief, for although the valley is wider, it is still dangerous. Soon the army is entering the valley of the Queyras, where the track is a mere lip cut in the steep flank of the mountain, with precipitous heights frowning above them, and the river far below. Then, once again, the trumpets sound the alarm. An avalanche of boulders rolls in thunder down the mountainside, taking its fearful toll, and in the confusion the Gauls appear again, leaping out of their hiding places, or storming down the crags and scree with the light-footedness of goats, And still the road climbs more steeply into the mountains.

Hannibal, with a body of picked horsemen, is riding ahead of the column, fighting off ambush after ambush in the hope of finding a point of vantage from which he can cover the advance of his army. At last he finds what he is seeking. At the eastern end of the Valley de Queyras a huge dome of rock rises from the valley floor, commanding the mouth of the mountain cleft. Today this crag is crowned by a high-walled medieval castle, but it may well be the "bare rock" which Polybius describes. To this place Hannibal leads his weary horsemen, and after throwing up rough defenses and setting guards, camps for the night. He does not think of sleep, for all night long he hears the stumbling steps of his shattered army making its way out of the mouth of the valley, to fall exhausted within the protection of the defenses.

Hours later Hannibal sees the dawn light silhouetting the somber eastern peaks, the final barrier which he has still to cross. As the light increases it reveals on the western side of the camp a sight which humbles even his stubborn spirit. Out of the jaws of the valley a slow-moving mass of weary men is moving in no order, but shambling onwards as if sleepwalking. Some stagger under the weight of wounded and dying comrades; others fall, then rise and stumble on. Many lie, unmoving. Some of the unwounded horses are carrying two or three riders; others, wounded, are being led, and right at the rear certain of the pack animals which have survived the attack pick their way across the stones, driverless, but still instinctively following.

No one speaks. The army moves in exhausted silence, save for the chink of accouterments, the shuffling of weary feet over pebbles, the morning song of birds, and the roar of the indifferent river.

9

THE LAST BARRIER

HANNIBAL had crossed the Rhône with nearly 60,000 men. The force that he was now mustering for the final assault on the Alps could not have numbered more than 40,000 of whom many would not live to see Italy. Of the missing 20,000 some were prisoners of the Gauls, some may have deserted, but the majority were dead. So were many hundreds of helpless animals which, in a modern army, would be represented by the unfeeling metal of tanks, carriers, and lorries. Not all of those 20,000 were killed outright by enemy weapons. Many, who in a modern army would have been saved by medical science, died of their wounds, or disease, or exhaustion. Those who still cherish the illusion that wars fought with sword and spear were more "romantic" and less ghastly than those fought with cordite and T.N.T. should reflect on these facts. I am convinced that if one of Hannibal's soldiers could be given the opportunity of watching a modern "conventional" army fight, and could see how it is provisioned, fed, and its wounded healed, he would prefer to take his chance in the twentieth century.

East of Chateauqueyras the valley opens out for a few miles. We were able to follow the road with difficulty, because in many places it had been washed away by floods, and landslides necessitated detours, sometimes into the river itself. At Aiguilles, where we camped for the night, the village lies at the foot of a gloomy canyon and the river's monotonous roar, booming back from the valley walls, becomes oppressive, particularly at night. At the half-ruined hamlet of Ville-Vielle we had seen evidence of its power. Many of the old houses had been split wide open by the floods, and stood deserted and partly unroofed, as if by bomb blast.

Farther east, towards Abries, the valley floor was an unbroken mass of boulders, pebbles and dried river-borne mud sending up clouds of blinding white dust which was sucked into the trailer as it pitched and rolled through the valley at about six miles an hour. We pass through Abries, a winter-sports resort with the usual wooden chalets, deep-eaved, with balconies, and tracks leading to the ski slopes; then the last vestiges of a road disappeared altogether. We bucked our way, yard by yard, over virgin rock, until at last it was obvious that to attempt to drive "Vairee Luvlee" any farther would be to invite a breakdown. So we parked, packed our rucksacks, and began to walk.

It was a relief to stop the laboring engine, and to climb down from the cab into fields bright with wildflowers and butterflies. This was alpine scenery—I was going to write "at its most magnificent" but "heavenly," though trite, is a better word. One thought of the Elysian fields . . . drifts of scented wildflowers, a rushing stream of crystal-clear water, sluicing and eddying over clean white stones and flashing like a million diamonds in the sun. On every side, green, pine-covered slopes rose as steeply as a house roof for thousands of feet until the pines became fewer and fewer and there was only rock; higher still, dazzling white against the blue, rose the snow-covered peaks of the Hautes Alpes.

So clear was the atmosphere one felt that a short, sharp walk through the pines would take one to the snow line. In fact, as we knew, those white slopes were vertically a mile above us. And they were only the lower peaks. The highest, Mount Viso, which overlooks the Col de la Traversette, is over twelve thousand feet high.

As we climbed towards the pass swarms of butterflies arose from the fine grass, like flowers which had freed themselves from their stems and learned to fly; red, brown, mottled yellow, and sky blue, they hovered in the sunshine or settled on the wet stones at our feet. Apart from the eternal river roar, the only sounds were the wind in the pines and the deep "tong-tong" of bells hung from the necks of the cattle. These gentle animals, with their sleek, sable-colored coats wandered along the lower slopes or stood in the shallow water, watching us with a mildly benevolent interest.

We continued to climb the pass for a mile or so until the whole valley lay before us, the valley along which I believe the Carthaginians came; and behind our backs rose the superb peak of Mount Viso, the mountain which saw Hannibal assault and conquer the last and most formidable barrier to his ambition. It was impractical for us to climb higher, since we were within a few miles of the Italian border which at this point has no frontier post. But armed guards are alert for smugglers, and although my rucksack contained only a few sandwiches and a copy of Polybius, it might have been difficult to persuade the sharpshooting frontier guards that we were only looking for Hannibal.

So, leaning comfortably against a rock, I took out the Greek's well-worn book and, with the sun warming my back and the river murmuring far below, reread his account of Hannibal's break-through into Italy. And once again the scene began to take shape.

It is now October, and near the setting of the Pleiades. Nearly five months have passed since Hannibal and his original 102,000 set out from Cartagena. Apart from a few plundering attacks by small bands which are easily repulsed, the Gauls leave the Carthaginians alone. Now the enemy is nature herself. As the army climbs towards the frontier ridge the landscape becomes increasingly grim, bleak, and hostile. First to disappear are the valley pastures and the homes of men; the tall pines overshadow the army for several miles, and then they, too, become thinner and sparser and finally fall away behind. Now there is nothing but bare rock and scrub, and the track winding endlessly up towards the snows. A piercing wind screams and whistles among the crags. During the night halts the resinous smell of pine-wood fires blows across the camp; the rocks are ruddy with the flames, against which the little dark men from Africa and Spain huddle for protection against the unaccustomed cold. But fuel is scarce and has to be strictly conserved. Many of the troops, especially those weakened by wounds, fall victims of disease, and every morning, as the army strikes camp, it leaves behind sick men who can march no farther.

Marharbal is worried about fodder for the animals, especially for the elephants, for there is little among those lifeless rocks which yields even the scantiest food, and much of the carried fodder has been lost with the pack animals. The men might be sustained in an emergency by the flesh of such animals as are unfit for further work, but the elephants are not flesh-eaters, being accustomed to live on bark, leaves, roots, and fruit. The great animals suffer severly, and some, worn out by hunger and the fatigue of that terrible climb, sink to their knees and die. Their flesh is cut up and eaten by the troops, and the carcases left to the vultures.

On the ninth day from the start of the climb a faint sound of cheering drifts down from the heights. The Carthaginian army, now reduced to about 35,000 men, drags for miles along a track so narrow and tortuous that a man can see only a few hundred of his comrades ahead and behind. The rest are hidden by the rocky flanks of the mountains, but the cheering continues, sometimes heard clearly, at other times blown away by the gale. It can have only one meaning. The vanguard must have reached the top of the pass, and, as the news is carried for mile after mile along the toiling ranks, men who seem to have reached the limit of exhaustion suddenly take fresh heart.

Staggering, stumbling, starving, blind and dizzy with fatigue, still they struggle on, up to the place where the last winter's snow, which had been creeping nearer and nearer down the slopes, covers the ground before them. They clamber on over the frozen ground, slipping, falling, rising and climbing on all fours. Rounding a rocky bluff they are met by a flurry of new snow, and for a time the peaks are lost in a storm of white flakes which, falling on the frozen snow of the previous winter, creates a new hazard. The skinny horses slip and slide, striving for a foothold, and many fall, but the great weight of the elephants gives them an advantage, as their feet pound the new-fallen snow into a compact mass. The cheering grows louder, and each man, as he struggles over the lip of the pass, sees what he had never hoped to see. *The road climbs no higher.*

Along the narrow ridge, surrounded by mountains, thousands of men are huddled, black against the snow. Many lie exhausted; others, spurred on by their officers, are lighting fires and making camp, and as more and more men breast the ridge and join their companions the air is full of hoarse, exultant voices, some shouting, some sobbing with joy, while others gather on a rocky platform from which they can see the track winding steeply downwards to where the pines begin again, and a river gleams. Among that group are Hannibal and certain of his officers. Wrapped in their cloaks, they watch silently, their faces strained with the agony of the long march. Beside them the Gaulish guides, who have accompanied them all the way from the Rhône, are chattering and pointing. But Hannibal, Maharbal, Gisgo, and the rest say little.

The snowstorm has blown away, and the sun, sinking behind

the mountains which the army has climbed, lays a swathe of golden light across the green plain eight thousand feet below. More and more men press forward and gather around Hannibal. Their dark faces are emaciated and their eyes have a mad glint. The skins of many are festered with sores—the result of starvation and disease—and their stench is nauseating, even in that wild and windy place. In that hour, all share something of the exultation of their leader, the sense of triumph which comes to men who have endured the ultimate in pain and fatigue and yet have survived, while others have perished. They cannot understand the gibberish the Gauls are pouring into the ears of their general, but one word, clumsily pronounced in a dozen different accents, spreads through the army. It is "Italia." After five months of marching, fighting, enduring, dying, the Carthaginians look down, at last, on the land of the Romans.

10

FIRE AND VINEGAR

For two days, they remained encamped on the summit; and rest was given to the soldiers, exhausted with toil and fighting; and several beasts of burden, which had fallen down among the rocks, by following the track of the army arrived at the camp. A fall of snow, it being now the season of the setting of the constellation of the Pleiades, caused great fear to the soldiers, already worn out with weariness and many hardships. On the standards being moved forward at daybreak, when the army proceeded slowly over all places entirely blocked with snow, languor and despair, strongly appeared on the countenances of all.

ANNIBAL decided that the time had come for another of his exercises in "psychological strategy." Assembling some of the troops on "a certain eminence whence there was a prospect far and wide, he points out to them Italy and the plains of the Po, extending themselves beneath the Alpine mountains." [1]

---

[1] Both Livy and Polybius state that the army could *see* the plains of the Po, which limits the possible passes to the following: Col de la Traversette, Col de Malaure, Col Clapier.

The Col de la Traversette,[2] which is a narrow ridge, could not accommodate 30,000 men in one compact body. But, as De Beer points out, it would not be necessary for all the soldiers to see the view simultaneously. Since in any case Hannibal would have to speak to them through their officers, it would be sufficient to address the latter, for whom there would be room on the "eminence" or "promontory." As Livy describes it, Hannibal said:

> "Soldiers! . . . You have now surmounted not only the ramparts of Italy, but also of the city of Rome. You are entering friendly country, inhabited by people who hate the Romans as much as we do. The rest of your journey will be smooth and down-hill, and, after one, or, at most a second battle you will have the citadel and capital of Italy in your power and possession."

He probably did not believe a word of his own peroration, which proved to be wrong on all counts. The descent, far from being "smooth," was in fact considerably worse than the climb, because the Italian side of the pass is even steeper than the French side, and the road was narrow, slippery, and precipitous. To quote Livy:

> . . . Neither those who made the least stumble could prevent themselves from falling, nor, when fallen, remain in the same place, but rolled, men and beasts of burden, one upon another. They came to a rock much more narrow and formed of such perpendicular ledges, that a light-armed soldier, carefully making the attempt, and clinging with his hands to the bushes and roots around, could with difficulty lower himself down. The ground, even before very steep by nature, had been broken by a recent falling away of the earth into a precipice of nearly a thousand feet in depth. Here when the cavalry had halted, as if at the end of the journey, it was announced to Hannibal, wondering what obstructed the march, that the rock was impassable.

[2] The Col Clapier could, however, give the full army a view, and some authorities prefer this Pass, but there are serious objections to it, *e.g.*, it cannot be approached from the valley of the Durance.

It is a dramatic moment, one which has excited the imagination of many historians. It is dramatic enough, even when read in cold print, but much more so when one has seen the type of obstruction which, detached from its parent rock, pitches down the mountainside and falls thunderously into the valley below. Along the lower slopes of the Col de la Traversette I saw several such monsters. One, which is illustrated in the photo section following page 114 must have weighed thousands of tons and was as big as a three-story house. If a similar rock had fallen in a narrow gully it could have effectively blocked the route of the Carthaginian army. Nowadays a few pounds of gelignite would have been sufficient to blast a way through, but Hannibal had no such resources.

For hours the army has been making its slow, painful way down the mountain track, sometimes halting, then struggling on, sometimes moving faster over the easier slopes, sometimes crawling, foot by foot down the frozen stretches, but still making steady, if slow progress. Hannibal, conscious of the nearness of the winter, and desperately anxious to bring relief to his half-starved army, urges them on with promises of the cattle-filled pastures, cornfields, and vineyards which lie almost within their grasp. The elephants, though painfully slow in descending the steep and narrow track, were in one way a help, for, Polybius says, by their very presence "wherever they went they rendered the army safe from the enemy," who were still active, though not in great concentration. Then comes a halt and for several miles the army is stationary, unable to move. Hannibal and his officers struggle through the immobile mass, seeking the cause of the delay. Eventually they find it.

Blocking the narrowest part of the track, between the mountain wall and a one-thousand-foot precipice, a huge rock bigger than a large house prevents further progress. It towers above the heads of the horses who stand idle, while their riders look at the seemingly impassable obstacle with despair on their faces. Some of the more agile troops have climbed the rock, using handholds, and are able to see over the top, but they report there are more and even larger rocks blocking the road beyond. Light-armed troops could scale these obstacles, but the horsemen, pack animals, and elephants are helpless. The Carthaginians seem, as Livy says, "to have reached the end of the journey."

At first Hannibal tries to lead his army round the rock, over nearby pathless and untrodden regions. But this, says Livy, proved impracticable,

> . . . for while the new snow of a moderate depth remained on the old, which had not been removed, their footsteps were planted with ease as they walked upon the new snow, but when it was dissolved by the trampling of so many men and beasts of burden, they then walked on the bare ice below, and through the dirty fluid formed by the melting snow. Here there was a wretched struggle, both on account of the slippery ice not offering any hold to the step, and giving way beneath the foot by reason of the slope; and whether they assisted themselves in rising by their hands or their knees, their supports themselves giving way, they would tumble again; nor were there any stumps or roots near, by pressing against which, one might with hand or foot support himself, so that they only floundered on the smooth ice and amid the melted snow.

After enduring days of this misery, with many losses both in men and animals, Hannibal has to admit that there is no practicable way round the obstacle. The only solution is to destroy it. But how?

They have by this time reached ground where a few trees grew. Hannibal gives orders to his engineers to fell a considerable number of pines and make a huge pile of timber around the rock. As soon as a wind rises and begins to blow through the valley, the word is given to light the wood. When night falls the scene is an inferno. For hundreds of feet up

the slopes the snow-covered rocks glow crimson as the flames
leap high around them, and as more and more logs are thrown
onto the fire, the great mass begins to glow a dull red. Still
more fuel is flung on to the fire, while Hannibal, who is well
grounded in Greek science, watches and waits for the decisive
moment. He has issued orders to some of the foot soldiers to
bring vinegar [3] in as large a quantity as possible. Now there are
hundreds of these men, each with his vinegar-filled wineskin,
silhouetted against the glow, waiting for a signal, while others
stand nearby, armed with heavy iron hammers and picks.

Suddenly Hannibal gives a command. The men rush
through the smoke and fling the liquid over the glowing mass.
Relay after relay springs forward and as each contingent
flings his burden into the flames, a deafening hiss rises and is
echoed by the watching mountains. Clouds of blinding steam
billow up from the rock and, through the cloud, the shapes
of the hammer-and-pick men are seen advancing, swinging
their iron tools above their heads. Above the roar of the flames
and the hiss of steam the sound of the hammers is like the
clangor of Vulcan's smithy. As blow after blow rains on the
tortured rocks, the Carthaginians, half mad with excitement,
shout encouragement.

The rock splits and crumbles. Almost before the shattered
lumps are cool enough to grasp, men are dragging them away
and hurling them down the valley-side. Hannibal turns to his
officers and laughs, his face ruddy in the glow of the dying
fire. Then he halts the hammermen and gives orders to throw
more fuel on the flames. So the process is repeated, hour after
hour, through day and night, and as some men fall exhausted,
others take their place. Within four days the seemingly impassable obstacle has disappeared, and Hannibal, besides hav-

---

[3] Vinegar, which contains from 3 to 9 per cent of acetic acid, was, in Hannibal's time "wine vinegar," *i.e.*, liquid of low alcoholic strength, produced
by leaving wine exposed to the air. Hannibal's vinegar was probably just
bad wine.

ing solved an immediate, practical problem, enjoys the prestige of having performed a feat, which, to most of his ignorant followers, must have seemed magical. Livy says:

> Four days were spent about this rock, the beasts nearly perishing through hunger; for the summits of the mountains are for the most part bare, and if there is any pasture the snows bury it. The lower parts contain valleys, and some sunny hills, and rivulets flowing beside woods, and scenes more worthy of the abode of man. There the beasts of burden were sent out to pasture, and rest given for three days to the men, fatigued with forming the passage; then they descended into the plains, the country and the dispositions of the inhabitants being now less rugged. . . . In this manner they came to Italy in the fifth month (as some authors relate) after leaving New Carthage, having crossed the Alps in fifteen days.

One of Hannibal's first actions, after he had assembled his scattered forces in the fertile plain beside the Po, was to make a roll call. When he crossed the Rhône he had nearly 60,000 troops, cavalry, and infantry: now he had 23,000. He had lost 36,000 men in that march, besides horses, mules, and elephants.[4] Moreover the survivors, weakened by wounds, disease, and exhaustion, were in no fit condition to do battle with the Romans, who were fresh, vigorous, and had the advantage of fighting in defense of their own homeland. Polybius says that Hannibal's men "had become in their external conditions more like beasts than men," and Livy mentions that "they now chiefly felt the disorders they had before contracted, in remedying them; for ease after toil, plenty after want, and attention to their persons after dirt and filth, had variously affected their squalid and almost savage-looking bodies."

[4] These are the figures given by Hannibal himself.

11

FIRST BLOOD

MEANWHILE, Publius Cornelius Scipio, having sailed from Marseilles after failing to intercept Hannibal on the Rhône, had landed at Pisae (modern Pisa), and advanced towards the plain of the Po with his troops. Hannibal, while his weary soldiers were resting and recuperating, made contact with the local Gaulish tribes, enemies of the Romans, hoping to supplement his meager force with fresh auxiliaries. The whole success of the operation depended on this factor. He came, he said, not as a conqueror but as a liberator. Rome formed the head of a federation of loosely allied states; once break that federation, and cause the allies to defect from Rome, and victory would be in sight. Now Hannibal, the warrior, must have had to use all his considerable diplomatic gifts to persuade the Gaulish chiefs that his sorry body of men were reliable allies against the hated Romans. Realizing that a violent demonstration of power would be more convincing than any amount of verbal persuasion, he allied himself with a tribe called the Insubres, who lived near the foot of the mountains, attacked the citadel of their enemies, the Taurini (modern Turin), and took it.

In Rome, Hannibal's arrival in Italy created exactly the moral effect he had desired. At first there was amazement, mixed with reluctant admiration, followed by consternation and alarm. It seemed only a few weeks since Scipio had reported to the Senate that the Carthaginians were on the Rhône; yet now they were advancing across the plains of the Po, and nothing but Roman arms could prevent them from attacking the capital itself. An urgent message was sent to another Consul, Tiberius Sempronius, who was then at Lilybaeum in Sicily, ordering him to abandon immediately his present plans and return with all possible speed. Tiberius, it is said, made his troops swear to be at Ariminium on a certain day; they kept their oath though it meant marching from the Straits of Messina up the length of Italy to Ariminium in forty days.

Scipio and his legions had already crossed the Po and were quite close to the Carthaginians. At first Hannibal refused to believe his own messengers, since it seemed to him impossible that the Roman general could have made the long coasting voyage from Marseilles to Etruria in so short a time. But soon he had definite information that a large body of Roman troops was encamped near Placentia (modern Piacenza) and realized that, whether his troops were sufficiently recovered or not, he must soon join battle. And he was well aware that the legionaries, the "iron men" who had defeated his father, were far tougher and more resolute foes than the undisciplined Celts.

Of the two Consuls opposed to him Scipio was a capable soldier, but Sempronius, judging from his subsequent actions, was rash, impetuous, and extremely jealous of his fellow Consul. How Hannibal gained this knowledge of his opponents we do not know, but he certainly possessed it.

Polybius tells us that he was extremely adept at disguises, and had a number of wigs which, with changes of clothes, altered his appearance so completely that sometimes he would appear as a young man, at other times middle-aged, and then again as an old man. He must also have been a considerable actor, for with the aid of these disguises he mingled, unknown, among the Gauls, picking up valuable information. After his experiences in the Alps he probably preferred to form an opinion of his Allies when they were off guard.

Rising in the Alps, the river Po winds its way eastward across the plains of northern Italy to lose itself in the Adriatic. Near Piacenza, it is joined from the south by a tributary, the Trebbia. The surrounding country is flat and dull, crossed by the main Bologna-Milan trunk road which, after passing through Piacenza, is carried across the Trebbia on an ugly iron bridge.

On the western end of this bridge a stone column, erected by order of the Emperor Francis the First, Archduke of Austria, bears Hannibal's name and the date of his battle beside the river. There is nothing else to strike the imagination or recall that first great victory for Carthaginian arms. The river, when I saw it in June, was a shallow stream wandering idly through an ocean of pebbles; but in winter it is a *"torrente,"* fast-running and extremely difficult to cross. On either side land is low but hummocky, and still crisscrossed with ditches and banks like those from which Mago sprang his devastating ambuscade. But that is to anticipate the story.

It is winter, the kind of northern Italian winter which troops who fought there in the Second Word War will remember well. Throughout the gray November days violent snowstorms soak the plain, swelling the Trebbia and other tributaries into violent torrents, turning the banks into acres of thick, squelching mud, which clings to the feet of the marching men. The Carthaginians, crouched in their tents, shiver in the cold; the legionaries of Tiberius Sempronius on their forced march along the road from Ariminium, curse the weather, and Hannibal.

The Carthaginian leader, knowing that Scipio is near at

hand, withdraws his troops from camp and marches downstream along the left (*i.e.*, north) bank of the Po, with the river on his right. Scipio, advancing upstream from the east, also along the left bank of the river, is eager to meet his enemy, but when the armies do meet, probably by accident, the Romans are at a disadvantage. The fast, light-armed Numidians, with their formidable javelins, are able to fall on the flanks and rear of the enemy, following their own method of fighting, which is to rush in, deliver their attack, retreat out of range, then return at the gallop to attack from yet another quarter. The Romans, engaged with Hannibal's heavy cavalry in their front, are helpless against this form of warfare, and, despite Scipio's personal bravery, are soon in rout. Scipio himself is severely wounded in the action and, according to one report, was saved from death by the bravery of his young son, also called Publius Cornelius. This boy is later to become the great Scipio Africanus.

Realizing that in such open country his army is at the mercy of the Carthaginians, the Roman general crosses the Ticinus (a northern tributary of the Po) destroys the bridge, and then passes over to the south bank of the Po and takes refuge under the walls of Placentia. Hannibal, hindered by the broken bridge, turns about and, retracing his steps along the left bank of the Po, crosses it higher up and then swings eastward again towards Placentia. He camps about six miles away.

So ends the first heavy skirmish which is sometimes dignified with the name "Battle of Ticinus." However, the bulk of the Roman army is still intact, and Scipio, who has narrowly escaped death in his first action with Hannibal, anxiously waits for the arrival of Sempronius. When the other Consul arrives he finds that Scipio has withdrawn from Placentia and occupied positions six miles away where the Trebbia issues from the hills to the southwest. It seems strange that Sempronius was able to make contact with the other Roman army without interference from the invaders. This may have been due to a combination of bad weather and bad intelligence, or is it possible that Hannibal was so confident of victory that he preferred to fight the combined armies, knowing that the moral effect of a victory would be all the greater? Whatever the reason, the two Roman forces joined, and Hannibal was faced with an enemy totaling more than 40,000 men, mainly heavy infantry, though with cavalry support. His own army, now supplemented by the Gauls, probably amounted to about the same number.

Polybius and Livy put into the mouths of the rival commanders the usual "eve-of-battle" orations which were the accepted convention of the time. Scipio, after recalling the fact that the Carthaginians were a defeated people who had dared to revolt, described their army as little better than slaves. He also pointed out, with truth, that the enemy was fighting far from his native land, and that after crossing the Alps he was so weakened by hardship and disease that he would be no match for a resolute Roman army fighting in defense of its own land. Hannibal's method, if we are to accept Polybius's account of it, reveals an almost diabolical understanding of primitive human psychology. According to the Greek writer,[1] Hannibal had brought with him, as prisoners, a number of young Gauls who had been captured while molesting his army during its march through the Alps. They had, we are told, been deliberately ill used.

Assembling his troops in a circle, he had the Gauls brought in and exhibited to the soldiers. Their fetters were struck off, and into the ring were thrown a number of suits of armor, "such as the Gaulish kings are wont to wear when engaged in single combat." Besides these Hannibal caused to be brought in a number of fine horses and rich military cloaks. According to Polybius, he then put to his prisoners the following question, "What would you rather do, remain in your present wretched state, or take up these arms and armour, and fight

[1] Livy tells a similar story.

with one another in single combat, the winner receiving as prizes the cloaks and horses, the losers being released by death from their present miseries?" As one man the Gauls begged to be allowed to fight. Hannibal then told them to draw lots. The two on whom the lot fell were to arm themselves and do combat.

> The young men, the moment they heard this, lifted up their hands and prayed to the gods, each eager to be himself one of the chosen. When the result was announced, those on whom the lot had fallen were overjoyed and the rest mournful and dejected, and after the combat the remaining prisoners congratulated the fallen champion no less than the victor, as having been set free from many and grievous evils which they were left alive to suffer.

When this grim charade was over, Hannibal dismissed the remaining prisoners and addressed his watching troops.

> "Fortune," he said, "has brought you to a like pass. She has shut you in on a like listed field of combat, and the prizes and prospects are the same. For either you must conquer, or die, or fall alive into the hands of your foes. For you the prize of victory is not to possess horses and cloaks, but to be the most envied of mankind, masters of all the wealth of Rome."

He then rammed home the lesson, first warning them of the fate which would overtake any who sought to escape death by flight. Polybius continues:

> "Think of the length of the road you have travelled," he told them. "Think of the enemies that lie between you and your native lands, and the size of the rivers you have had to cross. What hope has any one of you to escape by running away? You thought both the victor and the vanquished fortunate by comparison with those who were not allowed to fight. You are in exactly the same situation. Go into battle determined to conquer if you can, and if you cannot, then die fighting. I

implore you not to let the thought of living after defeat enter your minds at all."

This story, if it is true, provides one explanation for the fact that Hannibal's multiracial army fought bravely for him and never murmured against his authority. It is not the only explanation, of course, but Hannibal clearly understood the psychology of fear as well as more humane methods of persuasion. He was not a naturally cruel man, but on this occasion, the eve of his first battle on Italian soil, he may have decided that a grim object lesson was justified in order to stiffen the morale of his troops. With the lives of thousands at stake in the coming battle, those of a few Gaulish prisoners would hardly trouble his conscience.

12

THE BATTLE OF TREBBIA

HANNIBAL'S next object lesson was in military strategy and his pupils were the Romans. It was a hard lesson which took a long time to sink in. Field-Marshal Montgomery has stated that one of the most important factors in winning battles is to know your enemy. He went so far as to have photographs of his principal German opponent pinned up on the wall of his battle headquarters. The same principle was clearly understood by Hannibal, as we can see from his actions following the preliminary skirmish on the Ticinus. He knew that Scipio was badly wounded, and that for this reason the other Consul would probably have taken over command of the joint army. He knew that the mind directing the Roman forces would not be the cautious Scipio but the impatient and impetuous Sempronius, and made his plans accordingly.

That was the first consideration; the second was the relative condition of the two armies. Hannibal's men, though somewhat recovered from their alpine ordeal, were still not in the best physical condition, and coming from sunnier lands were unaccustomed to fighting in the bitter cold of a north

Italian winter. The problem was somehow to redress the balance by putting the Romans at a temporary but fatal disadvantage. Hannibal, conferring in his tent with his brother officers, outlined a plan which might make this possible.

He had noticed, says Polybius, "a place between the two camps, flat indeed and treeless, but well adapted for an ambuscade, as it was traversed by a water-course with steep banks densely overgrown with brambles and other thorny plants, and here he proposed to lay a stratagem to surprise the enemy." Summoning his brother Mago, who though still quite young, was "full of martial enthusiasm and trained from boyhood in the art of war," he outlined his scheme. Mago was to take 2,000 of the fittest and bravest troops, an equal number of horse and foot, and, stealing out under cover of night, occupy the water-course, making certain that they were completely hidden.

It might seem impractical to hide horsemen in such a shallow declivity, but here Polybius, warming to his subject with the relish of a former general, explains how it could have been achieved:

> Any kind of water-course with a slight bank and reeds or bracken or some kind of thorny plants can be made use of to conceal not only infantry, but even the dismounted horsemen at times, if a little care is taken to lay shields with conspicuous devices upside down (to conceal the prominent markings) and hide the helmets under them.

The horses would, of course, have been trained to lie prone and still at command.

Hannibal's next task was to lure the Romans out of their camp and draw them into a position from which Mago's hidden force could strike at the vital moment. Perfect timing was essential for this operation. Let us try to see it as Mago viewed it at dawn the following day. Crouched in the shallow ditch, their horses lying prone beside them and their weapons and helmets hidden, the young officer and his men look out across the sodden plain towards the swollen Trebbia. It is probably Mago's first important command, and in the excitement of that moment he hardly notices the cold and stiffness in his young bones. Suddenly there is a wild shouting and cheering from the direction of the Carthaginian camp, mingled with the sound of hoofs. Across the plain come several thousands of Hannibal's Numidians, moving at a fast pace towards the Roman camp. They clatter past the ambuscade, splash through the river and are soon lost in a flurry of mud. In the Roman camp the legionaries and their allies are hardly roused from sleep when there are cries from the sentries on the outworks and trumpets sounding the alarm.

The wounded Scipio limps to the door of his tent, and with Sempronius, watches the furious charge of the Numidians as they leap in among the forward defenses of the camp, flinging their darts, then wheeling in complex and bewildering maneuvers returning again and again, seemingly from all directions at once. The camp is in a turmoil; the centurions bark their orders through the mist, and the soldiers, still half asleep, shuffle and stumble into line. Darts and spears fall thickly among them and many fall. So do many of the Numidians as the Romans fight back. The African horsemen, relatively few in number, know that they have been sent on a desperate mission. Hannibal still waiting with his main army at his camp several miles away, has sent them with orders to skirmish up closely to the Romans, and if possible, draw them out into battle. Scipio, suspecting this, urges his colleague to be cautious. This, he says, is not Hannibal's main army. The Romans, cold, wet, and hungry after a soaking night, are not yet ready for battle. They have not breakfasted and if they march out now will have to cross the river and fight the Carthaginians on empty bellies.

But Sempronius will not listen. To wait any longer may be dangerous, he argues, for what if Hannibal's army has already left camp and is following close on the heels of the Numidians? Now, and not later, is the time to strike. He gives the orders and the army marches out of camp breakfastless, cold, and still harried by the hard-riding Numidians whose sting is like that of the picadors goading a bull. But seeing that the Romans are on the move, the horsemen gradually retreat, being careful to lead the enemy towards the spot Hannibal has selected as the place of battle. When the survivors, many wounded, ride back into camp they are able to tell their commander that their mission has been accomplished. He congratulates them and promises rich rewards.

Meanwhile, in the Carthaginian camp, the soldiers have eaten well and are now crouched around their fires, oiling their bodies as a protection against the cold and sleet. Hannibal is confident and unhurried as he gives Maharbal and Gisgo their final orders for the line of battle. Having taken the initiative and allowed himself ample time for preparation, he can now arrange his battle array on ground of his own choosing. The Romans, ill prepared, have accepted his challenge, as he guessed they would, but it will be Hannibal and not Sempronius who will dictate the place of combat: and that place is on the Carthaginian side of the Trebbia. The Romans, having first waded through the swollen current, will fight with their backs to Mago's hidden 2,000.

That young man watches from his hiding place in excited admiration as he sees his brother's plans fulfilled to the letter. He sees the Romans struggling breast-high through the fast-flowing river. Soaked and weary, they clamber up the bank, and under the barked orders of their officers, take up their positions in conventional order of battle, one of the standard textbook patterns which are all that their general knows. In the center is the infantry, numbering 16,000 Romans and 20,-000 of their allies. On each wing is the cavalry, about 4,000 in all. Thus, in the usual Roman order, Sempronius's troops advance across the sodden ground, "in imposing style" writes Polybius ". . . marching in slow step."

Facing them, the Carthaginians are strung out along a wide front, with 20,000 Spaniards, Celts, and Africans in a single line, flanked by more than 10,000 cavalry divided between each wing. In front of the heavy infantry are light-armed skirmishers, including slingers. The elephants, also divided into two formations, are stationed in advance of each cavalry wing, thus giving additional protection to the Carthaginian flanks.

Snow is falling as the two armies close. First the light-armed troops in the forefront of each army join combat, but the Roman spearmen, having marched from daybreak without food, are hard pressed by the Carthaginians, who are fresh and well fed. Moreover these spearmen are short of missiles, having already thrown most of them at the Numidians when they attacked the Roman camp. Soon the skirmishers retire through gaps in the Roman line left for the purpose, and their place is taken by the *hastati* and *principes* (heavy-armed infantry). As soon as this happens the Carthaginian heavy cavalry led by the elephants, charge into the Roman horsemen whom they greatly outnumber, besides having superiority in freshness and vigor. Gradually, remorselessly, the Roman cavalry wings are pushed farther and farther back, leaving their infantry, whom they were intended to protect, more and more exposed on either flank.

The legionaries, though newly recruited and only partially trained, fight with their usual stubborn courage, and at first hold their own with the enemy's foot soldier. For a long time the two lines of men fight desperately, hand to hand and foot to foot, struggling and sliding over the slippery, blood-soaked ground, while a gray curtain of sleet falls indifferently on friend and foe. Hannibal and his officers are fighting hand to hand with the rest, sometimes riding along the ranks to shout encouragement, sometimes plunging into a mêlée of struggling men to bring relief at a threatened point.

Mago, still hidden and unmoving, sees the Carthaginian heavy horsemen, who have driven back the Roman cavalry wings, wheel in on each side and attack the struggling Roman infantry on the flank. At the same time Carthaginian pikemen and Numidians, in a compact mass, dash past their own troops and fall savagely on the Romans on their unprotected sides, hindering them from dealing with the enemy foot soldiers who face them. Mago, remembering his brother's instructions, decides that the critical moment has come. Rising to his feet he shouts an order to the Numidians crouched in the ambuscade. From the ditch two thousand men struggle to their feet, and a thousand horses. Their riders, grasping weapons and shields, leap on their backs and rapidly make formation. A second order, and Mago is galloping ahead of a great crescent of charging, shouting warriors which slashes like a giant sickle into the backs of the hard-pressed Roman infantry.

It is the last feather in the scale which swings the balance. It is the moment when the wrestler, who has matched hold for hold, strain for strain, suddenly feels his muscles begin to crack and knows he is beaten; or when the boxer, who has traded blow for blow, throughout nine long rounds, reels under the final punch which brings him to his knees. The Roman line wavers and begins to break. Hunger grips the belly; exhaustion overwhelms the spirit. The sword arm can no longer thrust, nor the shield arm parry the blow. What had been a line of resolute fighting men, with courage and determination in their hearts, becomes a mob of fugitives whose only remaining strength is in their legs. Pursued by the triumphing Carthaginians they run blindly back to the Trebbia. Thousands are cut down, and many more are drowned in attempting to cross to safety.

Many of the Romans, however, do not lose their fighting formations. The vanguard of their center, forced to advance by pressure from the rear, actually defeats the Celts and Africans opposed to them, and breaks through the Carthaginian line. But seeing that both flanks had been driven from the field, and despairing of giving help, these men retire in good order to Placentia. The remainder of the infantry are killed by Hannibal's elephants and cavalry, though most of the cavalry get away and join the other fugitives in Placentia.

The Roman army, though not entirely destroyed, had been rendered temporarily impotent as a fighting force. The road to the south was now open, since Sempronius was incapable of preventing Hannibal from doing whatever he wished to do. What Scipio said to Sempronius at the end of that terrible day is not recorded, but one can imagine it. However, one must not be too hard on Tiberius Sempronius. He was a brave and resolute man and he had fought well, within the limits of his knowledge and capabilities. What neither he nor any Roman knew, or could have known until that day, was that they were faced with a military genius such as the world had not seen since the days of Alexander the Great.

13

THE BAIT

ONE of Hannibal's main problems at this stage was to secure the continued support of the Gauls. The tribes living along the Po basin had helped him, and some had fought beside him on the Trebbia, but his army was living off their land, consuming their food, imposing a great strain on their primitive agricultural economy. It was essential to remove that strain as soon as possible by transferring it elsewhere, to regions of Italy where other tribes might help feed his thousands in return for assistance in throwing off the yoke of the Romans. Unless he could break up the confederation of Italian States which were linked to Rome, and bring some, at least, of her allies over to his side, he could not hope to achieve his ultimate ambition, which was to destroy the power of Rome forever.

Although it was now winter, he decided on an attempt to cross the Apennines, hoping to bring the Etruscans over to his side, "either by force or favour," as Livy remarks.

But, defeated by the winter storms, he struggled back to the Po basin where his Gaulish hosts had to sustain his hungry thousands until the early spring of 217 B.C., when campaigning again became possible. He had lost all his elephants except one. Meanwhile the Romans, shocked and dismayed by Sempronius's defeat (which at first he tried to conceal), immediately made plans to counter the new threat from the north. Sempronius returned to Rome and the people resolved to elect as Consul a man who had already distinguished himself by brilliant victories in Cisalpine Gaul. His name was Flaminius, and he was elected Consul for the second time. With him they elected as the second Consul, a member of an old patrician family named Cornelius Servilius Geminus.

It is important to note that Sempronius was not dismissed and dishonored on account of his defeat. It just happened that the time had come for the annual election of the Consuls, and it is possible that he would not have been re-elected even if there had been no Trebbia. Servilius replaced Scipio and took command of his army, while Flaminius after his election was appointed to command what remained of Sempronius's forces. As both armies were thinned out by the defeat of Trebbia, four new legions were levied, containing an unusually large proportion of soldiers from the Italian allies. These new forces together with the remains of the former army, were divided equally between the two consuls and were placed near the line along which it was expected that Hannibal would advance in the spring.

We do not know by which route he crossed the Apennines. The easiest way would have been through the valley of the Magra, along which the modern road runs from Parma to La Spezia, from which he could have moved along the coast, crossing the Arno at Pisa, or further inland at Lucca, and so breaking through into the plains of Etruria (modern Tuscany). But Pisa was probably garrisoned and he would wish to avoid contact with any point from which his position and route could be reported to the Romans. The two Consuls waited, one at Ariminium on the Adriatic coast, guarding the eastern route, the other at Arretium on the western flank of the Apennines, overlooking the Val de Chiana and the Tuscan plain.

Hannibal preferred a straighter, though much more difficult line, probably down the valley of the Serchio for a while, and then, instead of descending on Lucca, swinging eastward over the mountains and descending on the valley of the Arno a little to the south of Florence. The Romans did not expect him to take this route, as it involved crossing the marshes which then lay on each side of the lower Arno.

Crossing the Apennines, even in summer and in a car, is not an easy journey. From Parma to La Spezia, a distance of some thirty-five miles, the road switchbacks over range after range of mountains, climbing, descending, climbing again, through endless forests of pines. On the lower slopes there are ranks of spearlike cypresses and olive trees in great numbers—a shimmering silver-gray haze veiling the landscape. There are also many vines, and in many places corn stooks stand in golden ranks in the spaces between the trunks of the olive trees. Often one passes creaking carts hauled by teams of white, large-eyed oxen, descendants of those which were sacrificed on Roman altars, or slaughtered by Hannibal in hundreds to feed his troops. Regardless of the stink and scurry of modern mechanized traffic, they plod patiently along the dusty roads, with their drivers sitting high on a pile of green fodder smoking pipes and waving a greeting.

If anyone asks how Hannibal fed his army, he has only to make a journey through Umbria and Tuscany today; no doubt the land is much more intensely cultivated than it was in Hannibal's time—though Botticelli's paintings of five centuries ago reveal an almost identical landscape. But the four essentials of that landscape—corn, the vine, olive trees, and cattle—are still as they were two thousand years ago.

However, the valley of the lower Arno is not the same.

Nowadays, drained and cultivated, it is as civilized as the rest of the landscape, but when Hannibal led his men down into the valley in the spring of 217 B.C., they floundered up to their waists in a fetid morass of water, mud, and slime. Nor was it, according to Livy, a short crossing, but took four days and nights.

The vanguard still followed the standards wherever the guides would lead them, through the exceeding deep and almost fathomless eddies of the river nearly swallowed up in mud, and plunging themselves in.

The Gauls, unused to enduring hardship and fatigue, suffered most.

They . . . could neither support themselves when fallen, nor raise themselves from the eddies . . . when, the water covering every place, not a dry spot could be found where they might stretch their weary bodies, they laid themselves down upon their baggage, thrown in heaps into the waters.

Hannibal, riding on the one remaining elephant to be higher out of the water, contracted an eye disease—probably opthalmia, from the unwholesome air of the marshes, and the transition from heat to the nocturnal damp. Having no time or opportunity to apply remedies, he eventually lost the sight of one eye.

At the beginning of the fifth day the army reached dry ground again, leaving behind many dead men, horses, and cattle. Camping for a time to rest his army, Hannibal sent out scouts who brought back the information that Flaminius was at Arretium. He next made his usual diligent inquiries, and from the reports of his spies was able to learn about the roads, the political situation in the country through which he was to march, the available sources of supplies and, most important, the character and temperament of the Consul. Flaminius, he learned, was a man of proud disposition, arrogant and overbearing with a confidence born of the victories he had won over the Gauls during his former consulship (this was his second term of office). Polybius calls him "a mob courtier and demagogue," and says he was also highly irritable and, when angered, "more likely to fall into the errors natural to him." Hannibal decided to irritate him.

Livy describes the country through which the Carthaginians now advanced as "among the most fertile in Italy, the plains of Etruria, between Faesulae and Arretium, abundant in its supply of corn, cattle, and every other requisite." This description is true in every respect today. From modern Fiesole, on its hilltop above the towers and domes of Florence, the road winds through mildly undulating country which repeats, for mile after mile, the same monotonous pattern of vineyards, cornfields, and olive groves. This land, now named Tuscany, was the former kingdom of Etruria, whence came the ancient Etruscans who ruled the land before the Romans.

Gradually the country becomes more hilly but is never mountainous; there are frequent stretches of wide level plain of which every square yard is cultivated. The main Apennine range lies well away to the east, but on the foothills near the modern road the ancient walled hill towns, Arezzo and Cortona, originally Etruscan, later Roman, still occupy their ancient sites.

Arezzo, a walled city with modern suburbs, stands near the edge of a broad river valley, crossed by two bridges, one ancient and broken, the other modern and carrying the main road. In a nearby war cemetery ranks of white crosses mark the graves of thousands of British and Commonwealth troops who died fighting near Arezzo in the Second World War.

Arezzo was ancient Arretium, where Flaminius and his large army waited to intercept the Carthaginians. To the Consul's surprise and annoyance, Hannibal did not pause to offer battle though he was well aware of the enemy's strength and intentions, but swept past the city, leaving Cortona high on its hill to the left, and moved on towards the central plains of Italy. Nor did he appear to be in any hurry. Frequently the helpless occupants of the hill towns saw the Carthaginians foraging far out across the plain, driving off the fat white cattle, looting all they needed, then burning and destroying what was left. Locustlike, they alighted on the rich plains of Etruria, and when they moved on, left a swathe of scorched earth behind.

All this, of course, was a deliberate act of policy intended to inflame Flaminius. Hannibal was not yet plundering Roman territory, which in some ways would have been a lesser evil, since men fight all the better in defense of their homeland. But he was attacking one of Rome's allies, and if the dominant power did not soon show itself capable of protecting its friends they might decide to break the tenuous alliance and throw in their lot with the invader.

Every day the smoke of burning villages plumed up from the plain. Every day came fresh reports of devastation, and waves of fugitives hammering at the gates of Arretium and demanding redress. Flaminius may have been moved by pity, but one suspects that his dominant emotion was outraged pride, and a determination to assert his authority. Like the unfortunate Sempronius, he lacked both common sense and self-control. What he should have done, and what his advisers urged him to do, was to send out auxiliary forces, such as light cavalry, and harry the plunderers, while reserving his main force until the other Consul, Servilius, arrived with his army from Ariminium.

It was impossible to argue with him. "Though every other person in the council advised safe rather than showy measures," writes Livy, "urging that he should wait for his colleague, in order that, joining their armies, they might carry on the war with united courage and counsels . . . Flaminius, in a fury, hurried out of the council and at once gave out the signal for marching and for battle."

Next day, when a fast-riding scout overtook Hannibal and

told him that Flaminius was on the move with his full force, the young Carthaginian, after inquiring concerning the distance separating the two armies, smiled and unhurriedly continued his march. He had set the bait. Now he would spring the trap.

14

THE TRAP

BEYOND Arezzo our road swept down to the northern shore of the Lago Castiglione, also called Lake Trasimene, the name by which the Romans knew it. It is an enormous expanse of blue water, more like an inland sea than a lake; so huge, in fact, that on a heat-hazy day one can scarcely see the opposite shore. Fishermen in long, flat boats still throw their nets, as no doubt they did in Hannibal's time. From the hills above Passignano one can see rocky capes thrusting out into the misty blue water which shades into mauve as it nears the mud flats along the shore. On each cape is outlined a fortified town with tall towers, and on the rocky spurs inland are other hill towns, originally Etruscan, later Roman.

Passignano, a tiny lakeside village, lies on the road which skirts the northern shore of Lake Trasimene and connects Cortona with Magione and Perugia. It is Hannibal's road—the road to Rome—and whatever arguments there may be concerning other parts of his route, there is no doubt at all that the Carthaginians came this way. In the little *ristorantes*, in the shade of hanging vines, Chianti bottles glow red on the white tablecloths and in the soporific heat of June one is lulled by the mellifluous murmur of Italian voices, while the lake shimmers in the heat and the distant town of Castiglione hangs like a mirage above the water.

A little to the south of the village the road and the railway squeeze into a narrow area, with cliffs on one side and the lake on the other. Beyond this the country broadens out, and the modern road climbs along the eastern side of a U-shaped cup in the hills, to the town of Magione, beyond which it begins to descend again. There is another, secondary road, which can be seen from the modern highway, following the valley bottom, and this seems to me most likely to have been the track of the ancient road.

Though there are some puzzling discrepancies, this place answers very closely to the description given by Polybius.

> The road led through a narrow strip of level ground with a range of high hills on each side of it lengthwise. This defile [1] was overlooked in front crosswise by a steep hill difficult to climb, and behind it lay the lake, between which and the hillside the passage giving access to the defile was quite narrow. Hannibal, coasting the lake and passing through the defile occupied himself the hill in front, encamping on it with his Spaniards and Africans; his slingers and pikemen he brought round to the front by a detour and stationed them in an extended line under the hills to the right of the defile, and similarly taking his cavalry and the Celts round the hills on the left, he placed them in a continuous line under these hills, so that the last of them were just at the entrance to the defile, lying between the hillside and the lake.

Livy's account of the topography of the battlefield is a little clearer. He says:

> The place, was formed by nature for an ambuscade, where the

---

[1] Actually "defile" is not an accurate description. There is indeed a narrow passage between the mountains and the lake, already described, but the place where Hannibal sprung his trap must have been the valley into which this passage led, and which has the lake behind and the hills in front and on each side. L.C.

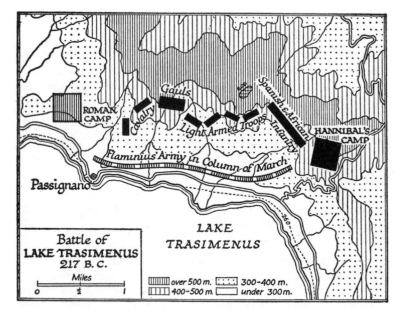

Battle of
LAKE TRASIMENUS
217 B.C.
Miles
0   ½   1

||||||| over 500 m. [:::::] 300-400 m.
|||||| 400-500 m. [   ] under 300 m.

Trasimenus comes nearest to the mountains of Cortona. A very
narrow passage only intervenes, as though room enough just for
that purpose had been left designedly; after that a somewhat
wider plain opens itself, and then some hills rise up.

Flaminius, at the head of his legions and auxiliary soldiers,
marched out of Arretium and set off along the road to Lake
Trasimene. Arriving at Passignano, near the entrance to the
narrow passage leading to the "defile," he camped for the
night but did not take the precaution of sending scouting
parties in front to reconnoiter. He was evidently convinced
that he would catch Hannibal in column of route, and at dawn
next day he safely passed through the narrow corridor between cliffs and sea, and the valley opened before him. Or it
would have, had he been able to see it.

Anyone who visits Passignano in summer, after reading Polybius's account of Hannibal's ambuscade, will probably be

as puzzled as I was. Where were all these troops hidden, the "slingers and pikemen . . . brought round to the front by a detour and stationed . . . in an extended line under the hills to the right"; and the "cavalry and the Celts" who were placed "in a continuous line" under hills to the left? Some, perhaps, could have been concealed, but not 30,000 men.

The answer lies in Polybius's line, "it was an unusually misty morning," and in Livy's words, "a mist . . . rising from the lake," but the word "unusually" suggests that the presence of the mist was a lucky accident which helped the Carthaginians. I do not believe this. I do not believe that Hannibal would ever have attempted to lay an ambuscade in the shallow, fairly open valley between Passignano and Magione unless he had *known* with a reasonable degree of certainty that there would be mist. He had evidently studied the lake as carefully as he studied everything else. He must have observed the frequency of morning mist at the time of year when he came to Lake Trasimene, and decided to make use of it.

A slight gamble was involved, of course, but Hannibal was a lucky gambler, and on this, as on so many other occasions, his luck held. When the Roman army emerged from the corridor and began to climb towards the hills they could see very little on their flanks, but ahead, where the road climbed above the mist-curtain towards the hills, they could see a considerable distance. And what they saw delighted Flaminius. It was, to all appearances, the rear guard of Hannibal's army moving away from them over the crest of the hills. Urged on by their commander, the legions pressed on up the slope. Hidden on that hill, unseen and unseeing, the Carthaginians must have heard their enemies through the fog: the heavy tramp of the legionaries, the shouts of the officers, and the clatter and whinnying of horses. But they themselves remained still and silent.

Now the forward ranks of the Romans are closing at the top of the rise with the Carthaginians, who turn and fight.

Here, near the top of the valley, there is more space to deploy, and soon 6,000 Romans are in hand-to-hand combat with Hannibal's Spaniards and Africans, whom they believe to be the rear guard of Hannibal's main force. The fight is bitter, but gradually the Carthaginians retreat, drawing after them the Roman vanguard, whose cheers are borne back to their comrades, still struggling up in a narrow column through the mist of the lower valley.

High above them, hidden in the mist, Hannibal gives a signal. A trumpet blast echoes from the heights. Another answers it, then a third. The Romans in the valley bottom, strung for miles in a long vulnerable column, look up in alarm. From above and all around them, comes a sound so terrifying that even the veteran troops stand frozen by fear; it is the massed war cry of some 30,000 men, Africans, Spaniards, and Gauls, as they rush down the slopes from every side. Before the Romans can grip the sword or raise the shield, the huge naked forms of the Gauls emerge from the mist, their broadswords swinging and slashing; from another direction the Spanish infantry, in their white and crimson tunics, thrust their spears into the unprotected sides of the legionaries who fall, groaning and vomiting blood. From yet another direction a shower of javelins brings men and beasts crashing to the ground, and the next moment the terrible Numidian horsemen, who ride without bridle or saddle, are in among the disordered column, howling for the kill.

Blinded by the mist, caught in column of route, surprised and outmaneuvered, the Roman soldiers still fight bravely. Again and again they charge their enemies while their officers, shouting above the tumult, try to organize them into the positions in which they are accustomed to fight. But to no avail; hemmed in on every side by the mountains, the lake, and the enemy, there is no hope of safety but in the right hand and the sword. There is no regular line, with *principes, hastati,* and *triarii.* [2] Men no longer fight in their own cohorts or companies.

> Chance collected them into bands; and each man's own will assigned to him his post; whether to fight in front or rear; and so great was the ardour of the conflict, so intent were their minds upon the battle, that not one of the combatants felt an earthquake which threw down large portions of many of the cities of Italy.

Caught in the trap, surrounded by the carnage which his own pride and rashness had helped to bring about, Flaminius fights beside his men with a courage which goes far to redeem his folly. Wherever the Consul sees his soldiers hard pressed and distressed, he is among them, but his splendid armor makes him an easy target. Again and again he is singled out for attack, his bodyguard defending him with their lives. Eventually a Gaul named Ducarius, recognizing him, calls out to his fellow countrymen, "See! This is the Consul who slew our army and laid our country waste"—recalling the time when Flaminius, during his former consulship, had devastated Cisalpine Gaul.

> Putting spurs to his horse, he rushed through a very dense body of the enemy; and first slaying his armour-bearer, ran the Consul through with his lance.

The body of Flaminius rolls from the saddle and falls sprawling among the dead and dying. It was never found, though Hannibal, wishing to give his enemy honorable burial, searched hard for it. The bones of the Consul may still lie somewhere beneath the olive groves above Passignano.

It is now three hours after dawn. The Roman vanguard of 6,000 men, unaware of what has happened in their rear, have given up the pursuit of what they thought was the Carthaginian

[2] The regular fighting formations of the Roman infantry.

rear guard. The enemy has fled into the hills, but there is no sight of his main army, which they had hoped to overtake. Bewildered, they re-form their ranks, and, marching back to the crest of the ridge, look down into the valley from which they have come. The sun has melted the last traces of the morning mist. The lake glitters in the calm morning light which reveals every detail of the scene below. Scattered along the valley bottom lie the bloody corpses of some 15,000 of their comrades, among which the Carthaginians move, stripping them of arms and armor. Along the muddy shores of the lake enemy horsemen are hewing down the last remnants of the Roman infantry which have tried desperately to escape by wading into the water. But weighed down by their armor, they cannot swim, and have to struggle back to the shore, where the Numidians are waiting for them.

The Roman vanguard no longer has any doubt as to where Hannibal's main army is. After losing only 1,500 men—one Carthaginian for every ten Romans—it is now re-forming to continue the march.

15

"THE DELAYER"

I T is impossible to overestimate the effects of this catastrophe
on the people of Rome. For many years they had been mili-
tarily irresistible, and their hold over their allies rested partly
on this fact. Now, in two great battles (three, if one counts
Ticinus), they had been decisively defeated with appalling
losses. How much longer could the alliance hold out? And
now that Hannibal had smashed his way through Etruria, could
anything stop him from attacking Rome itself? His present
force alone might still be defeated, but what if some of the
allies defected to his side, and joined in the attack?

According to Polybius:

> On the news of the defeat reaching Rome the chiefs of the state
> were unable to conceal or soften down the facts, owing to the
> magnitude of the calamity, and were obliged to summon a
> meeting of the commons and announce it. When the Praetor
> therefore from the Rostra said, "We have been defeated in a
> great battle", it produced such consternation that to those who
> were present on both occasions the disaster seemed much
> greater now than during the actual battle.

And Livy says:

> The matrons, wandering through the streets, ask all they meet, what sudden disaster was reported? What was the fate of the army? ... During the next and several successive days, a greater number of women almost than men stood at the gates, waiting either for one of their friends, or for intelligence of them, surrounding and earnestly interrogating those they met; nor could they be torn away from those they knew especially, until they had regularly enquired into every thing. .... The joy and grief of the women was especially manifested. They report that one, suddenly meeting her son, who had returned safe, expired at the very door before his face—that another, who sat grieving at her house at the falsely reported death of her son, became a corpse, from excessive joy, at the first sight of him on his return.

Hannibal, marching south with his triumphant army, must often have regretted that his great father, Hamilcar, was not alive to enjoy his revenge. But the Carthaginian's hatred, far from being slaked, burned more strongly than ever. When his forces had rounded up and captured the enemy which had escaped him at Trasimene, he immediately dismissed the Roman allies to their homes, repeating that he had come to re-establish the liberty of the Italian peoples, and restore to them the lands which the Romans had stolen from them. He kept the Roman prisoners in chains, giving them just sufficient food to keep them alive.

Meanwhile, the Romans were carrying on the war in Spain. Gnaeus Cornelius Scipio, brother of the Scipio who was wounded at Ticinus, landed at Emporion (Ampurias) and at other places along the Spanish coast, reducing by siege all the coastal towns as far as the river Ebro, then advanced into the interior. After winning over, or subduing a number of the inland cities, he was confronted by Hannibal's brother, Hanno, who had been left to guard Spain. At a place called Cissa,

Cartagena (New Carthage) from which Hannibal began his march.

The Ancient Greek city of Ampurias on the coast of Catalonia.

The Roman Theater at Vaison-la-Romaine.

View of "Les Barronies" from the Castle. These mountains formed the eastern limit of "The Island."

Maillane, Provence, where the skeleton of an elephant was discovered in 1777.

The Junction of the Rhône and Drôme where Hannibal probably turned east towards Italy.

Approach to the Col de Grimone.

The upper valley of the Durance — "easy marching country."

The Gorge de Guil, possibly the site of the second Gaulish ambush.

The Castle of Chateauqueyras, possibly built on the "bare rock" where Hannibal camped.

A thousand-ton boulder, dislodged by a landslide; the type of obstacle which Hannibal broke up with fire and vinegar. For scale note figure in foreground.

Flooding had destroyed the road to the Col de la Traversette.

MARIA . LVDOVICA
IMP. FRANCISCI . I . CAES. FILIA
ARCHIDVX . AVSTRIAE
DVX . PARM . PLAC . VAST .
. TREBIAE
CVM . HANNIBAL . AN . V . C . DXXXV.
LICHTENSTEINVS . AN . CHR . MDCCXXXXVI.
SVVOROFIVS . ET . MELAS . AN . CHR . MDCCXCIX.
BELLO . VICTORES
ILLVSTRABVNT
PRINCEPS . BENEFICENTISSIMA
FACTA . PONTIS . COMMODITATE
GLORIAM . FELICIOREM
ADIVNXIT
ANNO . MDCCCXX

The stone column at Trebbia commemorating Hannibal's first victory in Italy.

Lake Trasimene, where fifteen thousand Roman soldiers were trapped and killed by the Carthaginians.

The White Oxen of Tuscany which helped to feed Hannibal's army.

Terra-cotta figure of a Roman war-elephant found at Pompeii (first century A.D.). After the Hannibalic War the Romans also used these animals.

An aerial view of the hill of Cannae near which the battle was fought.

Air Ministry, Rome

A typical hill village in Campania, where much fighting took place.

Barnabys Picture Library

Calabria
in which
Hannibal
campaigned.

The harbor of ancient Tarentum, which Hannibal captured with the aid of a "fifth column."

Medieval fortifications.

Roman aqueduct.

A street in old Carthage.

An eighteenth-century artist's impression
of Scipio receiving the keys of Carthage.

Gnaeus defeated the Carthaginians in a pitched battle, capturing much valuable booty, including all the heavy baggage which Hannibal had left behind when he departed for Italy. Hanno himself was taken prisoner, and the Iberian tribes north of the Ebro deserted to the Romans. Hasdrubal, the Carthaginian commander, Hannibal's other brother, advanced from New Carthage with about eight thousand infantry and a thousand cavalry. Hearing that the Roman fleet which had tranported Gnaeus and his army to Spain was off its guard, he sprang a surprise attack on the crews who were enjoying themselves on shore, killed a large number and compelled the rest to take to their ships. Then he retreated, recrossing the Ebro, and, after first fortifying and garrisoning the Iberian towns south of that river, retired to New Carthage. No doubt Hannibal far away in Italy, eventually heard this news.

Back to Italy; Servilius, who is waiting at Ariminium, on the Adriatic coast, hears that Hannibal has invaded Etruria, but, unaware of the disaster at Trasimene, sends his second-in-command, Gaius Centenius, in advance with four thousand horse. Hannibal, hearing of this *via* his private "bush telegraph," sends Maharbal with a small force of pikemen and cavalry to intercept the Roman reinforcements. Half the Roman force is killed and the rest taken prisoner. When the news of this fresh disaster reaches Rome, says Polybius, "not only the populace but the Senate are thrown into consternation. Abandoning therefore the system of government by magistrates elected annually, they decide to deal with the present situation more radically, thinking that the state of affairs and the impending peril demands the appointment of a single general with full powers."

The man they chose as "dictator," *i.e.*, sole commander, was Quintus Fabius, a man of such admirable judgment and great natural gifts that in Polybius's own time, half a century later, he was still referred to as Maximus, the "Greatest." He was also to acquire another name, "Cunctator" meaning "Delayer," for reasons which will appear later.

Quintus Fabius Maximus towers above his contemporaries as Winston Churchill dominates the "Men of Munich." Compared with Fabius, such mindless hotheads as Sempronius and Flaminius were pigmies. Yet, like Churchill, Fabius had to endure a long period of misunderstanding and hostility. In the past the Romans had been accustomed to defeating their enemies in pitched battles in which they were usually victorious. Fabius realized, before anyone else, that in Hannibal they were faced with a different and more dangerous kind of enemy. He had introduced into warfare elements which gave him, for the time being, an overwhelming advantage. There was his heavy cavalry under the brilliant direction of Maharbal, one of the greatest cavalry commanders of all time. It provided a weapon to which the Romans, who were essentially infantrymen, had no answer. But even more important, they were faced by a mind of such powerful originality in military affairs that no conventionally trained Roman general could defeat it.

As Fabius saw the situation, there was only one way to defeat Hannibal, and that was to wear him down. The Carthaginian's weakness lay in the fact that, as the commander of an invading foreign army on Italian soil, he could only destroy the Roman State by enlisting the support of the peoples allied to Rome. As long as the allies remained loyal there was hope that the tide would turn, but every time the Romans lost a battle their allies' faith in them weakened. The answer to the problem was never to engage Hannibal in battle but always keeping at a discreet distance, to hang on the rear and flanks of his army, in sufficient numbers to discourage the allies from going over to the enemy, yet never challenging the Carthaginians to open combat.

It was a sound scheme but an unpopular one, because the Romans, accustomed to breaking their enemies' power by direct action on the battlefield, found it hard to stomach a policy which involved standing by inactive while Hannibal ravaged their country as he pleased. The methods of Fabius, "the Delayer," while acceptable to the wiser minds among the Roman government, irritated and eventually infuriated the man in the street. Such is the weakness of popular government, which rarely learns anything except the hard way.

Fabius took immediate steps to defend Rome should Hannibal decide to march at once on the city. Walls and towers were strengthened, the bridges over the Tiber broken down and citizens enrolled for defense. One is reminded of the rapid improvisation of defenses in Great Britain when, after the fall of France, it seemed that Hitler would invade the island. But, like Hitler, Hannibal deferred his attack, and instead of moving directly southward on Rome, swung eastward and laid siege to Spoletum (modern Spoleto) in Umbria. He was severely repulsed, and having no adequate siege train, with battering rams and storming towers,[1] had to retire from the walls and continue his march.

Spoletum may have been a trial attack. Livy remarks that Hannibal, "conjecturing from the strength of this one colony what was the size of the city of Rome, turned aside into the territory of Picenum, which abounded not only with every species of grain but was stored with booty, which his rapacious and needy troops eagerly seized." It seems that Hannibal, realizing that he was not yet strong enough to attack the capital, concentrated first on improving the health of his men by letting them forage at will in rich country. At the same time he tried to break the allegiance of the allies by proving that Rome was powerless to protect them. So far not one colony had defected, but one more decisive Roman defeat might well turn the scale.

Umbria, one of the smallest and loveliest of the Italian provinces, is the birthplace of St. Francis of Assisi and contains some of the finest Etruscan remains in the country. Its two principal cities, Perugia and Orvieto, both have medieval walls on Roman

[1] He had left it in Spain.

and Etruscan foundations, and, like other Umbrian cities, stand on high hills. To these the terrified peasants retreated as Hannibal's Gauls, Spaniards, and Africans ravaged the plain.

Hannibal moved on in a leisurely way across the Apennines in the direction of Ancona and descended on the district of Picenum; then, following the Adriatic coast, he entered the rich land of Apulia, near the "heel" of Italy. Short marches, long rests, enjoyable foraging raids which brought in slaves, women, cattle, corn, wine, oil; that was the pattern. The oil was used for anointing the skins of the soldiers, many of whom were still suffering from scorbutic disorders, and Hannibal found an unusual and interesting use for the less palatable wine. It was an old soldier's trick which he had probably learned from his father; he used the wine to bathe and tone up the skins of his horses and so improve their condition. Alcohol is still used today for the same purpose.

But while his army revels in ease and sunshine, Hannibal's cold hatred for the enemy remains unassuaged. Throughout these rich colonies of Rome live many officials, landowners, tax collectors, customs officers, farmers. Some have grown rich from the wealth of their colonies and live well in their pleasant villas on the slopes above the Adriatic. A few, who have had warning of Hannibal's approach, escape, but many are less fortunate. An official and his family are sitting under the colonnaded portico of their house, enjoying the sight of the vineyards and the distant sea, when a band of strange horsemen clatters up the road. Before the Romans have had time to think they are roughly grasped and led before a young Latin-speaking officer who questions them closely. As soon as he has established that they are Romans he gives his orders. The household servants, and the other non-Romans on the estate, are allowed to go. As for the rest, all men of military age are immediately killed. The women and children are taken away.

All along the smiling coast, from Pescara to Termoli and beyond, similar scenes are taking place. Rome has lost many thousands of her poorer citizens at the battles of Ticinus, Trebbia, and Trasimene. Now the rich and prosperous also feel the bitter edge of Hannibal's vengeance.

Before Fabius marched out of Rome with his army, he heard more grave news. The Carthaginians had again become active at sea. While their generalissimo was plundering far and wide in the Adriatic provinces, a Carthaginian naval force had cut off a whole convoy of Roman corn ships off the west coast, near Cossa in Etruria. These captured ships had been intended to supply the Roman army in Spain. Fabius gave orders that the former consul, Cornelius Servilius, should take all the ships at Ostia and in the Tiber and set to sea to protect the Italian coast. Meanwhile, with his Master of Horse, Marcus Minucius, Fabius marched through Campania and Samnium to Apulia, where Hannibal was operating.

Apulia is a country of green plains and gentle hills, richly fertile, in sharp contrast with the adjoining more mountainous regions of Calabria and Lucania. Its most important port, Bari, will be well remembered by troops who fought in Italy in the Second World War. The principal inland town, Foggia, is modern and dull, but Lucera dates from Roman times and Brindisi, also badly smashed in World War II, existed in Hannibal's time. But those who faithfully follow the path of the great Carthaginian will make their pilgrimage to the small undistinguished town of Canosa on the river Ofanto (formerly the Aufidius) for reasons which will become apparent later.

Now followed one of the most extraordinary episodes in the Second Punic War—or indeed in any war. There was no major clash of arms, no fiercely fought, decisive battle. The fascination is like that of watching two well-matched boxers at the start of a round, lunging, feinting, ducking, dancing on their toes, waiting for any loophole in their opponent's defense, yet never actually striking each other. It is not an exact parallel, of course, because in this case one of the opponents, Hannibal, was spoiling for a fight, while his adversary, Fabius, with a much larger army, was equally determined not to engage. And the "ring" in which they faced each other covered an area of thousands of square miles, from the Bay of Naples almost to the Gulf of Taranto.

Fabius, finding Hannibal in Apulia, encamped about six miles away and waited. He had the advantage of a much larger army, regularly and abundantly supplied with provisions. Whereas the Carthaginians had to send out foraging parties to gather food, thus exposing themselves to being cut off, the Romans never needed to scatter their forces. Remaining always at a safe distance Fabius kept Hannibal under constant observation. Every time the Carthaginian moved, Fabius moved also—at a distance. Sometimes the Romans were able to intercept one of Hannibal's raiding parties which had strayed too far from the main army. This gave the troops useful exercise and did something to mitigate the boredom of inactivity.

By remaining in the field, even without fighting, Fabius overawed the allies and discouraged them from revolting. Hannibal had hoped that the Apulians would join him: they did not. He recrossed the Apennines, moving through the country of the Hispanians and the Samnites, on the western slopes of the Apennines, above the bay of Naples. And as he moved, so "the Delayer" followed him, keeping to the high ground and marching parallel with the Carthaginians.

Beneventum, a great Samnite city which had once been at war with Rome, was not a Latin colony. Hannibal hoped that, by reviving the memories of former enmity, he could persuade the Samnites to join him in war against the Romans. But "the Delayer" was watching from the heights, and Hannibal found the gates of Beneventum closed against him. He laid waste its territory with fire and sword and then moved along the valley of the Calor until it joined the Volturnus (the modern Volturno). He ascended this river as far as Allifae, crossed it, and plunged down into the Falernian Plain, the richest part of the Campania, which was then and still is one of the most beautiful and fertile regions of the Peninsula. Millions of visitors to Italy, including those who fought there in the Second World War, know this region, stretching roughly from Sorrento in the south, past Vesuvius and the Bay of Naples, to the Gaeta Peninsula in the north. Its coast was studded with prosperous Greek and Roman colonies, of which Herculaneum and Pompeii are examples. Further north still lies the coastal plain of Latium, then the basin of the Tiber, and Rome.

Throughout his long wandering march, Hannibal had continually tried to sting Fabius into action. Livy tells us: "He began to provoke and try his temper, by frequently shifting his camp and laying waste the territory of the allies before his eyes; and one while he withdrew out of sight at quick march, another while he halted suddenly, and concealed himself in some winding of the road, if possible to entrap him on his descending into the plain." But Fabius refused to be drawn, though his troops, and especially his Master of Horse, Marcus Minucius, became increasingly restive and angry.

When the Romans arrived on the heights of Mount Massicus and looked down on the Falernian plain they saw "the most delightful country in Italy . . . being consumed by fire, and the farmhouses, on all hands . . . smoking from the flames," and their indignation broke into open anger. Minucius, who had been intriguing against Fabius and hoped to supplant him, saw in this an opportunity to win the soldiers over to his side. Addressing the officers, Livy says, he exclaimed:

> "Are we come here to see our allies butchered, and their property burned, as a spectacle to be enjoyed? And if we are not moved with shame on account of any others, are we not on account of these citizens, whom our fathers sent as settlers to Sinuessa, that this frontier might be protected from the Samnite foe; which now not the neighbouring Samnian wastes with fire, but a Carthaginian foreigner, who has advanced even this far from the remotest limits of the world, through our dilatoriness and inactivity?

Despite the unpopularity of his policy, Fabius remained unmoved, even though some men began to call him coward. Firmly pursuing his strategy of containment, he garrisoned Casilinum in the enemy's rear. The river Volturnus from Casilinum to the sea prevented any retreat southwards, and the colony of Cales barred the outlet from the plain. Between Casilinum and Cales the hills formed an unbroken barrier, steep and wooded, with only a few paths already secured by Roman soldiers.

Fabius had acted very cleverly. By all the rules of orthodox warfare, Hannibal was caught in a trap. He could not expect to winter in Campania, since once his army had exhausted its supplies it could not stay. It was without a single town in its possession, and with no means of pasturing its cattle and storing the masses of plunder it had accumulated. Besides many thousands of cattle, Hannibal was encumbered with numerous prisoners, plus the corn, oil, wine, and other provisions. His plan was to retreat across the mountains to Apulia, where there was an abundance of corn and open grassland which in winter was green and fresh, providing wide pastures for his cattle. Knowing his intention, we recognize a splendid insolence in the way Hannibal allowed Fabius to lock him within Campania, shutting door after door and apparently barring every escape route. One is reminded of the type of circus performer called an "escapologist" who, after inviting members of the audience to bind him in every possible way, even locking him in a box, manages in a few seconds to free himself.

Summer wore on and still the Carthaginian made no move, while his army reveled in the plenty of the richest region in Italy, and the Romans, greatly superior in numbers, watched anxiously from the hills. What would Hannibal do?

The only road along which his army can escape is that along which it came, and this narrow mountain pass is guarded by a strong detachment of Roman soldiers while Fabius, with the main army, is camped some distance away, watching the pass.

It is the third watch on a calm summer night in 217 B.C. Throughout the day there has been no unusual activity in the Carthaginian camp. Apart from the sentries and the men guarding the pass, most of the Roman army is sleeping. An orderly enters the tent of Fabius and wakes the dictator. As he rubs the sleep from his eyes and looks about him, he hears, in the far distance, the excited shouts of men. Is the camp being attacked? No, the sound is too far away for that. Throwing on his clothes Fabius leaves the tent and finds Marcus Minucius, his Master of Horse, gathered with other officers outside. They are all looking, not at the pass along which they expected Hannibal to attempt his escape, but at the hillsides above it.

The sight is enough to alarm and astonish them. Up the steep, dark slopes thousands of lights are moving, dipping and swaying, but all moving towards the heights. Some of the pin points of light are already nearing the crest of the ridge while below other flames, as if of torches, are massed in a glittering constellation, moving haphazardly, now right, now left, then up, as if carried by men seeking a way of escape from the blocked pass and over the hills.

"We've got them, Sir!" shouts the excited Minucius. "The

fool thinks he can get away over the hills at night, while we're asleep! But only a few have got away. Move the army down to the foot of the pass *now*, and we can stop the rest!" He implores Fabius to give the order, but the dictator remembers Sempronius at Trebbia, and Flaminius at Lake Trasimene. "No," he says gravely. "This is another Punic trick. We have a force guarding the pass. They'll deal with these men. *The army will not move. We shall stay here until dawn. Don't move. I forbid you.*" In vain Minucius and the other officers try to persuade Fabius to attack, while more and more glittering lights move up the dark hillside and over the crest.

Meanwhile, the Romans guarding the pass, seeing the lights and believing that the enemy are trying to outwit them, leave their posts and scramble up the hillside. It is hard going in the dark, for the mountainsides are steep and treacherous, and it is some time before the more agile soldiers come close enough to get to grips with their adversaries. A young centurion, sword in hand, runs towards one of the moving lights and then stops, bewildered. His companions, when they join him on the heights, look on in astonishment and disappointment before slowly they sheathe their swords. What they see before them is a huddle of cattle with burning brands tied to their horns. From above and below they hear the excited cries of their comrades who, like them, are climbing the heights in pursuit of imaginary enemies.

The cries change to shouts of disgust and anger. Realizing that they have been tricked, they begin to hurry down the hillside again, back to the posts they have deserted. Then they get another surprise. They blunder into dark shapes standing among the rocks, the shapes not of cattle but of men. Quietly, but with deadly efficiency, the small force of picked Carthaginian troops who have driven the cattle up the slopes, fall on the dismayed Romans and cut them down. No one knows whether the shadows around him conceal men or beasts. Leaderless, out of their accustomed formation, alarmed and terrified by the darkness and the uncertainty, the Romans wait for the dawn, remembering the stories they have heard concerning Hannibal, who now seems more like a god than a man.

But the god is far away. He is down in the unguarded pass far below, joking with Maharbal, Hasdrubal and the rest, as they move unmolested over the mountains to safety. Behind them march the thousands of Africans, Numidians, Gauls, loaded with the plunder of Campania, and driving before them some 2,000 cattle. Before dawn they will be out of danger and on their way to the lush grasslands of Apulia, to which their commander had promised to lead them.

When the dawn light seeps across the green Campanian plain, it reveals the Roman army still within its camp, where Fabius is still assuring his officers that this is yet another Punic trick. He is right, of course, and this time the victim is Fabius. When his scouts, whom he has sent to reconnoiter the Carthaginian camp, return, it is with despair and frustration on their faces. Hannibal has gone; and so has all his army with its booty.

I have not read every book on Hannibal, but in none which I have studied has the author pointed out what seems to me to be the brilliant facet of this maneuver. It was a clever trick *but one which was intended to be recognized as a trick*. Once again Hannibal had studied the mind of his opponent and taken his measure. Both Sempronius and Flaminius were rash fools who fell into the traps prepared for them, but Fabius was not a fool, and Hannibal knew this. If "the Delayer" had been as impetuous as either of the two Consuls whom Hannibal had already defeated, he would have been deceived, and would have led his army out of the camp in time to intercept Hannibal's main force. Being a cautious and prudent general, he stayed where he was and so allowed the Carthaginians to get away.

But in all three cases the result was the same. Hannibal made his opponents do what he wished them to do, and reaped the benefit himself.

16

A COMMAND DIVIDED

AFTER escaping from the trap set for them by Fabius, the Carthaginians had first followed the valley of the Volturnus as far north as Venafrum, thence into Samnium and across the Apennines towards Sulmo, where the rich Pelignian plain yielded a harvest of plunder, and finally back to their old quarters in Apulia on the Adriatic side. This leisurely, circuitous journey shows that Hannibal was still in no hurry, and exhibits a contempt for the Romans which only increased their fury against him and their distrust of Fabius. The moneyed classes particularly felt the pinch, because they could get no returns on their property; the wealthy graziers had to stand impotent while Hannibal drove off their cattle to provision his army; the farmers of revenue were hindered from collecting their gains. And the poorer classes chafed under the burden of constant military service throughout the winter, when there was no prospect of plunder.

All this anger and frustration eventually focused on the dictator. His cautious, defensive tactics might have been wise and in the end possibly successful, but in the meantime Hannibal wandered unhindered through Italy, plundering where he pleased. If he were not defeated soon, the sorely tried allies believing that Rome could not protect them, might go over to the enemy, and the Federation would be at an end. Yet, despite the agitation against him, Fabius continued to pursue his former policy. He followed Hannibal across the Apennines into Apulia, but camped on high ground in the neighborhood of the Carthaginian army which had established headquarters in the small town of Geronium. This also held the accumulated stores, while most of the troops were quartered in a fortified camp outside the walls. Hannibal, naturally confident of his superiority, kept only one-third of his army in camp under his own command, and sent the remaining two-thirds out in foraging parties. The Carthaginians pastured their numerous cattle on the slopes of the adjoining mountains, while other men reaped the corn and stored it within Geronium against the coming winter.

I was not able to establish the exact site of Geronium, but it was some way inland, on the north side of the river Fortore which enters the Adriatic near the Lago de Lesina. The hills rise steeply on the west, and Fabius could have camped somewhere in the region of Larino which was a Roman colony (Larinum). The modern town of Lucera, to the south, preserves the name of another Roman colony, Luceria. All this region of cornfields, olive groves, and pasture, lying between the mountains and the sea, was at that time allied territory; not Roman, but an abundant source of wealth to Rome.

During the autumn of the year 217 B.C. Fabius was recalled to Rome to attend to certain religious duties, leaving his Master of Horse, Minucius, in command. Fabius, before leaving, instructed his second-in-command to use only defensive tactics, to keep the enemy constantly in view, to cut off his foraging parties wherever this was practicable, but never to engage the main army in a pitched battle.

Minucius, an able officer, followed "the Delayer's" tactics but improved on them. Observing that Hannibal, in contempt of his cautious enemies, had sent out two-thirds of his army on foraging expeditions, Minucius sent cavalry and light troops to cut off the plunderers, killing many, and even dared to attack the Carthaginian's camp. Hannibal, left with only one-third of his men, was seriously embarrassed by this sally, and only the timely return of some of the foragers obliged the Romans to retreat. Minucius, greatly elated by his success, sent back to Rome a glowing report of his achievement.

The result, as the Master of Horse must have anticipated, was to turn the tide of popular feeling against Fabius. His second-in-command had managed better than Fabius himself. The dictator was unpopular. He belonged to the aristocratic party and had not been sparing in his condemnation of former generals. A bill was brought forward by one C. Terentius Varro, who had been *praetor* in the preceding year, urging that Minucius, a member of the popular party, be granted equality of rank with Fabius. The bill was carried, and when Fabius returned to his place in the hills above Geronium, he had to divide his army. One half remained under his command. The other half was led by Minucius, who camped a few miles away. Under the Roman system each general took command on alternate days.

The result could have been foreseen. It was not long before Hannibal learned from his agents that he now had to deal not with one united command, but two rival generals. One can almost see him rubbing his hands in delight at the news. It could be Trebbia all over again, and it very nearly was. Even the same trick was used: the concealment of troops in ravines and hollows, while, on a day carefully chosen because Minucius was then in command, the Roman army was tempted out to battle. In the middle of the action, while Fabius watched anxiously from the hills, five thousand Carthaginian troops suddenly appeared, as if by magic, from the ground, and smashed into the Roman rear. In a short time the army of Minucius was in flight but, fortunately for him, an older and wiser general was standing by with a formidable army. This time, "the Delayer" delayed no longer but led his legions down into the plain, and, after a sharp encounter, prevented the Carthaginians from repeating the success they had had at Trebbia.

Minucius, having learned his lesson, was honest enough to admit that he had been wrong. For the rest of the campaign, he gave up his equal and separate command and placed his army under control of Fabius. The rest of the autumn passed quietly, and after six months both the dictator and his Master of Horse resigned their offices in accordance with Roman custom. This custom is well summed up by Macaulay in one of his *Lays of Ancient Rome*;

> *In seasons of great peril*
> *'Tis good that one bear sway,*
> *Then choose we a dictator*
> *Whom all men obey.*
>
> *And let him be dictator*
> *For six months and no more*
> *And have a Master of the Horse* [1]
> *And axes twenty-four. . . .*

During the winter the army was put under the command of the Consuls: Gnaeus Servilius, who had commanded the fleet during the summer, and M. Atilius Regulus, who had been appointed in place of Flaminius.

This system of electing generals in the middle of a great war when the whole security of the State was threatened, seems ridiculous to the modern mind. It was absurd, but it had a sound basis in the Roman theory of government. The factor which in the end defeated Hannibal was not the military ability of the generals opposed to him but the political system which they represented. That system with all its faults was

[1] In the original, "Master of the Knights."

broadly democratic and therefore commanded popular support, even among the allies of Rome, who at this time had little or no representation in the government.

Within the Republic, rivalry between the aristocratic (patrician) and the popular (plebeian) parties also influenced the choice of leaders. The Plebs, having gained increased power, were able to insist that one of the two Consuls elected each year should be of the popular party. When, on the resignation of Fabius, new elections were held, one of the newly elected Consuls, C. Terentius Varro, was a plebeian. Varro is said to have been a butcher's son. Left a considerable fortune by his father, Varro succeeded in obtaining a number of public offices, which he filled ably. He was an eloquent speaker and enjoyed considerable popularity; and he had sponsored the bill which gave Minucius equality of command with Fabius. His own military experience was not great. The other new Consul, L. Aemilius Paullus, was a known partisan of the aristocracy, had held the consulship three years earlier, and was known to be a good soldier. On these two men, elected by popular vote, rested the security of the Republic in the fateful spring of 216 B.C.

After the elections, which were held in the winter, the new Consuls did not immediately join their army, which was camped a little to the south of Hannibal's winter quarters at Geronium. Gnaeus Servilius and Marcus Atilius, formerly Consuls, retained their command as Proconsuls for some time after Aemilius and Varro took office. Polybius writes:

> Aemilius, after consulting with the Senate at once enrolled the soldiers still wanting to make up the total levy and dispatched them to the front, expressly ordering Servilius on no account to risk a general engagement, but to skirmish vigorously and unintermittently, so as to train the lads and give them confidence for a general battle; for they thought the chief cause of their late reverses lay in their having employed newly raised and quite untrained levies.

This petty skirmishing went on throughout the winter, and there were one or two minor engagements, but nothing decisive. In the meantime the Roman government raised a new army of unprecedented size, hoping to secure success by overwhelming strength in numbers. "They decided," Polybius tells us, "to bring eight legions into the field, a thing which had never been done before by the Romans, each legion consisting of about five thousand men apart from the allies." As each legion was accompanied by an equal number of allied troops, both infantry and cavalry, the total strength of army which faced Hannibal in the summer of 216 B.C. could not have been much less than 90,000 men. He himself had only 50,000.

But before the Consuls arrived with the main army, Hannibal took the initiative, as usual. While the Romans were still in their winter quarters, he left his camp at Geronium where his winter supplies were now almost exhausted and descended swiftly on the Roman citadel of Cannae, modern Canosa, which overlooks the low flat lands beside the river Aufidus. This was a particularly astute move, since Cannae contained important storage magazines from which the Roman army drew supplies of corn and other provisions. At one stroke, therefore, Hannibal provided his own troops with fresh supplies and denied the Romans access to theirs.

He had also placed himself, on the eve of the early harvest, between the Romans and their expected source of supply, for in southern Apulia, which is low-lying and warm, the corn ripens much earlier than in the higher lands to the north and west. The Proconsuls, Servilius and Atilius, sent urgent messages to Rome asking what they should do. They had only three alternatives; (a) to retreat; (b) to offer battle, or (c) to draw their supplies, with great difficulty, over a long distance. The Senate decided on battle, but ordered the Proconsuls to wait until the Consuls arrived with the newly raised army.

It was not until June that Aemilius and Varro reached Apulia with their legions, and, joining force with the army already encamped there, moved southward in search of the Carthaginian. After two days' marching, they found him on the left bank of the Aufidus, about nine miles from the sea. They camped about six miles away, and looked down over the vast sunny fields of golden corn which the Carthaginians were happily reaping. Surveying the ground, so favorable to cavalry, in which Hannibal was superior, Aemilius counseled a move to hillier country where infantry would have the advantage. Once again the curse of dual command operated against the Romans. Varro, impatient for battle and confident in his superior numbers, would not accept the advice of his more experienced colleague. And on the very next day, when it was his turn to take supreme command, he moved the whole army down the river, intending to deploy his forces on the plain beside the Aufidus and offer battle to Hannibal.

The Carthaginians attacked the Romans in column of route and caused some losses; but the forces of Terentius Varro, by advancing some of their heavy infantry and afterwards sending forward their spearmen and cavalry, beat back their enemies and were able to take up their position beside the river. Next day, when it was the turn of Aemilius to take command, he judged it inadvisable either to fight or withdraw but camped with two-thirds of his force on the river bank, and sent the remaining portion to fortify a position on the other side of Aufidus, "to the east of the ford." The purpose of this second camp was to cover the foraging parties from the main camp and harass those of the enemy.[2]

Hannibal, seeing that a major battle was now certain, briefly addressed his troops, exclaiming, according to Polybius:

"What greater gift could you ask of the gods . . . than to fight the decisive battle on such ground as this, where you are greatly superior to the enemy in cavalry? Thank the gods,

[2] Authorities differ as to the bank on which the battle was fought, but the majority favor the left bank.

then, and then thank me, your commander, for compelling them to fight, which they can no longer avoid, and to fight here where we have the advantage!"

In this, of course, Hannibal spoke the truth, as his soldiers knew. He did not mention that they were outnumbered by nearly two to one, since they could see that for themselves. Then he told them that it was unnecessary for him to exhort them to fight well, as he had done in the past.

"Now you have beyond dispute beaten the Romans consecutively in three great battles, what words of mine could confirm your courage more than your own deeds? For by those former battles you have gained possession of the country and all its wealth, as I promised you, and not a word I spoke but has proved true; and the coming battle will be for the cities and their wealth. Your victory will make you at once masters of all Italy, and through this one battle you will be freed from your present toil. You will possess yourselves of all the vast wealth of Rome, and will be lords and masters of all men and all things. Therefore no more words are wanted, but deeds. . . ."

17

CANNAE

CANNAE is one of those names—like Blenheim, Austerlitz, Gettysburg, Ypres, Alamein—which have a permanent place in this history of warfare. It appears in modern military textbooks, and will probably go on appearing as long as men, and not missiles, fight battles. The theory of "double envelopment," which was the basis of the massive German offensive in 1914—the Schlieffen Plan—was based on the tactics Hannibal employed beside the Aufidus over two thousand years before. His battle plan was one of the simplest that he ever employed, but the results were as deadly as an atom bomb.

On the day following his speech to his troops, says Polybius, Hannibal "ordered all his men to look to their persons and accoutrements and on the following day he drew up his army along the river with the evident intention of giving battle as soon as possible." But Aemilius, who commanded on that day, kept quiet, not liking the ground, and hoping that the Carthaginians would soon have to move their camp to obtain supplies. Seeing that the enemy did not intend to fight, the Carthaginian withdrew his forces to their camp but sent a party of Numidians to skirmish up to the Roman camp and molest the water carriers.

When the Numidians came up to the actual palisade of the camp and prevented the men from watering not only was this a further stimulus to Terentius Varro, but the soldiers displayed great eagerness for battle and brooked no further delay. For nothing is more trying to men in general than prolonged suspense. . . .

Next day Varro was in command, and on that day Cannae was fought. Shortly after sunrise the Consul led his forces out of both camps, and crossing the river, drew up his army facing south, with the river on his right flank. The diagram on page 137 shows the battle order of the two armies. Beginning with the Romans, let us follow their line from right to left. On the extreme right near the river, Varro stationed the Roman cavalry which was under the command of the other Consul, Aemilius. Left of them he placed the Roman foot but marshaled them in closer ranks than was customary, the depths of the maniples (units of 120 men) being many times greater than their front. On the extreme left was the allied cavalry which he commanded himself. The two Proconsuls, Servilius and Atilius, commanded the infantry in the center. In front of the whole force stood a screen of lightly armed troops, some distance ahead of the foremost rank of the main army.

This great army, by far the largest that the Romans had put in the field, stretched for several miles across the plain. There were about 80,000 foot and rather more than 6,000 horse. The sun, rising on their left, glittered on their helmets of polished brass, above which rose a forest of waving red and black plumes, a foot and a half high. The legionaries, each with shield on his left arm, throwing-spear in his right hand, and short sword on his right thigh, dressed ranks under the orders of the centurions. On either wing the cavalry horses stamped and snorted, or stood patiently waiting, while their armored riders patted them. The long months of waiting and wandering were over. Each man knew that, before the sun set, the issue would be decided, one way or the other.

About a mile away, facing the Romans, the Carthaginians were also forming into line of battle. They were far fewer, about 50,000 against the Romans 86,000, and about half their number were Celts (Gauls), both mounted and on foot. We will now look at their ranks, again from right to left, *i.e.*, the Roman right to the Roman left. This is not the orthodox way of describing a battle plan, since obviously any army's "right" faces its enemy's "left" and vice versa, but it is less confusing for the moment to look at the two armies from one direction, which is from the Roman ranks, gazing towards the Carthaginians.

Although Hannibal has deployed his army in a broadly similar formation, with cavalry on the wings and infantry in the center, he has positioned the various races within his army according to their particular fighting qualities, intending to employ both their strength and their weakness to carry out the maneuver he has planned.

In the center, facing the legionary foot, the strongest element in the Roman army, he has stationed his weakest troops, the Spaniards and Celts. On either side of these soldiers are solid blocks of heavily armed African infantry, now armed in the Roman fashion with weapons captured from the enemy. On his left wing, facing the Roman right, stand his Spanish and Celtic horsemen commanded by Hasdrubal. They will be opposed to Aemilius. On his right wing, facing Terentius Varro, are the dreaded Numidians, under Maharbal.[1] Hannibal himself, with his brother Mago, commands the foot soldiers in the center. The composition of the army is about 40,000 infantry against the Roman 80,000, and 10,000 horsemen against 6,000 Roman cavalrymen. And in front of the Carthaginian ranks are pikemen and slingers from the Balearic Islands.

At first Hannibal forms his troops into a straight line, but having done this he executes an unusual maneuver, described thus by Polybius:

[1] Livy says Marharbal commanded the Numidians, Polybius gives Hanno.

After thus drawing up his whole army in a straight line, he took the central companies of Spaniards and Celts and advanced with them, keeping the rest of them in contact with these companies, but gradually falling off, so as to produce a crescent-shaped formation, the line of the flanking companies growing thinner as it was prolonged, his object being to employ the Africans as a reserve force and to begin the action with the Spaniards and Celts.

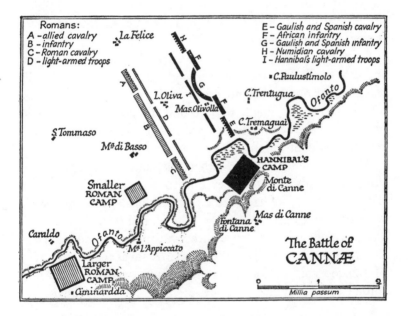

Romans:
A – allied cavalry
B – infantry
C – Roman cavalry
D – light-armed troops

E – Gaulish and Spanish cavalry
F – African infantry
G – Gaulish and Spanish infantry
H – Numidian cavalry
I – Hannibal's light-armed troops

The Battle of CANNÆ

A glance at the diagram will make this formation clear. The final battle array is now a bow-shaped formation of Celts and Spaniards bulging forward in the center, with wedges of heavily armed Africans standing back on each side of the bulge, while they in turn are flanked by the cavalry. The river runs past the Roman right and the Carthaginian left, and on its other side are, first, the Carthaginian camp, and farther upstream, the larger Roman camp; but the Romans also have a smaller camp on the same side as, and just behind, their army.

Concerning this moment, when the outnumbered Carthaginians faced the Romans at Cannae, Plutarch relates one of those rare anecdotes which reveal the character of the young Carthaginian. One of his lieutenants, Gisgo, began to bewail the numbers of the enemy, like "cousin Westmoreland" at Agincourt.

Hannibal turned to him and said seriously, "Yes, Gisgo, you are right. But there is one thing you may not have noticed."

"What is that, Sir?" asked the puzzled officer.

"Simply this; that in all that great number of men opposite there isn't a single one called Gisgo."

Gisgo's face broke into a reluctant smile. Hannibal laughed and other officers joined in the laughter. Then, Plutarch tells us, the ranks of men behind, seeing their general in such a good humor, began to laugh, too, feeling his confidence both in himself and in them. They gripped their weapons and waited for the word of command.

The trumpets sound on either side, and the lightly armed skirmishers advance to meet each other, while the Balearic slingstones ring like hail on the Roman shields, and one missile wounds the Consul Aemilius. The skirmishers, having discharged their missiles, retire through gaps in the ranks. Then the trumpets sound again, the standards advance, and the roar of 140,000 voices rolls across the plain as two armies crash in thunder. As Polybius describes it:

> When the Spanish and Celtic horse on the left wing came into collision with the Roman cavalry, the struggle that ensued was truly barbaric; for there were none of the usual wheeling evolutions, but having once met they dismounted and fought man to man. The Carthaginians finally got the upper hand, killed most of the enemy in the mêlée, all the Romans fighting with desperate bravery, and began to drive the rest along the river, cutting them down mercilessly, and it was now that the heavy infantry on each side took the place of the light-armed troops and met.

In the center, the massed plumes of the legionaries, who are fighting in close disciplined ranks, tower above the towheaded, long-haired Gauls who fight naked to the navel, and the white tunics of the Spaniards, now soaked in blood. Urged on by the two proconsuls, Servilius and Atilius, who are fighting stoutly among the ranks, the Roman infantry is forcing its enemies farther and farther back. The Celts and Spaniards, quickly wearying after the first charge, cannot stand up to that moving wall of shields and the short, sharp stabbing-swords which flash from between them. The convex "bulge" is first smashed flat, and then caves inward, as the legionaries hack and thrust their way deeper and deeper into the faltering ranks of the enemy foot.

As in all great battles involving great masses of men, the individual soldier knows nothing of what is happening more than a few yards beyond him. He fights shoulder to shoulder with comrades in his own century; he follows the standard, obeys his centurion, and that is enough; enough that he is still alive and fighting, and that his unit is resolutely attacking. What is happening to the massed thousands in front, behind, and on either side he does not know. He does not know, for instance, that the protecting wing of cavalry far away on his right has been killed or driven from the field by Hasdrubal's horsemen. He does not know that on the other flank Maharbal's Numidians are in deadly combat with the other Roman cavalry wing, drawing them off and attacking from all sides at once. And he does not know that, in pursuing the celts and Spaniards, he and his comrades have wedged themselves deep between the two wings of heavy African infantry, who up to now have taken little part in the action.

Suddenly there is a change. Still facing the enemy in front, he hears, to right and left, the war cries of the heavy African infantry as each wing makes a quarter turn, the right wing swinging to the left, and the left wing to the right, in order to take the Romans on the flanks. It was, says Polybius, almost an automatic action, "the situation itself indicating to them how to act. The consequence was that, as Hannibal designed, the Romans, straying too far in pursuit of the Celts, were caught between the two divisions of the enemy, and they no longer kept their compact formations but turned singly or in companies to deal with the enemy who was falling on their flanks." The Africans were fresh and vigorous but the Romans were exhausted by their attack on the Celts and Spaniards.

Such was the tactic of "double envelopment." The Roman infantry were caught in a giant vice which was slowly crushing them to death. Aemilius, whose cavalry had been defeated in the action on the right wing, galloped his horse back onto the battlefield, and seeing what was happening to the Roman foot, rode along the center of the line, where, says Polybius, "he not only threw himself personally into the combat and exchanged blows with the enemy, but kept cheering on and exhorting his men. Hannibal, who had been in this part of the field since the commencement of the battle, did likewise."

Meanwhile Maharbal's Numidians were still fighting the cavalry on the Romans' left, with little advantage gained on either side. Then Hasdrubal, having defeated the Roman right, brought his horsemen across the battlefield, behind the struggling infantry, and prepared to charge the still undefeated Roman horsemen opposed to Maharbal. But seeing Hasdrubal approaching, they turned and fled. The Carthaginian, leaving the Numidians to pursue the fugitives, then checked his own men, and swinging round, attacked the Roman infantry in the rear.

Livy has a story of how one of the military tribunes, Gneaus Lentulus, who had fought among the defeated Roman cavalry, came upon a man sitting on a stone, and covered with blood. He recognized the Consul, Aemilius. "Lucius Aemilius!" the young officer cried. "Take this horse while you have strength, and I am with you to strengthen and protect you. This battle has been calamitous enough without the death of a Consul."

Aemilius refused. After thanking Lentulus, he told him to take his opportunity of escaping from the enemy. "Tell the fathers of Rome," he said, "to fortify the city, and garrison it strongly. . . . Tell Quintus Fabius that Lucius Aemilius lived, and now dies, mindful of his injunctions. For myself, I would rather die among my slaughtered troops than be accused for a second time after my consulate, or stand forth as the accuser of my colleague [Varro], in order to defend my own innocence by incriminating another."

At that moment a mob of flying fugitives stormed across the place where the two were standing. Lentulus's horse, borne away in the throng, carried its rider to safety. But the Consul was never seen alive again. And at that moment Terentius Varro, his cavalry wing having been defeated, was flying with the survivors from the battlefield, thus saving his life.

The other commanders did not desert their troops. The two former Consuls, Servilius and Atilius, and the hotheaded Minucius, the former Master of Horse under Fabius, fought side by side with the Roman foot soldiers, until all three were killed. On that day there died beside them two *quaestors* (Financial Officers), twenty-one military tribunes,[2] and eighty Senators.

Now the vice was closing, tighter and tighter, on the doomed legionaries. At first, when they could turn and present a front to their enemies, they held out, but gradually, as their outer ranks were cut down and the rest were jammed in a tight mass around their standards like cattle in a corral, they were helpless. Still they would not surrender and, like the Spartans at Thermopylae when their weapons were useless, fought with their nails and teeth. At the end of the day, out of

---

[2] Military tribune is difficult to define in modern terms. He was a young officer of good family receiving military training; rather like a modern A.D.C. but he sometimes commanded large bodies of men.

the original 80,000 Roman infantry, about one man in ten was still alive.

Seventy thousand Romans and their allies perished at the battle of Cannae. The Carthaginians lost in all about 6,000 men killed of whom 4,000 were Celts, 1,500 Spaniards and Africans, and the remainder cavalry. The total death roll was, therefore, nearly 80,000 men. This ghastly toll of lives, the result of a few hours' fighting, is greater than the total number of men killed in the Royal Air Force throughout the First and Second World Wars. It represents just under one-third of the total number of American soldiers, sailors and airmen killed in four years' fighting during the Second World War.[3] My earlier statement, that Hannibal's strategy at Cannae was as deadly as an atom bomb, is therefore not an exaggeration. No living man has seen, or ever will see, a large-scale battle of the ancient type fought with sword and spear. When, in films or plays, modern actors wear the ancient weapons and armor, they usually seem unreal, "romantic" or faintly comic. When, on the motion-picture screen, we see a "reconstruction" of some ancient conflict employing thousands of "extras," we may be awed and excited by the spectacle but are not receiving even the dimmest impression of the reality. My own belief is that it was more horrible than anything that can be imagined, save, perhaps by those who fought at Stalingrad or on the battlefields of Flanders.

Some of the ancient writers occasionally lift a corner of the curtain. Here is Livy, for instance, describing Cannae on the morning after the battle:

> On the following day, as soon as it dawned, they set about gathering the spoils and viewing the carnage, which was shocking, even to enemies. So many thousands of Romans were lying, foot and horse promiscuously, according as accident had

[3] The actual figures, as given by Chambers' Encyclopaedia, are: R.A.F. casualties 1939-1945, 70,000; 1914-18, 4,000. U.S.A. deaths on all fronts between 1941-1945, 252,000.

brought them together, either in battle or flight. Some, whom their wounds, pinched by the morning cold, had roused, as they were rising up, covered with blood, from the midst of the heaps of slain, were overpowered by the enemy.

Some too they found lying alive with their thighs and hams cut, who, laying bare their necks and throats, bid them drain the blood that remained in them. Some were found with their heads plunged into the earth, which they had excavated; having thus, as it appeared, made pits for themselves, and having suffocated themselves by overwhelming their faces with the earth which they threw over them. A living Numidian, with lacerated nose and ears, stretched beneath a lifeless Roman who lay upon him, principally attracted the attention of all; for when the Roman's hands were powerless to grasp his weapon, turning from rage to madness, he had died in the act of tearing his antagonist with his teeth.

Livy does not attempt to describe the total scene. One may have seen a slaughterhouse but not one extending over a square mile. One may have seen, in one sector of a huge modern battlefield, some thousands of human bodies shattered by shells, bombs, and grenades, but I doubt if anyone living today has seen 76,000 mutilated corpses heaped in an area roughly the size of Central Park in New York. That was the reality of Cannae.

One's first natural reaction to this holocaust is pity for the victims and revulsion from the conqueror. Yet I think it would be unjust to regard Hannibal as a prototype of Genghis Khan and Attila, barbarians who delighted in slaughter. He had been brought up from boyhood as a soldier, and death on the battlefield was familiar to him; yet there is nothing in his actions which suggests that he enjoyed killing for killing's sake; indeed by the standards of a cruel age he was less cruel than most. Livy says that the carnage was "shocking, even to enemies."

Like all generals, his aim was to destroy the enemy's power to fight, but this did not necessarily mean killing all his opponents. The reason for the high death rate at Cannae, apart from the fact that many men died from wounds who would have lived today, was the method of fighting. When an enemy was in flight, it was easier to take prisoners. They could be surrounded, made to throw down their weapons, and then led away; but in the middle of a pitched battle this was difficult, if not impossible. In a modern battle a large group of soldiers, once disarmed, is helpless and can be guarded by one man with a Sten gun. One has only to try to imagine this in the infantry mêlée at Cannae to realize its absurdity.

If you forced your enemy to throw down his weapon, there was nothing to prevent his picking it up again—or taking another from the heaps of dead and wounded—and attacking you while your back was turned. This actually happened at Cannae, when a number of Numidians pretended to surrender, throwing down their spears, but retaining swords hidden under their clothes. At a suitable moment they attacked their captors from behind; no doubt this was one of Maharbal's pleasant little stratagems.

Personally I believe that even Hannibal's iron nerves were shaken by the slaughter, which may have returned to his mind many years later, when he tried to persuade his opponent, Scipio, not to do battle with him. For whatever reason, Hannibal did not seize the opportunity presented to him and immediately march on Rome. Arnold has a splendid passage on this which I cannot forbear quoting:

Maharbal, seeing what his cavalry had done, said to Hannibal, "Let me advance instantly with the horse, and do thou follow to support me; in four days from this time thou shalt sup in the Capitol." There are moments when rashness is wisdom; and it may be that this was one of them. The statue of the goddess Victory in the Capitol may well have trembled in every limb on that day, and have dropped her wings, as if for ever. But Hannibal came not; and if for one moment panic had unnerved the iron courage of the Roman aristocracy, on the next their inborn spirit revived; and their resolute will striving beyond its present power, created, as in the law of our nature, the power which it required.

Arnold does not quote Maharbal's reply, when he realized that his general would not allow him immediately to march on Rome. To me this is the most critical moment in the tremendous drama, when the great cavalry captain and the young general, both bloody from the slaughter, look out across the plain, one eager, the other doubtful. And then, seeing the hesitancy in his commanders' eyes, Maharbal says:

"Truly the gods have not bestowed all things upon the same person. You know how to conquer, Hannibal; but you do not know how to make use of your victory."

18

THE TURNING POINT

IN 216 B.C., immediately after Cannae, neither the triumphant victor nor the despairing enemy could have foreseen that the war would drag on for nearly half a generation; nor could either have known that, in fact, the turning point already had been reached, less than two years after the Carthaginians crossed the Alps. Yet, looking back, we can see it clearly. One is reminded of the fulcrum of a balance in which one arm is short but heavily weighted, the other long but unweighted.

The short arm of the balance represents the first two years of the war when Hannibal, by a series of brilliant victories achieved in a short space of time, had brought the Romans almost to their knees. The long arm represents the fourteen years of campaigning, during which Hannibal, still irresistible in battle, marched up and down the length of Italy, defeating the Romans whenever he could bring them to battle, dominating the country in which his army was quartered, yet never able to force the door which stood between him and complete victory. The key to that door was possession of the towns. So long as the majority of Rome's allies remained faithful to her and their fortified cities stood secure, the invader might ravage as he wished and inflict widespread suffering, but the Roman State could not be destroyed. Eventually, as we shall see, the gods hung one additional weight on the long arm of the balance, thus forcing it down. That weight was the genius of young Publius Cornelius Scipio, son of the Scipio whom Hannibal had defeated at the battle of Trebbia.

In a book of this length it would obviously be impractical to describe every battle, march, shift and maneuver which took place during that long campaign. It is equally impractical to continue following Hannibal's path, since he marched thousands of miles and frequently covered the same ground again and again. I shall therefore content myself with outlining the broad pattern of events, highlighting only those which are especially significant.

The immediate effect of Cannae was to bring the Roman State nearer to total collapse than at any time in its history. In this, her third and most humiliating defeat at the hands of Hannibal, Rome had lost the largest army she had ever put in the field. Seventy thousand of her finest troops were dead, and the rest—mainly those who had been left to guard the two camps—taken prisoner. It was total catastrophe, comparable, in modern times, to the fall of France in 1940. Nor is this merely a story of steady recovery leading to military victory. In Italy, Rome was beaten again and again, year after year, by the Carthaginians. Abroad she was attacked by Sicily and Macedon, and Spain supplied arms to her most dangerous enemy. Yet the Republic survived. The factor which, in the end, defeated the invader was not the ability of Rome's generals, but the strength and vitality of her political institutions.

After Cannae, as after the battle of Lake Trasimene, Hannibal sought among the slain for the bodies of his distinguished opponents and gave ceremonial burial with military honors to Lucius Aemilius Paullus and others. When news reached Rome of the utter destruction of both consular armies and the deaths of Aemilius and the two proconsuls and eighty Senators, the grief and alarm were so overwhelming that even Livy felt himself unable to describe it. In three battles Rome had lost a fifth of the entire population of citizens over seventeen years of age. Every house in the capital was in mourning.

Although he was no longer dictator, Fabius took virtual command of the city, for whatever resolutions he proposed in the Senate were immediately adopted. He sent out light horsemen to gather information about the enemy's movements. He gave orders to members of the Senate, acting as magistrates, to "stop all loud or public lamentations"—which recalls the laws against "spreading alarm and despondency" which the British Parliament passed at the beginning of the Second World War. The city gates were to be closely guarded so that no one might attempt to fly from Rome, but all stand together against the common danger. All public meetings were temporarily suspended, for, as Arnold says "at such a moment, had only one tribune uttered the word 'peace' the tribes would have caught it up with eagerness, and obliged the Senate to negotiate." At this crisis it was the aristocracy who saved the Republic.

Eventually the panic ceased and news reached the Senate from Terentius Varro, who had escaped from the battle, that he had rallied the few thousand men at Canusium, and that Hannibal to all appearances was not preparing immediately to advance on Rome. Hope was rekindled; the Senate began to meet again, and measures were taken to continue the war. Meanwhile Varro handed over his troops to the praetor Marcellus when he arrived at Canusium, and himself returned to Rome to face the Senate. In this he showed a moral courage which had not been in evidence on the battlefield. He had not perished gloriously in the fight, like Flaminius at Trasimene and Aemilius at Cannae. He was a fugitive, whose only folly had been partly responsible for the annihilation of the Roman army, but he returned to face public disgrace.

He was a plebian and had no friends among the aristocracy,

yet, when he met the Senate in the Campus Martius, party feeling was suspended. Some of his officers, at Canusium, had talked of leaving the country, but Varro had preferred to submit to the judgment of his countrymen. Arnold says, "The butcher's son, the turbulent demagogue, the defeated general, were forgotten." The Senate voted him its thanks "because he had not despaired of the commonwealth." It is incidents such as these which go far to explain why, in the end, the Roman Republic was victorious.

If this story shows that the Republic could be magnanimous to its servants, there is another which illustrates its severity. Most of the Romans who had escaped from the battle had taken refuge in their two camps. They were a mere half-armed multitude without leaders and could see little hope of further resistance. Then a message was sent by the troops in the larger camp to those in the smaller, urging that they should attempt to break through the Carthaginian lines at night and join the soldiers in the larger camp. It was urged that as the enemy would now be exhausted by the battle, or overcome by feasting, it should be possible to execute this maneuver. But most of the soldiers in the smaller camp refused, pointing out that the intervening space was crowded with the enemy. Then a young military tribune, Publius Sempronius Tuditanus, got to his feet and harangued the men, pointing out that they were the fellow countrymen of Lucius Aemilius who had preferred an honorable death to infamy. Says Livy:

"Before the light overtake us," he urged, "and more numerous bodies of the enemy beset our way, let us break through those disorderly and irregular troops who are making a noise at our gate. . . . By the sword and courage, a road may be made through enemies, however dense. . . . Come with me, therefore, ye who wish the safety of yourselves and the State."

Six hundred men agreed to follow him.

Having thus said, he draws his sword, and forming a wedge, goes through the enemy; and as the Numidians discharged their javelins on their right side, which was exposed, they swung their shields to the right hand, and thus escaped, to the number of six hundred, to the greater camp; and setting out thence forewith, another large body having joined them, arrived safe at Canusium.

Those remaining in the camps surrendered to the Carthaginians on the following day. Hannibal then called the prisoners before him, and addressed them in terms which suggest to me that he was, in fact, sickened by the carnage at Cannae, and wanted nothing further than the end of the war on terms which would satisfy his honor. Many authorities will, I am sure, disagree strongly, alleging, with the Roman historians, that the terms offered were just another "Punic trick." They could have been, but I believe that Hannibal meant what he said:

> "I am not carrying on a war of extermination against the Romans. I am contending for honour and empire. My ancestors yielded to Roman valour. I am endeavouring that others, in their turn, will be obliged to yield to my good fortune, and my valour. You may have your liberty, in return for ransom; five hundred denarii for a horseman, three hundred for a foot soldier, and one hundred for a slave."

The phrase, "my good fortune," suggests a modesty and an intellectual honesty not invariably found among generals.

The prisoners, overjoyed by the news, asked that they might elect ten of their number to go to Rome and plead with the Senate to provide ransom; the only guarantee of their fidelity was their oath to return, which Hannibal accepted. The ten delegates set off for the capital accompanied by "a noble Carthaginian named Carthalo," who hoped to negotiate terms of peace.

Carthalo's journey was wasted. He was not allowed even to

see the Senate, but was informed, through one of the lectors, that he must leave the Roman territories before night. Next day the delegates were received by the Senators, who listened to their story of how, after being deprived of water and beset by the enemy, the prisoners had agreed upon terms that they might be ransomed and let off; and that they had surrendered their arms, in which there was no longer any protection, to the enemy.

Many of the Senators were sympathetic, and urged that the ransom should be paid. Rome, desperately short of men, needed every fit soldier she could get, but after listening to a speech by one of the Senators, Titus Manilius Torquatus, the tide of sympathy turned against the delegates. Recalling the desperate deed of Sempronius, who had cut his way out of the camp with his six hundred men, Manilius, according to Livy, upbraided the prisoners:

"What would you do if you had to die for your country? Fifty thousand of your countrymen and allies on that very day lay around you slain. If so great carnage did not move you, nothing ever will. . . . Too late you now endeavour to evince your regard for her when degraded, and become the slaves of the Carthaginians. . . . You did not listen to Sempronius, your countryman, when he bid you take arms and follow him; but a little after you listened to Hannibal, when he ordered your arms to be surrendered and your camp betrayed. . . ."

Swayed by the eloquence of the old Senator, a man whom even Livy says was "a man of primitive over-rigorous severity," the Senate voted that the delegates should be sent back to Hannibal with the message that the prisoners would not be ransomed. Thus the Romans lost more than 10,000 fit men whom they could have ransomed; nor did the fact that these men included members of the Senators' families have any effect on the issue. Such a gesture was cruel, unrealistic, and not even logical, since later the Romans had to employ slaves in the place of their lost thousands. Yet there is also a splendor in it, since this pitiless insistence on the duty of a citizen to die for his country was one of the pillars of Rome's greatness. But the effect of this refusal to negotiate was to prolong the war for a further fourteen years.

Not once, in all those years, did any Roman army ever camp in front of Hannibal on open ground.

At Canusium, where the wreck of the Roman army was camped, the situation was desperate. Some of the young noblemen, convinced that Cannae meant the end of Rome, had determined to escape from the country while there was time. The chief of these was a young officer named Caecilius Metellus. Some of his companions were for immediate flight. Others wanted to call one of the Consuls to deliberate on the matter. Among the officers still loyal to the State was one who determined to stop the rot if he could. With a few chosen companions, Livy tells us, he entered the quarters of Metellus and his friends, drew his sword, and holding it in readiness, addressed the group.

> "I swear to you," he said, "that neither will I desert the cause of the Roman Republic nor will I suffer another citizen of Rome to desert it. If I knowingly desert my oath then, O Jupiter, supremely great and good, may you visit my house, my family and my fortune with most horrible perdition! I require you, Lucius Caecilius, and the rest of you present, to take this oath. And let the man who shall not take it be assured that this sword is drawn against him."

The alarmed officers, writes Livy, were "terrified as though they were beholding the victorious Hannibal himself." They all took the oath and delivered themselves into custody. The name of this young man was Scipio "the Younger," who had saved his father at Ticinus. He was twenty-one years of age.

When the delegation returned from Rome, and informed Hannibal that the Senate refused to ransom the prisoners he was understandably angry. He sold most of the prisoners as slaves, which was the accepted custom of war at that time.

As they had refused to ransom Hannibal's prisoners, the Romans decided to make up their losses by enlisting such slaves as were willing to serve. Eight thousand were recruited, arms being provided by taking down from the temple walls the spoils won in former wars. Eventually a force amounting to about 25,000 men marched into Campania under the command of the new dictator, Marcus Junius. He made his headquarters at Teanum, with the Latin colony of Cales on his front, and communicated by the Latin road to Rome. M. Marcellus with another army camped above Suessula on the right bank of the Volturnus, ten or twelve miles east of Capua. The reason for this concentration was that Capua, second largest city in Italy, was known to contain many who were sympathetic towards Hannibal though the aristocratic party remained faithful to Rome.

During this time Hannibal reaped the fruits of his victory. Arpi and Salapia opened their gates to him, as did Bruttium and Lucania. He himself remained for a time in Apulia which became his adopted home in Italy. When he moved into Samnium the popular party at Compsa went over to him. He then instructed his young brother, Mago, to march to Bruttium with a division, embark from this port, and carry news of his victory to Carthage. Mago was also to bring back reinforcements as soon as possible. (For geographical details see end papers.)

Meanwhile, Hanno [1] with another division moved into Lucania to protect the Lucanians who had rebelled against the Romans and joined the Carthaginians. Hannibal, with the main army, descended into the Campanian plain and received the surrender of Capua. The Romans were unable to stop him. Thus he gained control of practically the whole of southern Italy at a blow. Samnium, Lucania, Apulia, and now Campania—

[1] Another Hanno; not Hannibal's brother.

including its key city of Capua—were his. Capua, a city capable of raising an army of 30,000 foot and 4,000 horse, now formed the head of a powerful coalition of southern Italian states hostile to Rome. Hannibal had access to their towns and supplies, and an ample recruiting ground for more soldiers. But these new allies also brought responsibilities since he had to divide his army to provide garrisons to protect them. That is why he had sent Mago back to Carthage to collect reinforcements.

But the Romans had learned their lesson. They developed the delaying, hampering tactics which Fabius had taught them, and which, they now realized, were the only means of wearing down and eventually defeating the invader. So the rest of the war becomes rather like a group of lesser animals following a wounded lion. Every now and then the beast turns, and they scatter. Sometimes it conceals itself and then, leaping out, tears its tormentors to pieces. Afterwards it moves on alone and unmolested for a while, but before very long it hears once again the stealthy pad-pad of footsteps following some way behind.

The campaign of 216 B.C. ended with Junius camped at Teanum, Marcellus at the mountain camp above Nola, while Hannibal and his main army wintered pleasantly in Capua, a city of such wealth and luxury that censorious Roman writers pretended that the Carthaginians were "ruined" by the sensual enjoyments of Italy's second city. If this is true, one can only comment that the corruption required a very long time to take effect.

19

LAKE OF THE DEAD

I N Chapter Fifteen we described the activities of Scipio in Spain; this was Gnaeus Cornelius Scipio, brother of the Publius Cornelius Scipio who was wounded at Ticinus. In 215 B.C., the year following the battle of Cannae, P. Cornelius Scipio returned to Spain and took over command from his brother who had been successful in defeating the Carthaginians and taking Hanno [1] prisoner. After this defeat, the Carthaginian army in Spain was in great difficulty, largely because many of their Spanish subjects went over to the Romans.

Saguntum, which Hannibal had captured before his march into Italy, was regained by treachery, and so many Spaniards were won over by the Scipios that Spain, formerly a nursery of soldiers for the Carthaginian army, was now more of a liability than an asset. With the reinforcements brought by Publius Cornelius, the Roman forces must have been about equal in strength to those of Hasdrubal,[2] Hannibal's brother-in-law, who had been left in command of Spain.

[1] A third Hanno. The name was very common.
[2] Not to be confused with the other Hasdrubal, who was serving with Hannibal in Italy.

In the same year, 215 B.C., new officers were appointed to command the Roman armies. To avoid too much detail, I shall give the names only of the principal generals. One of these we already know: Quintus Fabius Maximus—"the Delayer." Fabius, who was one of the Consuls, took over from the former dictator, M. Junius, and moved his army from Teanum to Cales at the northern extremity of the Falernian plain, less than ten miles from Capua, which Hannibal held. The other Consul, Tiberius Gracchus, stationed himself at Sinuessa on the Appian road, at a point where the Massic hills run out as a bold headland into the sea. Marcellus the prætor still lay near Nola, with two new legions, while his old army went to Sicily to relieve the legions there. These legions returned to Italy and formed a fourth army, commanded by M. Valerius Laevinus. The small force which had been led by Varro was sent to Tarentum, the important naval base now known as Taranto, on the Straits of Messina. C. Fulvius Flaccus commanded in Rome, and there were other small armies in Sicily and Sardinia, where the Carthaginians were again causing trouble. The Roman State was, therefore, fully extended when, at the beginning of the campaigning season, Hannibal marched out of Capua and took up his position on the hill known as Tifata, where he overlooked the Campanian plain.

His immediate opponents were Fabius, Gracchus, and Marcellus, all with formidable armies watching Campania. They waited to see what he would do. The Carthaginian must have felt extremely confident during that summer. Apart from having secured most of southern Italy, including several of its most important cities, he had been in communication with the popular party in Tarentum, who were prepared to desert the Romans and go over to his side. He had also made alliances with Syracuse, in Sicily, and with King Philip V of Macedon who was about to declare war on Rome and wanted Hannibal as an ally. The Romans, according to Arnold, were also having trouble in Cisalpine Gaul.

Seeing the result of his work thus fast ripening, Hannibal sat quietly on the summit of Tifata, to break forth like the lightning flash when the storm should be fully gathered.

But the storm did not break, either in that year or the next. To adopt Arnold's "storm" simile, the period 215-214 was more like one of those gray, sultry summer days when the clouds lie thick over the land, and occasionally one hears a roll of thunder or sees an odd lightning flash, yet the tension remains; the longed-for relief never comes. Or to change the image completely, the marches and countermarches of the rival armies were like the complex, slowly meditated moves of two expert chess players. The positions of the pieces were shifted, sometimes by slow progression, other times by swift leaps. One or other is swept from the board, when one town or another is taken. After some hours the players still face each other in furrowed concentration; the principal pieces are still intact, and neither opponent seems able to make headway against the other.

By this time the Roman generals had learned their business, and the men who commanded after Cannae were far more able and efficient than their predecessors. They had come to realize that in open ground Hannibal's cavalry was irresistible, but if they stayed among mountains or behind walls, they had the advantage over him. Whatever move Hannibal made he was unable to checkmate them. Fabius initiated a "scorched earth" policy, enforcing stern laws designed to prevent the enemy from obtaining his supplies; e.g., green corn was not to be left standing but reaped and brought to his storage magazines. Hannibal then made a sudden move, capturing Casilinum, so that Fabius was forced to move his camp to Suessula where he joined Marcellus. Gracchus advanced towards Capua, Marcellus garrisoned Nola, and three Roman armies were camped along the left bank of the Volturnus, threatening Capua.

As long as Hannibal remained watching from the heights of

Tifata, Capua was safe. In an endeavor to make him unclench his grasp, a move was made against his allies, the Samnites, who appealed to the Carthaginians for help. Fortunately the long-expected reinforcements, mainly cavalry and elephants, had just arrived at Bruttium. As soon as Hannibal had news of this, he moved his army from Tifata and appeared before the Roman-held town of Nola, timing his arrival to coincide with that of his reinforcements. The Romans could do nothing to prevent the junction of the two armies, nor were they able to attack Capua.

Hannibal overran the territory of Nola and tried to take the town, but Marcellus sallied forth from the gates and drove him back. Meanwhile Fabius ravaged the country around Capua, carrying off the corn to his quarters at Suessula. As winter approached, Hannibal moved to his old quarters in Apulia; Gracchus, with one of the Roman armies, followed him at a safe distance, but did not engage. And so the campaigning season ended, with little advantage gained by either side, though the Romans had won two important tricks. T. Manilius Torquatus, commanding in Sardinia, had frustrated a Carthaginian-inspired revolt, and the Roman fleet had captured the returning ambassadors of the King of Macedon, thus learning of the plot and delaying the alliance by about a year.

The strain on the Roman economy was now so great that soldiers and sailors went destitute and unpaid, loans had to be raised, and a heavy property tax levied to help finance the war. As a patriotic gesture the officers of the equestrain (noble) class refused to accept pay, and their example was followed by the centurions (company officers).

In the following year, 214 B.C., the Romans had to sustain a fresh burden when Philip of Macedon brought his powerful fleet into action against them. In order to protect the Italian coast, and hinder Hannibal's communications with Carthage, they had to raise a fleet of 150 warships. Ten legions were employed in Italy alone besides two in Sardinia, two in Sicily, two in Cisalpine Gaul, and two in Spain. With the coming of spring, the deadly chess game began again.

The headquarters of the two Consuls were at Cales, the camp above Suessula, in Campania. Gracchus, with two legions, had been wintering in northern Apulia, keeping an eye on Hannibal who was at Arpi. Fabius was ready to march into Apulia as soon as Gracchus was to advance into Lucania and Samnium, and thus threaten two of the Carthaginian's allies. Hannibal's strategy appears to have been to hold on in Italy for an indefinite time, knowing that the Romans, for all their numerical superiority, would not dare to attack him on his own ground. He hoped that Carthage would renew her attempts to conquer Spain and Sicily, and that his new ally, Philip of Macedon, would add to the pressure. Meanwhile, he watched the Romans' cautious maneuvers and waited for the chance to strike a lightning blow.

For a long time he had had his eye on the rich and important city of Tarentum which lay in the extreme south. His agents had been active there, and though the Tarentine aristocracy were pro-Roman, there was a strong popular party which favored him. Had it not been for his Campanian allies, threatened by the presence of the two consular armies, he would probably have marched on Tarentum early in 214 B.C. As it was, in order to encourage the Capuans, he broke up his winter quarters at Arpi, returned to Campania, and took up his old position on the hill of Tifata.

Then he did something which most historians refer to only in passing, but which to me has fascinating dramatic interest. It may also throw light on Hannibal's character. In Homer's *Odyssey* there is a wonderful and somber passage which describes the hero's visit to Hades. After he had performed the sacrifice which Circe had instructed him to make, the wraiths of the dead came to him.

Then from out of Erebus they flocked to me, the dead spirits of those who had died. Brides came and lads; old men and men of sad experience; tender girls aching from their first agony; and many fighting-men showing the stabbed wounds of brazen spears—war victims, still in their blooded arms. . . .[3]

There came to Odysseus the shades of men slain in battle, his companions, Aias and the swift-footed Achilles, who cried out:

"Ingenious son of Laertes, Odysseus of the seed of Zeus, daring unhappy soul! How will you find some madder adventure to cap this coming down alive to Hades among the silly dead, the worn-out mockeries of men? . . . Would that I were on earth a menial, bound to some insubstantial man who must pinch and scrape to keep alive! Life so were better than King of Kings among these dead men who have had their day and died."

Hannibal, who had received a Greek education,[4] and probably knew large parts of the *Odyssey* by heart, would certainly be familiar with this famous passage. He also knew, with the rest of the ancients, that the entrance to the Underworld was located by tradition at Lake Avernus (now called Averno) situated between Cumae, Puteoli, and Baiae, in Campania. This somber stretch of dark water, a mile and a half wide, lies in the crater of an extinct volcano. In places it is 200 feet deep and is almost completely enclosed by steep and wooded heights. It got its ancient name, Avernus, meaning "birdless" because it was believed that the sulphurous fumes rising from the lake killed any birds which attempted to fly over it. Here, according to ancient beliefs, the realms of the dead came nearest to those of living men, and here the offerings paid to the gods of the dead were most surely acceptable. Here lived the Cim-

---

[3] All quotations from Homer in this book are from *The Odyssey of Homer*, translated by T. E. Lawrence, Oxford University Press, London, 1935.
[4] He also wrote books in Greek; now, alas, lost, with everything else he wrote.

merians in their deep caverns, creatures who never saw the light of day; here were the Elysian Fields, the grove of Hecate, and the grotto of the Cumaean Sibyl (prophetess). It was one of the most sacred places on earth.

Leaving some of his best troops at Tifata to protect the immediate neighborhood of Capua, Hannibal descended with his cavalry and light-armed troops, into the country overlooking the Bay of Naples. The Romans had established a fortified post at Puteoli, and this he hoped to take, while at the same time he could ravage the territories around Cumae and Neapolis (Naples) which were loyal to Rome. I believe with Arnold that his real reason for the move was to sacrifice Lake Avernus. That he did this not merely as a mask to disguise his intended attack on Puteoli, but in a spirit of sincere devotion, since offerings to the spirits of the dead formed an important part of the Carthaginian religion.

It is a dramatic and somewhat eerie picture. The young general, in whose mind the culture of Greece is mingled with the dark religion of his ancestors, rides, with a few chosen companions, through the thick woods to the shores of the sinister lake. No doubt there would be a temple in which due sacrifice was made. Livy only mentions the bare fact that Hannibal visited the lake. We are left to imagine what ceremonial acts he performed there. Like Odysseus, he was a wanderer and a cunning warrior, and his hands also were stained with the blood of many men. Did he, perhaps, make the same sacrifice as the Greek hero, which Homer describes?

I drew the keen blade from my hip, to hollow that trench of a cubit square and a cubit deep. About it I poured the drink-offerings to the congregation of the dead, a honey-and-milk draught first, sweet wine next, with water last of all; and I made a heave-offering of glistening barley; invoking the tenuous dead, in general, for my intentions of a heifer-not-in-calf, the best to be found in many manors when I got back to Ithaca. . . . I took two sheep and beheaded them across my pit in such manner that the livid blood drained into it. Then from out of Erebus they flocked to me, the dead spirits of those who had died.

Most of Hannibal's recorded statements have a hard practical realism—not to say cynicism—which make him appear almost modern by the standards of his contemporaries. Yet in matters of religion, he was a man of his time.

20

TARENTUM

WHEN Hannibal was sacrificing at Lake Avernus five noble citizens of Tarentum came to him, offering to surrender the city. They had seen his standards approach the walls. Tarentum was the richest and most important town in southern Italy; its port and fine harbor would be invaluable to Hannibal both for his communications with Carthage and for the fleet of his Macedonian allies. He promised the envoys that he would soon be at Tarentum, and they returned to prepare for his arrival.

After failing to take Nola (for a third time) he returned to Tifata, remained there just long enough to allow the Capuans to get in their corn, and then he set off for the south. None of the Roman armies attempted to stop him. Gracchus laid siege to Casilinum, while Hannibal, to quote Arnold, "swept on like a fiery flood, laying waste all before him from Tifata to the Ionian Sea." He did not plunder the lands of his own allies either in Samnium or Lucania, but when he marched near the Latin colony of Venusia the Lucanians and Samnites in his army were careful to point out those districts belonging to the Roman colonists.

When at last he arrived before the walls of Tarentum there was no welcoming party. The gates remained closed and no citizens came out to greet him. The Romans had got there first. An officer named Livius had been in contact with the aristocratic party, which was favorable to the Romans, and the popular party which supported Hannibal was forced to send hostages to Rome, and to guard the walls. After a few days the Carthaginians retreated, but Hannibal kept his temper and did not waste the Tarentine territory, leaving it exactly as it was. He carried off the corn from the territory surrounding the Greek cities of Metapontum and Heraclea and then retired to his winter headquarters in Apulia.

In the meantime the Romans managed to capture Casilinum by treachery, and Gracchus intercepted Hanno, who was leading the reinforcements which had arrived in Italy. Hannibal had sent him with about 17,000 foot and 1,200 Numidians to march to a place near Beneventum. Gracchus met Hanno and defeated him with the loss of all his infantry, though Hanno himself escaped with the cavalry. Marcellus returned to Nola, Fabius moved into Samnium, and joining forces with Gracchus, took many towns. As winter approached, the armies divided again, Fabius moving to his winter camp above Suessula, Gracchus staying in Campania while another Fabius (the praetor) wintered in Lucania. So the year 214 B.C. ended with no decisive advantage gained by either side.

It was during this winter of 214-213, certain Roman writers allege, that Hannibal fell passionately in love with an Apulian girl who became famous for her influence over him. Whether or not his passion for her made him careless of everything else, the fact is that he lost the town of Arpi to the Consul Fabius and some of its Spanish garrison deserted to the Romans.

The satirist Lucian, who may have had access to writings now lost to us, makes Alexander the Great, in the Underworld, reproach Hannibal for allowing a woman so to captivate him that he neglected his military duties. The story may be only a legend, but I see no reason to disbelieve it. Such incidents in the lives of great commanders have a way of being remembered, and the story fits my conception of Hannibal's character. One cannot imagine the stern Fabius or the inhuman Marcellus exhibiting such weakness, but Hannibal, after five years' hard campaigning, may well have permitted himself the relaxation of a love affair. It is especially easy to imagine this taking place in Puglia, surely one of the loveliest and most relaxing regions of Italy.

With the coming of spring Hannibal marched from Apulia, leaving Fabius behind him. He took the road to Tarentum, but although he spent the entire season near the city, and managed to capture a few small towns in the vicinity, the Tarentines made no move to welcome him. News now reached them that the hostages they had sent to Rome had been cruelly killed while attempting to escape. This treachery strengthened the hands of the pro-Hannibalic party by releasing the Tarentines from any moral obligation to keep faith with Rome. Then followed one of the most extraordinary stratagems which Hannibal ever used to capture a city. Reading it, one is reminded of a commando raid in the Second World War, with the Resistance working inside to help the liberating army outside.

Two young Tarentine noblemen managed to get in touch with Hannibal and reached an agreement with him. Hannibal promised that if he took the city he would respect the liberty of the Tarentines and plunder only the houses of those known to be favorable to the Romans. One of these two men, named Philomenus, was very fond of hunting and had a secret arrangement with one of the guards in charge of the gates. Philomenus rarely returned to Tarentum at night without bringing back some game, which he usually gave to the guard. This was one of the reasons why he was allowed to enter the city at a time when the gates were closed. The same young man was also much in favor with the Governor of Tarentum, a man named Marcus Livius Macatus of whom Arnold primly observes that he was "a man too indulgent and fond of good cheer to be the Governor of a town threatened by Hannibal."

Livius was so far from expecting any danger that on the very day which the conspirators had fixed their attempt he had invited a large party to meet him at the Temple of the Muses in the market place, and from an early hour he and his friends were drinking and dining. Perfect timing was essential to the success of the operation which Hannibal had planned with the two Tarentines, who of course were acting on behalf of a large party favorable to Hannibal. Obviously it would not be possible for the Carthaginians to advance with a large force on the walls of Tarentum. If this had happened the alarm would have been given and the walls manned by the strong Roman garrison. But a small force might creep up to the gates without being observed, and if, by some means, one or preferably two of the gates could be opened at the precise moment of the enemy's arrival it might be possible to take the city.

To understand the operation which Hannibal carried out it is necessary to visualize the layout of ancient Tarentum which can still be partially recognized in modern Taranto. The city stood on low and practically level ground, surrounded by the usual walls and gate-towers. On plan it formed a triangle of which one side faced the Mediterranean. Of the other two, one was protected by a small landlocked basin now called the Little Sea. This inlet, like a Norwegian fiord, has a narrow entrance but runs deep inland. The third side faced the land. Almost at the mouth of the Little Sea is a small rocky knoll, forming the apex of the triangle; this eminence was crowned by the citadel, the most strongly defended part of the fortifications which could still resist even if the main part of the city was taken. Many of the Romans were in the citadel, though others were quartered in the town itself.

Another essential point to bear in mind is that the Tarentines, obeying the instructions of an oracle, buried their dead within the city walls. There was a large space, occupied by tombs, between the walls and the inhabited part of the town.

It is a calm Mediterranean night. The air is warm and soft. In the guard-towers along the walls the sentries do not need their cloaks, and, as they make their routine patrols, they see, on one side the harbor, lights dancing on the black water. On the other side other lights shine from the windows of houses, and groups of twinkling torches light the noble guests on their way to the Temple of the Muses, where Livius, the Governor, is holding feast. Sometimes the sound of laughter is carried on the soft breeze, and occasional drunken shouts. At the entrance to the harbor the sentries can just make out the black bulk of the citadel, on its rock, but not very clearly, for there is no moon, only a scatter of starlight. The citizens of Tarentum, greatest city in southern Italy, are secure behind their high walls. The heavy gates are bolted and barred against the night, and no one is allowed to enter or leave the town until dawn.

Now, round about midnight, a great number of torchbearers begins to assemble on the steps of the Temple; the darting flames light up the deep colonnade as the Governor and his friends leave the building. The party is breaking up and the revelers are being escorted home. Livius, who has wined and dined extremely well, is in riotous mood. As he and his friends make their unsteady way to their houses, other men join the throng, staggering drunkenly and exchanging jokes with the Governor's party. But these newcomers are, in fact, cold sober. They are part of Hannibal's "Fifth Column"—young Tarentines who have plotted to destroy their Roman overlords and make the Carthaginian master of the city. They alone know that Hannibal, with his army, is only a few miles away.

They escort the Governor to his house and watch until the last of the revelers has gone to bed and the sounds of merriment have died away. Now the town is asleep and all the streets are silent and deserted, save for the conspirators. These then divide into three parties. One is posted near the Governor's house. Another guards the approaches to the market place. The third makes its way to the cemetery, where ranks of tomb-stones stand between the walls and the inhabited part of the city. And there they wait, looking out from the wall to the darkness beyond.

Expressed in this way the story sounds, perhaps, like a schoolboy adventure. In fact many of the conspirators are sweating with fear and anxiety, for if the plot miscarries few will live to see another day. So they wait, peering into the darkness and keeping well in the shadows lest the guards see them.

Suddenly a little tongue of flame leaps up far out in the blackness beyond the city walls. Immediately one of the young men lights an answering fire at a point where Hannibal's hidden scouts will see it but the guards will not. After a few moments the distant fire flickers and disappears. As soon as this happens the men watching from inside the walls put out their own fire. The agreed signal has been exchanged. Now is the time for action. Swiftly the conspirators converge on the gates, kill or overpower the guards, and, with the tools they have brought, hack through the heavy wooden bars which bolt the doors. No sooner have the doors been swung open than a column of Carthaginian soldiers marches under the gates. The operation has been timed almost to the second.

Hannibal's cavalry remains outside the walls while a selected body of his infantry, marching in a regular column, advances through the quarter of the tombs and on towards the inhabited part of Tarentum. So far the plot has succeeded, but it was also necessary to make a simultaneous entry through one of the other gates. This is where the hunter Philomenus plays his part. He has obtained permission, as usual, to leave the city and hunt for game outside the walls. Just as the Carthaginians are enter-ing through the gates near the cemetery, Philomenus appears before the gate which he is accustomed to use when returning from his nightly expeditions. He gives a low whistle. The guard, quite unaware of what had happened on the other side of the town, unsuspectingly opens the gate. Philomenus enters, carrying a magnificent boar. As the guard bends down to admire it, thirty Africans, who have been waiting outside, rush in, overpower the guard, and then go swiftly to the main gate. With the advantage of complete surprise they soon master the gatehouse and towers, kill the guards, and, cutting through the bars, open the gates to 2,000 more Africans. These marching in regular order, advance quietly towards the market place.

But the city still lies asleep and unsuspecting. The Governor is snoring in his bed as, through the darkened streets, Hannibal and his Carthaginians, approaching from different directions, converge on the market place near the center of the city. As soon as the troops have reached their appointed places Hannibal detaches three groups of Gaulish soldiers and posts them along the principal streets leading to the market place. He tells the officers commanding these detachments to kill every Roman who comes their way, but to each party he attaches a number of the Tarentine conspirators, to warn any of their own countrymen to return to their homes and remain quiet. So the trap is laid, and now Hannibal springs it.

The conspirators have secured a number of Roman military trumpets. In the early hours of the morning the few citizens who are still awake hear the shrill blast of the "alarm" sounding from several quarters. The legionaries quartered in the town hurriedly arm themselves and stumble into the streets. One by one the Gauls cut them down. More trumpets sound and again more Romans fall before the swords of the Gauls. The Governor is lucky. The alarm reaches him in time, but as Polybius says, "he felt the fumes of wine were still overpowering him." Hurrying to the harbor, he gets on board a boat and is carried to the safety of the citadel.

When dawn comes its still does not clear up the mystery of the night alarm. The Tarentines are still safe in their houses.

Nobody has been massacred. Nobody has been plundered. All they have heard is the sound of Roman trumpets, yet the streets are littered with dead, while Gaulish soldiers are robbing the bodies. Then the citizens hear the public criers going through the streets, calling on them, in Hannibal's name, to assemble in the market place. Other shouts mingle with those of the criers: "Liberty! Liberty!" People who are still attached to Rome hurry to make their escape to the citadel. The vast multitude streams into the market place. There, to their astonishment, they see ranks of Carthaginian troops drawn up smartly in parade formation and on a rostrum stands the great general of whom they have heard so much, but have never seen.

"Liberty! Liberty!" the cries continue, led, of course by the conspirators. Hannibal raises his hand for silence and then addresses the people in their own language—Greek.

He tells them that he has come to liberate the inhabitants of Italy from the tyranny of Rome. "You have nothing to fear," he says in *The Histories*, "Go home, and each one of you write over his door 'A Tarentine's House.' Those words alone will be sufficient security; no door so marked will be violated. But the mark must not be set falsely on the door of any Roman house; [anyone] guilty of such treason will be put to death, for all Roman property is the normal prize of my soldiers."

The Tarentines returned to their homes, rejoicing in the liberality of the conqueror. He kept his promise, for such was his power over his troops that only the houses of the wealthier Tarentines who were attached to the Roman alliance, were plundered. The ruse by which Hannibal captured Tarentum was treacherous; indeed he himself admitted as much, yet by these means he had made himself master of the richest city in southern Italy, at the cost of only a handful of lives compared with the number who would have perished in a conventional attack.

The citadel was still occupied by the Romans. It threatened the town and prevented the Tarentine fleet from being used, since it guarded the harbor. Hannibal overcame this difficulty by ordering the Tarentines to drag their ships overland through the city streets from the harbor to the outer sea. As the land was flat the task was not too difficult. Then, leaving the citizens themselves to deal with the Roman garrison, he marched out of Tarentum with most of his troops and made his way to his winter quarters on the edge of Apulia.

In the early spring of 212 B.C., the Romans decided that in the coming campaign they would make a determined effort to recapture Capua. Hannibal was still far away in the south, probably besieging the citadel of Tarentum. Four powerful Roman armies prepared to move into the country around Capua and lay siege to the city. The Capuans sent word to Hannibal, warning him that if they were to withstand a long siege they must be adequately provisioned. Hannibal sent Hanno, who was encamped at Bruttium, to move into Samnium which adjoined Capuan territory, collect corn and other supplies from his Samnite allies, and transport them to Capua.

This was a particularly difficult operation, as Hanno had to evade Gracchus's army, which was in Lucania, on his line of march; the two consular armies were at Bovinium, and Cornelius Nero with two legions lay in the camp above Suessula. But somehow Hanno managed to slip through, and arrived safely near the town of Beneventum. He sent word to the Capuans, urging them to send every wagon and beast of burden they could muster to his camp in order to carry away the corn which he was going to provide for them. All would have gone well but for the ineptitude of the Capuans, who had failed to provide enough transport, and in any case were not ready.

Hanno's message to them on this occasion had a cutting edge. "Not even hunger, which excites dumb animals to exertion, can apparently stimulate the Capuans to diligence." He then named another day on which they were to collect the corn which he had taken so much trouble to provide. In the meanwhile, precious time had been lost and the Romans had heard of the

operation. Fulvius Flacchus marched with his army to Beneventum, and attacked Hanno's camp at a time when, as Livy
tells us, "Two thousand wagons had arrived together with an
undisciplined and unarmed rabble." If the camp had been on
level ground it would probably have been taken at the first
assault, but Hanno had been careful to site it on high ground,
and defend it with earthworks.

In spite of being hampered by thousands of unarmed rustics,
and even women and children, the Carthaginians managed at
first to fling back the attackers and chase them down the slopes
leading to the camp. Eventually, however, one of the centurions, named Titus Pedanius, snatched a standard from the
hands of the standard-bearer, and, crossing the ditch, began to
climb the defenses, calling out, according to Livy, "Soon this
standard, and this centurion, will be within the rampart of the
enemy; let those follow who would prevent the standard's
being captured by the enemy." His example stirred the Romans to action, and, attacking at several places at once, they
stormed the camp and captured all the wagons and stores.
Having done his utmost to help the allies, Hanno and his army
retired in disgust.

Hannibal, in the meantime, had mastered the whole of the
southern Italian coast from the Straits of Messina to the mouth
of the Adriatic, for the towns of Heraclea, Metapontum and
Taurii had also fallen to him. The only Roman stronghold left
in the south was the citadel at Tarentum.[1] The Romans, making use of their naval superiority, sent a strong garrison to the
citadel with ample provisions. With a powerful enemy force
in such a strong position, Hannibal was not able immediately to
march back to Campania when the Capuans again implored his
help. He did not neglect them, but detaching two thousand of
his best Numidian cavalry, ordered them to make their way
past the Roman armies and enter the city secretly. This they
did, but how they did it no one will know. Again and again,

[1] See end papers.

when studying Hannibal's campaigns, one notices how he gives the toughest operations to the Numidians. One would have given much to have read an account of this operation by the officer who commanded those 2,000 horsemen. . . .

The sequel, to me, is one of the most dramatic episodes in the Hannibalic war. The two Roman Consuls have almost completed their preparations for the siege of Capua. Not content with their own two armies they have sent a message to Gracchus, who is in Lucania, ordering him to bring up his cavalry and light troops to Beneventum to add to the force which is weak in cavalry. However, Gracchus is drawn into an ambuscade before he can leave his own province, and is killed. Knowing that Hannibal is far away, the Consuls march boldly down onto the Campanian plain and begin to gather in the green corn in order to stop the Capuans getting their supplies. To their horror, the great gates open and the Capuans ride out; and not only the Capuans. Right at the head, gathering speed for one of their devastating charges, are Hannibal's dreadful Numidians.

There are only 2,000 of them, and Hannibal is hundreds of miles away, but the mere sight of his cavalry is enough. In a moment the foragers are driven in, and before they can take up their legionary formation the horsemen break in among them like a whirlwind. With tremendous loss and confusion they are driven back behind their entrenchments. Then the Numidians ride back into Capua and wait. They do not have to wait long; nor do the Romans. A day comes when Fulvius Flaccus, the Consul, comes out of his tent in the early morning and sees, on the mountain of Tifata, a very unwelcome sight. Thousands of men are gathered on the slopes. There is no need to ask who they are. Hannibal, with his main army, is back again and the Romans have to watch helplessly as he rides triumphantly into Capua where the citizens flock into the streets to greet him with tears of joy.

Now there was nothing the Romans could do but to make

their formations, strengthen their earthworks, and wait for the inevitable shock of his attack. When it came the Numidians once again struck terror into the Roman line. Only the sudden arrival of Gracchus's long-awaited cavalry, which had been brought in by an officer named Cornelius, forced the armies to break off the engagement, since neither side knew whether the newcomers were friends or foes. Later, the bewildered Roman commanders must have pondered how Hannibal had managed to reach Capua so quickly. Although Cornelius and his cavalry set off from Lucania before Hannibal had left the south coast of Italy, the Carthaginians had arrived three days before Cornelius who had a much shorter distance to travel.

Dumfounded and disheartened, the Roman armies had to fall back. Fulvius retired down the coast to Cumae, and the other Consul, Appius Claudius, retreated in the direction of Lucania. For the time being Capua was saved. When the citizens looked out from their walls and saw the Roman camps deserted the joy was great and, as Arnold says, "there needs no witness to tell us with what sincere and deep admiration they followed and gazed on their deliverer, and how confident they felt that with him as a shield no harm could reach them."

Hannibal's movements after his departure from Capua are puzzling. One would have thought that, when all the south save the Tarentine citadel was his, he would have stayed in Campania to prevent Flacchus besieging Capua. Instead he returned to Tarentum, and then remained inactive for the rest of the year in his favorite region, Apulia. He may have decided that, after the many furious forced marches and battles fought at close intervals, the troops deserved a period of rest and recuperation. Devoted as they were to their leader he would not wish to press their loyalty too far.

His absence in the south gave the Romans the chance for which they were waiting. Like an old fox in his lair, Fulvius Flacchus wanted only the opportunity to steal out on his prey. Once they knew that Hannibal was far away, he and the other

Roman generals closed in remorselessly on the city. They built a fort near the mouth of the Volturnus and another at Puteoli, near Naples, which could be provisioned by sea. They had acquired a great store of corn to feed the besiegers. Then they began the siege, enclosing the city in a double ring of earthworks designed to repel the strongest force which might attempt to relieve it. Over 60,000 Roman troops lay before Capua. Appian says that the siege lines were so huge and elaborate that they looked like a large city enclosing a much smaller one. The Capuans, who had some good troops, especially cavalry, attempted several times to break through the lines, led by a brave and competent general named Jubellius Tauria. But although their cavalry was often successful, their infantry was ineffective against the Roman legionaries. However much they might struggle, the Capuans were caught like fish in a net.

Once again they sent to Hannibal for help. Once again the Numidian horsemen cut through the Roman lines and carried the Capuans' message to their leader. And once again he responded. Leaving his heavy baggage and main army behind, he marched swiftly northwards with his cavalry, light infantry, and thirty-three elephants. He evaded Beneventum, destroyed a Roman post, and, after camping behind the ridge of Tifata, came boldly down into the Capuan plain. This time he was unsuccessful. First he rode his cavalry scornfully along the Roman lines, hoping to tempt his enemies to battle, but the Romans stayed behind their earthworks. He then flung his army in a direct assault on the siege works, while the Capuans sallied out and attacked from the other side. Again the Romans stayed behind their ramparts. Having no artillery, Hannibal could not breach the defenses, nor could he maintain his cavalry, because the Romans had taken away all the fodder. Finally, having failed to punch a hole in the net, he decided to adopt another method.

21

MARCH ON ROME

HANNIBAL realized that there was only one way by which he might relieve the pressure on Capua; and that was to march on Rome. Once the capital was threatened the consular armies would be forced to release their grip on Capua and march to the aid of the sacred city. Unfortunately none of the ancient writers describes the course of Hannibal's great march, which was long and yet rapid. At one moment we see him encamped on the hill of Tifata; at the next he is riding up to the Colline Gate and flinging his javelin over the walls. Arnold says:

> Before the sweeping pursuit of his Numidians, crowds of fugitives were seen flying towards the city, while the smoke of burning houses rose far and wide into the sky. Within the walls confusion and terror were at their height; he had come at last, this Hannibal, whom they had so long dreaded. He had at length dared what even the slaughter at Cannae had not emboldened him to venture. Some victory greater even than Cannae must have given him this confidence; the three armies before Capua must be utterly destroyed or dispersed, and three other armies had gained possession of the entire south of Italy,

176

and now he had stormed the lines before Capua and cut to pieces the whole remaining force of the Roman people and had come to Rome to finish his work. So the wives and mothers of Rome lamented as they hurried to the temples. There, prostrate before the gods, and sweeping the sacred pavement with their unbound hair, in the agony of their fear, they remained, pouring forth their prayers for deliverance.

Within the city every able-bodied male hastened to man the walls and the citadel, while the Senate, outwardly calm, met in the Forum as usual, and remained assembled there in order to direct every official, on the instant how best to fulfill his duty. By a fortunate chance there happened to be in Rome at that time two newly recruited legions. With some 10,000 troops, even though many of them were raw, the city could put up a very strong defense. Nor could Hannibal, without powerful artillery, hope to breach those enormously thick walls and towers. All he could do was to ravage the country around, carrying off the crops and cattle, while the Romans watched helplessly from their ramparts. The citizens could not know, of course, that their dreaded enemy was powerless to attack them; for all they knew he had destroyed their one remaining strength, the armies encamped around Capua. To the pessimists among them it would have seemed only a matter of time before he starved them into surrender.

Meanwhile, Quintus Fulvius with a small force detached from the armies besieging Capua, marched back to Rome. Carefully avoiding the Carthaginians, he managed to enter the city. Enraged by the sight of Hannibal's army freely plundering within sight of the walls, he sent out a force of cavalry hoping to cut off the Carthaginian foraging parties.

Next day, according to Livy, Hannibal crossed the Anio and drew up his forces in order of battle. Fulvius, with the full agreement of the Senate, marched out and assembled his army to try the issue of battle. Rome was to be the prize of the victors. Here one feels suspicious; Livy, not the most accurate of historians, may have polished up the facts to make a dramatic story. However angry Fulvius may have been, it seems impossible to me that the Senate would have permitted him to risk a general engagement when the walls of Rome provided protection. The story may be true, and if so its sequel is even more astonishing. Again according to Livy, battle was prevented by "a violent shower of rain mingled with hail" which "created such disorder in both the lines that the troops, scarcely able to hold their arms, retired to their camps. . . . On the following day likewise a similar tempest separated the armies marshalled on the same ground; but after they had retired to their camps the weather became wonderfully serene and tranquil. The Carthaginians considered this circumstance as a Divine interposition, and Livy reports that Hannibal was heard to say, 'Sometimes I want the will to make myself master of Rome, at other times the opportunity.'"

One is fascinated again by the enigma of Hannibal's character. *Why* did he "want the will" to conquer Rome? What held him back? My own guess, as I have explained, is that it was a half-conscious revulsion from mass slaughter at Cannae. This was not pacifism—an inconceivable concept to a man of Hannibal's time—but perhaps a stubborn belief that he could satisfy his honor and achieve his ambition without the necessity of further blood baths. No doubt the psychiatrists, given enough material to work on, would provide a neat explanation, but without an insight into Hannibal's thoughts, such as his own writings might have provided, we are unlikely to read his case history. There seems to be a consistency even in the inconsistency of his actions, as if he swung from one extreme to the other. At one moment the professional soldier is in command, contemptuously destroying his less intelligent opponents. At the next, he is looking down, "for a long time without exaltation" (Livy) at the body of one of his bravest antagonists, Marcellus, and giving orders for the corpse to be

ceremonially burned, according to the Roman custom, and
the ashes sent to the dead Consul's son.

I wonder if Shakespeare ever considered Hannibal as a subject for a tragedy? Had he done so, he might have discovered
in him many elements of Hamlet. But this is mere speculation.
Most probably Hannibal had no intention of attempting to
take Rome on this occasion, but appeared before its walls only
in order to draw away the besiegers of Capua. He made no
attempt to besiege the capital or to storm it. There is a story
that shortly before he left the plain of the Tiber, Hannibal
rode with a party of his Numidians up to the Colline Gate and
along the outer walls, seeing as much of the city as he could.
Taking a javelin from one of his companions, he balanced it in
his hand and flung it high above the walls. That fragile shaft,
hurled from the hand of Rome's greatest enemy, may have
been a symbol of hate, frustration and defiance, or intended as
a warning of terror still to come. It was the only offensive action Hannibal ever made against the citadel of Roman power.
When, not long afterwards, the citizens saw the Carthaginians
leaving their camp and marching away to the north, they
were watching the retreat of an enemy who would never
return.

The Romans tried to harry Hannibal's retreat, but he
brushed them off like flies. He continued his march, with the
enemy following him at a respectful distance and always keeping to the higher ground in fear of his cavalry. In five days he
got as far as the country of the Marsians and then crossed by
the Forca Carossa to the plain of the Pelignians, and so back
through Samnite territory to Capua. There he heard, to his
chagrin, that the Roman armies were still in their lines, and
that his stratagem had failed. So he changed his plans. He
knew that he would have to abandon Capua, but up to the
present had not considered it worth the trouble of interrupt-
ing his march to attack the army which was shadowing him.

Now that he realized that he could not relieve the besieged city, he decided to deal once and for all with his unwelcome followers. He made a night attack on their camp; very swift and very deadly. By the morning the Romans who had not been killed or captured were flying in terror to the mountains, and Hannibal continued his march without further irritation.

He turned eastward towards the Adriatic, intending to consolidate his power in the east and south, where the Roman citadel at Tarentum was still holding out, though the city itself was in Carthaginian hands. But Rhegium (modern Reggio, in Calabria), was another Roman ally which might be surprised and taken, since its citizens would not suspect that Hannibal was so near. He succeeded in capturing many of its inhabitants who were working in the fields outside the city, and treated them kindly, hoping that Rhegium itself would surrender. But it remained faithful to Rome and closed its gates against the invader.

And now, with Hannibal far away in the "toe" of Italy, the Romans pounced on Capua. Quintus Fulvius hastened back from the capital to the siege lines. Mercy was promised to any Capuan who would defect to the Roman side before a certain day. None appeared, which suggests, says Dr. Arnold, "that the Romans were faithless as well as cruel." Judging from the Roman treatment of the citizens after their surrender the Capuans were justified in their fears. They tried once again to send messengers to Hannibal who had saved them on several occasions. This time the Numidian horsemen were captured when trying to penetrate the Roman lines. They were sent back to Capua, cruelly scourged and with their hands cut off.

The Capuan government, unable to restrain its starving people, opened their gates to the Romans, who discovered that several of the leading Senators, after enjoying a splendid banquet at the house of one of their number, had taken poison. The surviving Senators were put in chains, and commanded to surrender all their gold and silver. Fulvius Flacchus marched to the neighboring town of Teanum, took his seat in the Forum, and had the prisoners scourged and beheaded in his presence. He did the same thing at Cales, and sent the Senators and leading citizens of other revolted towns to die of starvation in the Mammertine prison. Thousands more, with their women and children, were sold as slaves, and the whole Campanian plain was forfeited to the people of Rome.

In this same year, 211 B.C., Rome met with disaster in Spain. Unfortunately there is very little reliable information about it, though one can trace a broad outline of events. Apparently the Carthaginians in Africa were having trouble with Syphax, king of the Numidians, and withdrew Hannibal's brother, Hasdrubal, to Africa to deal with this threat. The two Scipios, seeking to take advantage of this, advanced south to the Ebro into the heart of Spain. At first they were successful, since the two Carthaginian generals left in the country—Mago and Hasdrubal, the son of Giscon—were engaged in plundering raids in the western part of Spain, forfeiting the allegiance of their Iberian and Celtiberian allies. Publius Cornelius Scipio was admired by the Spaniards, and managed to draw many of them into alliance with Rome.

Then the great Hasdrubal returned, and such was his influence over the Celtiberians that they abandoned their Roman allies and returned home. The two Roman Scipios, while at a great distance from their resources, were left to the mercy of Hasdrubal. Unable apparently to join forces, they were attacked independently. Their armies were defeated and both the Scipios died fighting. What was left of their shattered legions escaped to the towns of their Spanish allies, but were betrayed. Thus in one year the fall of Capua, and the capture of Syracuse in Sicily, which fell to Marcellus with great slaughter, was balanced by the complete destruction of all the Roman forces in Spain. And Hannibal, their greatest enemy, still roved unhindered throughout central and southern Italy.

22

A SECOND HANNIBAL

DURING the following two years, 210-209 B.C., the grim chess game continued. Hannibal took several important pieces from the board, in the form of armies and towns, while in Spain the position was reversed, and the Romans, recovering from their defeat, inflicted a great defeat on the Carthaginians. But at the end of those two years neither opponent had gained a decisive advantage which would have meant victory. In 209, when the Romans had gained complete control of Sicily, they sent Laevinius, who had commanded there, to Africa; this was not so much to engage the Carthaginians in battle as to seek information. The news he brought back was ominous indeed. Hasdrubal, Hannibal's brother, had recruited men, and there was a firm rumor that he intended to invade Italy and join Hannibal. That same year twelve Roman colonies revolted, refusing any longer to help support the war. The Roman State was staggering under the burden of the war, now in its ninth year. Citizens were crushed by even heavier taxation, their allies were drained of resources and man power, armies went unpaid, and with each defeat more men, arms, equipment, and provisions had to be found to replace those lost. The Senate was eventually reduced to taking gold from the sacred treasury to pay the armies, but neither threats nor appeals would move the twelve rebellious colonies. According to Arnold, they told the Romans, "We are exhausted. We can neither supply men nor provisions. You can send your armies if you wish. They will find nothing." But the other eighteen colonies still remained loyal.

The Consuls for that year were Fabius and Marcellus. The latter, a courageous and energetic officer, had been praetor in 216 B.C., becoming Consul two years later, and then commanding in Sicily, where he won both fame and notoriety for his taking of Syracuse. His cruelties on that occasion made him unpopular among the more liberal Roman Senators, who remembered the long period during which Hiero of Syracuse had been a loyal ally of Rome. He was also boastful and inclined, in the words of his critics, "to turn his defeats into victories," but no general had been more ardent and unwearying in fighting the Carthaginians. In de Beer, Hannibal is quoted as saying: "Marcellus is the only general who, when victorious, gives his enemy no rest, and, when defeated, takes none himself." Comparing Marcellus with his other great opponent, Fabius Maximus, Hannibal remarked: "I feared Fabius as a schoolmaster, but regarded Marcellus as an antagonist, for the one prevented me doing any mischief, while the other made me suffer it."

These few fragments of Hannibal's conversation, if authentic, give us a faint glimpse of his mental quality. He seems to have had a gift for the epigrammatic phrase.

Marcellus had been re-elected Consul in 211 B.C., and it was as Consul that he took the field in 209 B.C. Fabius advanced on Tarentum while Marcellus, leaving his camp at Venusia, dogged Hannibal's army from a distance, using the "Fabian" tactics which his fellow Consul had invented. The Romans had overwhelming superiority in numbers, and the Carthaginian, while holding on to Apulia and Bruttium, could not retain

Samnium and Lucania into which Fulvius was marching with yet another powerful army. So he turned fiercely on Marcellus whose army met him bravely, but in two engagements the Romans were savagely mauled. Eventually the Consul was forced to retire to his camp at Venusia, where he remained for the rest of the campaign.

Meanwhile, "the Delayer" had arrived before the walls of Tarentum, followed by Hannibal, who was hoping to deal with Fabius as he had dealt with Marcellus. A shock awaited him. When he arrived at Tarentum, it was to find the Roman army looking at him from inside its walls. The city had been betrayed by the Bruttian commander of the garrison. Carthalo, the Carthaginian commander, had been killed in the fighting, as had the conspirators Philomenus and Nicon. It was a stunning blow, but Hannibal remained calm and outwardly unmoved.

Before he retired, however, he tried to trap Fabius with a ruse which almost succeeded. He persuaded certain citizens of the Greek city of Metapontum to go to Fabius and offer to surrender their city to him if he would appear with his army before its walls. Livy tells us that Fabius at first accepted their offer and was prepared to go to Metapontum to receive the surrender. Roman superstition then intervened to prevent him. The omens were threatening, and the priest, on inspecting the sacrifice, warned the Consul to "beware the hidden arts of the enemy." Suspicion fell on the Metapontine ambassadors; when they revisited Tarentum to find out the cause of the delay they were closely questioned. Under the threat of torture they confessed the truth. It was as well for Fabius that they did, for had he marched out to Metapontum he would probably not have returned. Hannibal's army was lying hidden in ambush not far from its walls.

Little is known about the rest of that year's campaigning, save that the Romans took no further action against the

Carthaginians, who ravaged far and wide before retiring to their winter quarters which, as usual, were in Apulia.

In Italy the Romans had no reason to be pleased with their commanders, and Marcellus was bitterly attacked in the Senate. A motion calling for the Consul to surrender his command was defeated, but news from their armies in Spain raised Roman hopes. An old familiar name was on the lips of the citizens—Scipio. Publius Cornelius Scipio, who fought Hannibal at Ticinus, and Gnaeus Scipio, his brother, had both been killed in Spain. The Scipio who now sprang suddenly to fame was the son of Publius Cornelius; the same young man who at seventeen had saved his father's life at Ticinus; the same who, after Cannae, had prevented Metellus and other despairing young noblemen from fleeing the country. His name also was Publius Cornelius Scipio "the younger."

In his early manhood he attracted great favor and was made *aedile* at an early age; this was one of the lower rungs on the ladder of promotion which Roman citizens had to climb to reach the higher offices of State. For a time, Scipio served under Cornelius Nero in Spain. Nero, of the same family as the later Emperor, had been sent there to take command of what was left of the Roman army after the death of the two elder Scipios. Nero could do little more than hold his ground at first, though it is said that he ventured to act on the offensive and penetrated into the southern part of the country as far as Baetis. But the story, as given by Livy, is full of improbabilities, and the chronology is so muddled that it is clear that the historian, drawing from different sources, had his dates mixed.

However, if we disregard the wilder improbabilities, and do not attempt to correlate exactly the events in Spain with those taking place in Italy, certain basic facts emerge. Hannibal's brother Hasdrubal was busy recruiting troops for his impending invasion of Italy, and was spending some time in Africa. The Carthaginian generals, Mago and Hasdrubal, the son of

Giscon, were only anxious to enrich themselves by the plunder of Spain. Having no further fear of the Roman armies, they moved around the country, plundering as they wished, rousing the hatred and disgust of the Spanish chiefs. Polybius tells us that these two Carthaginian generals distrusted each other and had only one thing in common—a hatred and dread of the great Hasdrubal, son of Hamilcar.

The Romans decided to exploit the opportunities so provided, and appoint a new commander of their armies in Spain. To the surprise of the Senate and the people, Scipio the Younger, then only twenty-seven years of age, offered himself for the post though he had up to that time held no higher office than that of aedile. Livy writes:

> The eyes of the whole assembly were directed towards him, and by the exclamations and expressions of approbation, a prosperous and happy command was at once augured to him. Orders were then given that they should proceed to vote, when not only every century but even individuals to a man, decided that Scipio should be invested with the command of Spain. But after the business had been concluded, and the ardour and impetuosity of their zeal had subsided, a sudden silence ensued, and a secret reflection on what they had done; whether their partiality had not got the better of their judgement? They chiefly regretted his youth. . . .

So the young Scipio found himself in command of the Roman armies in Spain, at almost the same age as Hannibal when he invaded Italy nine years earlier. Like Hannibal he must have been a man of great charm and authority and a compelling speaker. How otherwise could he have persuaded the Senate and people to entrust him with such responsibility?

The Senators had taken a chance, but unlike many gambles, this one succeeded beyond expectation. Before the year was out, Scipio the Younger had carried out an operation of such skill and daring that men who were dispirited and bowed down by the misfortunes of that year took fresh heart. At first they could hardly believe the news, which was that New Carthage itself, the Carthaginian capital in Spain, the city from which Hannibal had begun his great march, had fallen to Roman arms.

Scipio had had ample opportunity to study Hannibal's methods. Unlike most of the older Roman generals who, though brave and resolute, were unimaginative and trammeled by tradition, he was alert, sagacious, and resourceful. Youth was on his side, of course, and perhaps education, too. Like that of his great opponent, the mind of the younger Scipio had been opened to the culture of Greece; and the vitality and intellectual curiosity of Hellenic civilization were strong in him. Throughout his life he remained a pro-Hellene, a fact which aroused the hatred and suspicion of the older generation of Roman leaders such as Cato. Dour, puritanical, and narrow, they drew their strength from the immemorial traditions of Rome, with their insistence on honoring the country's ancient gods, and adhering strictly to the customs and usages of the founding fathers of the Republic.

Ruse and stratagem in war did not come easily to the conventional Roman generals. Scorning "Punic trickery" they preferred what Captain Liddell Hart happily describes as "honest bludgeon-work." Scipio had no such inhibitions. As for the gods, we are told that he was careful to honor them, even spending hours alone in the temples in order to enjoy communications from the divine wisdom. But Polybius, with the rational skepticism of the educated Greek, believed that Scipio did this only "to impose on the credulity of the vulgar" and that, in fact, the only oracle he consulted was the judgment of his own clear mind.

He had his critics, of course, who alleged that in his youth he had been overfond of wine and women, rather like the young Prince Hal of Shakespeare's *Henry IV*. Dr. Arnold prefers to skate delicately over this, since to the Victorians a hero had to be "pure." Most people today would take a more tolerant view of Scipio's youthful excesses, which make him a more human person than most of his colleagues. I imagine that he had been what the eighteenth century described as "a blade" and we, with less elegance, call a playboy.

During the winter following his arrival in Spain, Scipio obtained as much intelligence as he could concerning Cartagena; he studied its geographical position, the strength of its defenses, both natural and artificial, and the number of men guarding it. He neglected no reliable source of information, from whatever quarter. For instance, he talked to the fishermen of Tarraco, his Spanish base, who told him certain facts about the tides and currents in the harbor of Cartagena which were vital to his plan of attack. Yet during that winter, while making his plan, he revealed his true intentions only to one man, his close friend Laelius, who commanded the fleet. In this he showed an appreciation of the importance of military secrecy which few of his colleagues understood.

If Roman generals such as Marcellus and Fabius could have known what his plan was they would have been shocked and dismayed. Orthodox strategy demanded then—as it does sometimes today—that a commander should seek out his opponent's strongest concentration of force and try to destroy it, but Scipio recognized that there are times when this rule could be ignored, and this was one of them. The three Carthaginian armies were in places equally remote from each other and from their Spanish capital. Hasdrubal, Hannibal's brother, was besieging a city in central Spain, near modern Madrid. The other Hasdrubal, son of Giscon, was near the mouth of the Tagus, and Mago was far away in the west, near Gibraltar.

None of these officers dreamed, of course, that the Romans would attempt to take their chief city when the Carthaginians controlled nearly the whole of Spain. They had left only 1,000 garrison troops at Cartagena; with the city's almost impregnable defenses these were considered sufficient to ward off any attack. But within the huge high walls were thousands of tradesmen, artisans, and sailors, mostly civilians with no military experience.

This, says Polybius, "he [Scipio] considered to be a thing that would tell against the city if he appeared suddenly before it," a fact which shows that the young general understood the value of moral as well as military factors. Some of the earlier historians suggested that Scipio's move was little more than a piece of youthful impetuosity, a lucky gamble which succeeded. But the careful preparations he made, and the systematic manner in which the attack was mounted, support Polybius's statement that it was a piece of masterly calculation.

When spring came Scipio moved from Tarraco, and with a force of 25,000 foot and 2,500 horse, marched to Cartagena in seven days—a distance which Polybius gives as 350 Roman miles, roughly 300 American miles. To achieve this the troops would have had to march at more than three American miles an hour for twelve hours a day, which seems impossible. Although Arnold doubts the truth of Polybius's statement, I notice that Captain Liddell Hart, in his book *A Greater than Napoleon*, does not query it. Perhaps in fact the distance was not quite so great, but it must have been one of the fastest forced marches of history. Speed was vital to the success of Scipio's plan, for if any of the Carthaginian generals, each of whom was about ten marching days from New Carthage, got to hear of it he could have reached the city in time to intercept the Romans.

Scipio had already sent Laelius, with the fleet, along the coast with orders to anchor near New Carthage. It was to be a combined operation, with the army and navy co-operating as did the Allied forces in the Second World War. Neither force could have succeeded without the help of the other, for New Carthage was built in such a way as to be protected on two sides by the sea, and on the west by a lagoon, with only a narrow neck of land giving access to it. Captain Liddell

Hart likens the harbor to "a circular bottle, its mouth corked by an island, while Cartagena itself was like a candle stuck in the bottom of the bottle, the city standing on a narrow, rocky spit of land protruding from the mainland. This small peninsula bore a distinct resemblance to Gibraltar, and the isthmus joining it to the mainland was *only some four hundred yards across*.[1] . . . Here was a hard nut to crack, seemingly impregnable to any action save a blockade, and this time prevented."[2]

Scipio, twenty-eight years of age, in his first command had set himself the task of swiftly capturing the capital of the Carthaginian dominion of Spain, garrisoning it, and then retiring before the numerically superior Carthaginian armies could stop him.

Modern Cartagena gives us few clues as to the original appearance of New Carthage. It is no longer on an isthmus, as it was in Scipio's day, since the marshy lagoon which protected it on one side has been drained and built upon. And of its towering walls, so high that ladders brought to scale them broke under the weight of men, hardly anything remains above ground. And yet, as Rose Macaulay says:

> . . . the clash and echo of the siege, of the scaling of the walls, the shouting and the slaughter, and the Carthaginian rout, still tremble on the hot air, and the great harbour seems full of Roman galleys.[3]

Arriving at the city Scipio lost no time in making his preparations. First he raised a palisade across the isthmus, stretching from sea to sea, to protect his army against any attack from the landward side. On the side facing the town he did not erect any defenses, to as to give freedom of maneuver to

---

[1] My italics.
[2] All quotations attributed to Hart in this book are from Liddell Hart, Captain B. H., *A Greater than Napoleon*, William Blackwood and Sons, Edinburgh and London, 1926.
[3] Macaulay, Rose, *Fabled Shore*, Hamish Hamilton, London, 1949.

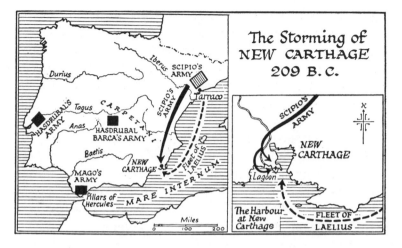

his assault troops. Next day Laelius encircled the town with his ships, which fired a constant barrage of missiles from their *catapultae* and *ballistae* (spring guns). At the third hour after sunrise, 2,000 picked Roman troops advanced along the narrow tongue of land, bearing scaling ladders. The cramped situation placed them in a vulnerable position, but this Scipio turned to advantage. The Roman trumpet sounded the assault. The landward gates of Cartagena swung open, and the defenders sallied out. Polybius says:

> But as the assistance sent to either side was not equal, the Carthaginians arriving through a single gate and from a longer distance, the Romans from close by and from several points, the battle for this reason was an unequal one. For Scipio had purposely posted his men close to the camp itself in order to entice the enemy out as far as possible, well knowing that if he destroyed those who were, so to speak, the steel edge of the population, he would cause universal dejection, and none of those inside would venture out again.

The Carthaginian commander, Mago—yet another officer of this name—had armed 2,000 of his strongest citizens and posted them behind the landward gate for a sortie. These were the men whom the Romans drove back with great slaughter, and in such flight that at one moment it seemed as if the pursuers would enter the city before the gates could be closed. Mago had divided his regular troops into two parties: 500 to man the citadel, and the remainder to occupy a hillock on the eastern side of the city.

Scipio, during this time, was in front of the walls with his troops, but he was careful to provide himself with reasonable protection against the missiles which were showered from the walls. Three strong young men made a wall of shields before their commander, so that he could be seen by his troops and thus encourage them, and at the same time be in a position to direct operations personally. These sensible precautions were taken, not, we may be certain, from cowardice but because Scipio knew that he was much more useful to his soldiers alive than dead.

By throwing in his reserves in waves, he had succeeded in pushing back the Carthaginians and discouraging them from further sorties. The ladder bearers had attempted to scale the walls, but such was the height of the ramparts, and so determined was the defense on the landward side, that the Romans were beaten off. But Scipio had succeeded in his first objective, which was to wear the defenders down. Now followed the next stage of his plan.

Months earlier, while wintering in Tarraco, he had talked with fishermen who knew the tides around Cartagena. The lagoon which protected one side of the city was tidal, and at a certain hour of the day, when the tide retreated, the water was sufficiently shallow in places for a determined body of men to wade across. Naturally his troops did not know this, nor did Scipio choose to tell them, knowing that when the phenomenon occurred they would regard it as a miracle, an intervention by the gods with whom, as we know, Scipio was in frequent communication. He assembled about 500 picked men on the shores of the lagoon, at the same time reinforcing his army in the isthmus with men and ladders; enough, as Liddell Hart observes:

> . . . to ensure that in the next direct assault "the whole extent of the wills should be covered by the escaladers"—an early example of the modern tactical axiom that a "fixing" attack should be on the broadest possible front in order to occupy the enemy's attention and prevent him turning to meet the decisive blow elsewhere.

Then, Polybius says:

> . . . the tide began to ebb and the water gradually receded from the edge of the lagoon, so that to those who were not prepared for the sight the thing appeared incredible. But Scipio had his guides ready, and bade all the men told off for this service, to enter the water and have no fear. He indeed possessed a particular talent for inspiring confidence and sympathy in his troops when he called upon them. Now when they obeyed and raced through the shallow water, it struck the whole army that it was the work of some god . . . their courage was redoubled.

With their long scaling ladders they rushed through the breast-high water and, led by their officers, swarmed over the walls at a place which the Carthaginians—who had never expected an attack from this quarter—had left undefended. Marines from the fleet scaled the walls at another point; in fact after the battle soldiers and marines almost came to blows when disputing who was first over the wall. Meanwhile Scipio had mounted another escalade from the landward side, and as the soldiers and citizens were repelling this, the Romans who had crossed the lagoon suddenly appeared from behind, taking the Carthaginians completely by surprise. In a short time the defenders were overcome. The Romans forced open the gates from inside the city, and in a few moments the troops which Scipio had kept in reserve for this purpose marched, in regular formation, through the streets, while their colleagues turned to massacring the townsmen after the usual custom of the time.

From the citadel, Mago saw that the battle was lost, and surrendered. No sooner had Scipio seen this happen than the trumpets sounded again. Such was the discipline of his soldiers, that they immediately sheathed their swords and began the more congenial task of plunder—the reward, sanctioned by long custom and tradition, of those who had risked their lives to take a town. Cartagena, the strongest, richest, most important city in Carthaginian Spain, had fallen, in a few hours. Scipio showed great magnanimity to the defeated. All the citizens of New Carthage were immediately set free. The artisans, numbering some 2,000, he declared "the property of the Roman people" but promised them freedom if "they showed goodwill and industry in their several crafts." Of the remainder, the sailors were conscripted for service with the fleet, and Mago, the defeated commander, and his officers were shown due respect.

There were numbers of Spanish hostages in New Carthage, whom the Carthaginians had kept as a guarantee of their allies' loyalty. These Scipio released and sent home. There is a story concerning some of the women hostages which throws an interesting light on Scipio's character. Some of his young officers, knowing his fondness for women, brought before him a girl of such surpassing loveliness that all turned to look at her. Scipio, writes Polybius, "was overwhelmed and astonished by her beauty, and he told them that had he been in a private position no present would have been more welcome, but as he was the general it was the least welcome of any. So he expressed his gratitude to the young men, but called the girl's father, and handing her over to him, at once bade him give her in marriage to whoever of the citizens he preferred. The self-restraint and moderation Scipio showed on this occasion secured him the warm approbation of his troops."

Livy has a slightly different version. He says that the girl was betrothed to a young Celtiberian nobleman named Allucius, and that Scipio, on hearing this, called for the young man and presented her to him. Later, when the girl's grateful parents made Scipio a handsome gift of gold and silver, the Roman general gave it to Allucius as a dowry from himself. A few days afterwards Allucius rode into Scipio's camp with 1,400 horsemen as reinforcements.

Scipio's imagination, energy and resourcefulness remind one inevitably of Hannibal, and in strategy he had begun to show promise of outstripping his master. After Fabius had recaptured Tarentum the great Carthaginian is reported to have said, "So the Romans also have a Hannibal. . . ." This was true, but neither he nor the Romans knew that the second Hannibal was not behind the walls of Tarentum, but far away, in Spain.

23

HASDRUBAL INVADES ITALY

AMATEUR strategists such as myself might well ask the question, "What was the use of Scipio capturing Cartagena when there were three active Carthaginian armies in the field ready to retake it?" The answer is given very succinctly by Captain Liddell Hart who points out that (*a*) the Carthaginians could not retake it if it was adequately garrisoned and supplied by sea, and (*b*) its possession gave Scipio the strategic initiative, since if the enemy moved on Cartagena he would lie on their flank with his main striking force; if they moved against him he could choose his own ground, while Roman-held Cartagena threatened the enemy rear, and if they remained passive they would be denied the use of their base, depot, and main line of communication with Carthage. Scipio, in fact, "had it all ways," and the outcome was that during the following winter three of the Carthaginians' most powerful allies went over to the Roman side, and Hasdrubal, the son of Giscon, faced with this change in the balance of power, was forced to take the offensive against Scipio. In the following spring he fought the Romans at Baecula on the upper reaches of the Guadalquivir river, and was skillfully beaten. He lost some 20,000 of his best troops, of whom eight thousand were killed.

But it is time to return to Italy. In 208 B.C., the year of Scipio's victory at Baecula, the Consuls were Marcellus and a new man, T. Quinctius Crispinus, an equally brave soldier, who had been Marcellus's lieutenant at the taking of Syracuse. Like Marcellus, he was a general of the "honest bludgeon work" school, and his record like that of his colleague was not distinguished except for stubborn courage. He tried to take Locri, a Greek colony on the south coast, but Hannibal forced him to give up the siege. He then joined forces with Marcellus at Venusia, the two armies camping about three miles apart. The total Roman force must have been over 40,000 men, nearly twice the force Scipio commanded at Cartagena, and considerably larger than that of Hannibal. But it could do nothing to prevent the Carthaginian from continuing his ravages, since the Consuls dared not meet Hannibal on open ground.

All that Marcellus did was to get himself killed. After the two armies had joined forces they decided to camp on a small wooded hill nearby, or at least to occupy it with an entrenched post, from which they might observe the enemy's movements. The two Consuls decided first to reconnoiter the ground, and with a force of only 200 cavalry, climbed the hill and entered the wood. Why the commanders in chief of the entire Roman force should have decided to risk their lives in such a trivial operation passes comprehension. Conspicuous in their red military cloaks and glittering armor, they rode under the trees, while a party of Hannibal's Numidians, who always kept a routine watch on the hill, looked on in astonishment. Marcellus had with him his son, also named Marcellus.

A short time afterwards the sentries guarding the Roman camp were amazed to see the scattered remnants of the scouting party, many wounded, galloping up to the ramparts, led by Crispinus and the younger Marcellus, both covered in blood. Having observed the Roman party from a distance, the Numidians had screened the wood, and then, advancing under cover of the trees, attacked the astonished enemy. A spear pierced the body of Marcellus, killing him instantly. His son and the Consul Crispinus were both severely wounded, but managed to escape.

As the survivors were telling their story, Hannibal having been informed by his Numidians of what had happened, was riding through the wood to find the fallen body of his enemy. Livy tells us that, after dismounting, he stood looking down at the dead Marcellus without speaking or showing any emotion. As Arnold describes the scene, one can almost see him shaking his head in astonishment.

> Marcellus, six times Consul, the bravest and stoutest of soldiers, who had dedicated the spoils of the Gaulish king, slain by his own hand, to Jupiter Feretrius in the Capitol, was lying dead on a nameless hill, and his arms and body were Hannibal's.

The Carthaginian gave orders for the body to be ceremonially burned with military honors, and the ashes sent to the Consul's son.

Not long afterwards Crispinus also died of his wounds, and the Republic was deprived of both its Consuls. Truly Hannibal had been right when, addressing his army before the battle of Trebbia, he said, according to Polybius, "You are fighting an enemy who is blind to the arts of war." Nevertheless, after ten years of fighting during which he had never lost a pitched battle, he seemed as far from conquering the Romans as he had been when he crossed the Alps. Bowed under a crushing load of taxation, with twelve of its colonies in revolt, its generals slain, its territory ravaged, and the flower of its manhood killed or taken prisoner, still the Republic would not surrender.

But Hannibal was now to play his trump card. After long, long delays his brother Hasdrubal was advancing across Gaul to join him. The Romans were already aware of this dreaded possibility, since their Greek allies, the Massiliots, had sent messages that Hasdrubal was in the interior of Gaul recruiting men. They had no idea of his route or when the blow would fall. Hasdrubal, after his defeat at Baecula, had re-formed his army and crossed the western Pyrenees where Scipio dared not follow him for fear of abandoning the seacoast, where he enjoyed the protection of the fleet. Hasdrubal was moving through territory which the Romans hardly knew, along the shores of the Atlantic near modern San Sebastian and thence into Gaul somewhere near Biarritz. One wishes the ancient writers had told us more of this epic march, when the son of Hamilcar, the second greatest of "lion's brood," with his elephants, his horsemen, and his infantry, was moving beside the wild, gray northern sea which the ancients called simply "Ocean," the limit of their world.

By making this huge sweep to the north, Hasdrubal ensured that any news of his movements would take so long to reach the Mediterranean shores that the Romans would be kept in the dark. The toadying Greeks of Massilia might scurry to their masters to tell them that he had been heard of in the north of Gaul, but, in days before radio, no one in Italy could possibly know when and where he would strike. We may be pretty certain, however, that his brother knew.

Turning eastward, and avoiding the Mediterranean, Hasdrubal probably crossed the Rhône somewhere near Lyons, and then joined Hannibal's original route in the plain of Dauphiné. We are told that he found parts of the roads, and some of the bridges, which Hannibal had built, still usable, and since the journey was made without heavy losses, it seems clear that on this occasion the Gauls did not impede his passage. He would certainly not have used the high and difficult pass into which Hannibal was led by treacherous guides, but may have entered Italy via one of the easier passes, such as the Mont Cenis or the Montgenèvre.

As soon as they knew that Hasdrubal was moving towards Italy the Romans prepared to meet the shock of two Carthaginian armies in their territory. Hannibal was in the south. Hasdrubal would obviously approach from the north, but unless he could be intercepted in the Po Valley he would have a choice of several routes. Hannibal had slipped past Flaminius after the battle of Trebbia, and Hasdrubal might well succeed in evading an intercepting force. And if the two greatest sons of Hamilcar Barca managed to combine their armies in the heart of Italy, then the outlook for the Romans would be black indeed.

To meet this double threat, the Republic made the most gigantic effort in twelve years of bitter fighting. Two new Consuls were appointed to replace Marcellus and Crispinus. One was C. Claudius Nero, who had served throughout the war as lieutenant to Marcellus in Sicily, as praetor and propraetor at the siege of Capua, as propraetor in Spain, and again as lieutenant to Marcellus in the year 209 B.C. He was by no means a notable captain, and had been accused of want of vigor when serving under Marcellus, and want of ability during his command in Spain. The other Consul was an old, soured man named Marcus Livius, who hated Nero and bore an undying grudge against the Roman Senate for having unjustly accused him of corruption when he had been Consul twelve years earlier. It might well be asked why, in such a dire emergency, Rome should choose two such men to lead her armies. The answer is that she had no choice. Old Fabius Maximus was now too frail and infirm to hold command. Gracchus was dead; so were Flaminius, and the bold and unwearied Marcellus. Looking around among the available experienced officers, whom could the Senators choose? Varro was still alive, but after the disaster of Cannae could hardly be expected to enjoy the trust of the people. Scipio, far away

in Spain, was still too young and untried, despite his triumph
at Cartagena.

In the winter of 208-207 B.C., they elected Claudius Nero
and Marcus Livius, one to command an army in the north,
the other in the south. Meanwhile Hasdrubal, with his elephants, his formidable African cavalry, and his infantry, Spanish, African and Gaulish, was moving unhindered across the
Alps and preparing to march down into the valley of the Po.

The army of the north, commanded by Livius, consisted of
two legions (10,000 men) with an equal force of Italian allies.
The southern army, commanded by Nero, was of the same
strength, but each consular army was also supported by two
others. In the north, assisting Livius was an army commanded
by L. Porcius, one of the praetors, while in Etruria a second
army led by Terentius Varro, overawed a region which was
notoriously unreliable. In the south the other Consul, Claudius
Nero, was supported by old Quintus Fulvius Flaccus at Bruttium, and yet another army lay in the neighborhood of Tarentum. In Italy alone fifteen legions, representing 75,000
Roman citizens, were under arms, besides an equal number of
allies. In addition there were eight legions serving abroad, two
in Sicily, two in Sardinia and four in Spain. Yet in that year
the total number of Roman citizens of an age to bear arms
totaled only 137,108 men, according to the census. Such was
the size of the Roman war effort.[1]

It seems certain that Hasdrubal did, in fact, arrive in northern Italy earlier than had been anticipated, in the early spring
of 207 B.C. Crossing the Po he advanced upon the colony of
Placentia close to the place where Hannibal won his first battle
against the Romans. Placentia was one of the eighteen faithful
colonies, and closed its gates against the invader. Hasdrubal,
having no artillery to reduce it, waited only long enough to
recruit sufficient of the Gauls and Ligurians, and pressed on

[1] Though these figures should be treated with some caution, they represent
the mightiest effort the Romans had made up to this date.

southward towards Ariminium (Rimini). Porcius, with an inferior force, retreated before him, and even when the Consul Livius arrived with his own two legions, the armies were apparently incapable of resisting Hasdrubal's advance. Leaving Ariminium to its fate they fell back behind the river Metaurus and camped under the walls of Sena, on the coast.

Hasdrubal meanwhile wrote a letter to his brother, informing him of the whole of his plans. He gave it into the care of four Gaulish horsemen and two Numidians, ordering them to ride south, evading the Roman armies, and deliver it to Hannibal. To us, accustomed to coded radio messages, this procedure seems unbelievable, yet there was no other way by which Hasdrubal could give his brother the information he needed if the two armies were to meet. From Placentia, Hasdrubal had a choice of roads: he could advance down the Adriatic coast, or he could cross the Apennines into Etruria, as Hannibal had done twelve years before, in the hope of winning over the Etruscans to his side, and then march south. It was obviously essential for Hannibal to know by which route his brother intended to march, so that he could meet him. And this vital information, committed to writing, lay in the wallet of one of the Gaulish or Numidian cavalrymen who set off from Placentia to ride the length of Italy in search of Hannibal. And the letter said that Hasdrubal was marching, not through Etruria, but upon Ariminium, and that he would join his brother's army in Umbria, on the Adriatic side of the country.

Hannibal, who had been wintering as usual in Apulia, learned that Claudius Nero, with 40,000 troops, was near at hand, and that another 20,000 Romans were in his rear at Tarentum. Faced with an army of 60,000 he evidently decided to augment his numerically inferior force by gathering all his garrisons into one mass, and if possible by raising additional troops from his old allies in Lucania and Bruttium. Hence his movements, which Livy describes, from Apulia into

Lucania, back into Apulia, and from there into Bruttium. He moved thus, baffling Nero's pursuit, or beating off his attacks, until he had amassed sufficient forces, and then moved northwards and halted near Canusium, waiting for news from Hasdrubal. Today a coded message, crackling in the headphones of a radio operator, would have given him all the information he needed. But this was 207 B.C. and Hannibal could do nothing but wait for the arrival of those six horsemen who at that moment, were riding through the mountains, traveling mainly at night, and avoiding any area in which the Romans were known to be concentrated.

Military skill, armaments, the effective disposition of armies and navies, military and civilian morale, all play a major part in deciding the issue of any conflict, but there is another element—luck—which sometimes swings the scale, in war as in other affairs of life. And this time luck—or "the divinity that shapes our ends"—was on the Roman side. The six horsemen succeeded in evading the Romans and made their way unharmed through the entire length of Italy. They arrived safely in Apulia, but found that Hannibal had moved swiftly into Bruttium. Attempting to follow him, they passed too close to Roman-held Tarentum, and were captured by a few foragers from the army of Quintus Claudius. And here follows one of those tantalizing questions which can never be answered. Why did not the messenger entrusted with the letter destroy it? Perhaps he did not have time. Or did he hope to conceal it from his captors? Or was he just stupid? A second and even more puzzling question: Why was this letter, in which Hasdrubal had revealed his exact line of march, and on which the entire Carthaginian fortune depended, *not written in code?* Such codes existed in Hannibal's time. Yet the message was in the normal Punic writing, which could easily be interpreted. The result was that Hannibal, waiting in Apulia, never received his brother's letter. The Roman Senate did.

So the last act of the tragedy—for so it was to the Carthaginians—began. Claudius Nero, who up to this moment had not shown any particular brilliance as a general, was inspired to execute a maneuver which was almost Hannibal-like in its skill and audacity. Two powerful Carthaginian armies were in Italy. The main essentials were (a) to prevent either marching on Rome; (b) to prevent their meeting, and (c) if possible to destroy one or both of them independently. It was little use hoping to destroy Hannibal, who had been unbeaten in twelve years, but if the latter could be kept inactive in the south, while the Romans brought a concentration of force to bear on Hasdrubal, they might defeat him. Speed was essential, for if Hannibal learned where his brother was he would immediately execute one of his terrifying forced marches, join with Hasdrubal, and then the Romans would be doomed. Nero made his plans quickly. He sent the letter to the Senate, advising them to call out every Roman who could bear arms, and move the two home legions forward to defend the narrow gorge of the Flaminian road. At the same time he told the Senate what he himself intended to do.

He picked out 7,000 men, including 1,000 cavalry, the flower of his army, and told them to be ready to march with him on a secret expedition into Lucania to surprise some of Hannibal's garrisons. Then, leaving his lieutenant, Q. Catius, in command of the main force, he set out at night with his chosen 7,000.

But he did not march towards Lucania, and when, from the direction they were taking, this fact could not be hidden from the soldiers, Nero called them together and told them his real intentions. He intended to march, day and night and as fast as possible, to join his colleague Livius at his camp before Sena. By combining his forces with those of Livius his hope was to crush Hasdrubal while Hannibal, still waiting for the letter, remained in Apulia. When the soldiers heard this they were overjoyed.

Cornelius Nero had taken care to send horsemen ahead of him along the road to Picenum and Umbria, with orders to the inhabitants to bring provisions to the roadside, together with horses and draught animals and even carriages to help transport his weaker or wearied troops. The life or death of the Republic depended on the speed of the march, and it seemed that the people realized this. As the 7,000 marched towards the camp at Sena, the local population crowded to the roadside, bringing meat, drink and clothing, while women knelt at roadside altars and prayed for the army's safe and victorious return. The troops were so deeply aware of how much depended on them that they would scarcely stop to eat and drink, and when they did, took their food standing in their ranks. Day and night they moved onwards, allowing themselves little rest until, in seven days, the march was accomplished, and the tents of the other consular army lay before them.

They arrived at night, for Nero's plan was that his reinforcements should join Livius's army under cover of darkness and share the tents of his soldiers, lest the appearance of new tents should warn Hasdrubal of his enemy's increased strength. The ruse succeeded, and when dawn came, the camp looked to Hasdrubal's scouts exactly as it had appeared on the previous day. (The Carthaginian camp was only half a mile away.) Livius and Porcius both urged Nero to give his men some rest before engaging in battle, but the Consul was adamant. Probably he already saw, in his imagination, Hannibal's army marching along the road he had traveled, eager to catch and destroy him. Nero was determined to give battle immediately. Livius reluctantly agreed; the red ensign was flown above the tents, and the Romans marched out and formed in line of battle.

The Carthaginian army came out to meet them but Hasdrubal, riding forward to reconnoiter, noticed the increased numbers of the Roman army, and became suspicious. Leading his troops back to their camp, he sent out some of his horsemen to gather information. The Romans also returned to their overcrowded tents. To all appearances their camp seemed unchanged. Only one thing, noted by the Carthaginian scouts and reported to their general, gave the secret away. Familiar as they were with Roman military routine, the scouts knew the trumpet calls which sounded at intervals as a signal for the various duties of the day. The camp of the praetor, Porcius, and that of Livius adjoined each other, but although the trumpet only sounded once in the camp of Porcius, it sounded *twice* in that of Livius indicating the presence of two consular armies.

Fearing the worst, unable to understand how Nero had been able to move from Apulia without Hannibal knowing, Hasdrubal gave orders to put out the campfires, and that night he moved his troops to a greater distance from the enemy, falling back rapidly towards the river Metaurus. The Romans followed.

The Metaurus today (modern Metauro) is not an impressive river, except briefly during the winter floods, and the country around it is open, fertile, and well cultivated. There are many farms and villages, set among the Umbrian plains, across which the spurs of the Apennines march in parallel ridges separated by deep ravines. Through one of these flows the Metaurus, past Fossombrone northeastward to enter the sea south of Fano. Two thousand years ago much of this land was thickly wooded, the trees clothing the heights and sweeping down to the edge of the ravine. Now that the woods have been largely cleared, and the river is smaller than it was in Hasdrubal's day, it is not easy to see why he failed to cross it, though the cliffs which overhang it at certain points do present an obstacle. After a long, wearisome march, Hasdrubal was forced to camp without having found a crossing place.

The Gauls in his army, always weakest in retreat, became unmanageable. That night they drank heavily and on the following morning many lay drunk in their quarters, incapable of moving. Eagerly following up their advantage, the Romans, who greatly outnumbered the Carthaginian forces, advanced in line of battle, and Hasdrubal had no alternative but to meet and fight them where he was.

Polybius tells us that he drew up his whole force along a narrow front, with such of the Gauls as were fit for action on his left, in a strong natural position which was unassailable from the front. He himself commanded his own Spanish infantry on the right. There is no mention of his cavalry, but his ten elephants were stationed in front of the army. Livius, who commanded the Roman left, opposite Hasdrubal, attacked vigorously, but Hasdrubal's Spanish foot fought well, and for a long time neither side gained an advantage. Meanwhile the other Consul, Nero, finding he could make no headway against the Gauls, wheeled round behind Livius's army, fell on the right flank and rear of the enemy. The elephants, galled by the Roman spears, did almost as much harm to their own ranks as to the enemy's. It seems to have been a disorderly battle, with only elementary tactical skill shown by either side, and in the end it was the Roman numbers which were victorious.

Hasdrubal, when he saw that all was lost, spurred his horse into the middle of a Roman cohort and, sword in hand, died fighting. It was, as Polybius says, a heroic gesture, but a pointless one, since the son of Hamilcar Barca, alive, was morally worth several armies; nor would it have been difficult to recruit more men if Hasdrubal had escaped and joined his brother. As it was, Hannibal was left with his single army to continue the war alone.

Ten thousand of the Carthaginian army were killed or taken prisoner, while 2,000 Romans fell in action; six of the elephants were killed, and the rest captured, and the plunder of the camp was rich. Nero, with almost as much speed as he had approached Sena, marched back to Apulia, where he found Hannibal still quiet in his camp, having heard nothing. His first intimation of the disaster on the Metaurus came when a group of Roman cavalry, riding up to the walls of his camp at night, flung something down and rode away. Some of his own soldiers went out to fetch the object in to Hannibal.

It was the head of his brother.

24

APHRODITE

WHEN I reflect on Nero's savage gesture, the point which strikes most forcibly is not so much its barbarity as its vulgarity. Hannibal would certainly not have treated a fallen foe in this way; witness the respect he showed to the bodies of Aemilius and Marcellus. One feels the younger Scipio, so like Hannibal in background and temperament, would, also have deplored Nero's act. Yet perhaps the Consul's vindictive triumph was more truly representative of Roman feeling than Scipio's urbanity, for to the mass of his people war was not an art, still less a game to be played according to the usages of good breeding. For twelve years they had struggled and suffered against an enemy who seemed invincible; their treasuries were almost exhausted, the country laid waste, and thousands of their young men had been killed by the invader. When, at last, the tide began to turn it was natural that they should express their joy in an act of vicious hatred; few, if any, would recollect what they themselves had inflicted on the Carthaginians. Such is the inevitable consequence of all armed conflict.

Hannibal, of course, was still undefeated; indeed he was

never beaten in a pitched battle while he remained on Italian soil. But now another and perhaps an even greater general began to put into practice the strategy which the Carthaginian had adopted when he first invaded the Roman homeland. Hamilcar Barca and his sons had seen clearly that the only hope of forcing Rome to release her grip on Carthaginian territory was to strike directly at the heart of the enemy. Scipio's triumphs in Spain, first by the taking of Cartagena and later by the subjugation of the entire country, was only a rehearsal for a much more ambitious plan—to draw Hannibal away from Italy by attacking Carthage itself. So, in time, the positions were reversed and the attacker became the defender.

Looking back over 2,000 years we can see this clearly. It was not clear to the majority of the Senate or the Roman people. At first only Scipio and his friends saw it, and Scipio was still not thirty years of age and initially had little influence in the higher councils of State. Fortunately he combined military genius with great charm, patience, and diplomatic address. For years he had had to conceal his frustration as he watched his superiors wasting the resources of the State in futile, if honest "bludgeon work." He knew that, given the chance, he could find an answer to the problem. But gradually, as he won more and more victories in Spain, he gained increasing Senatorial support. At Ilips, near modern Seville, he out-generaled Hasdrubal, the son of Giscon, and killed some 60,000 of his finest troops. After that victory he won over many of the Carthaginian's most powerful Spanish allies. Then, at great personal risk, he accepted an invitation from Syphax, king of the Massaeylians, whose territory neighbored that of Carthage, and by charm and diplomacy won his promise of support.

Hasdrubal, after first trying to capture Scipio's warship as it stood becalmed outside the harbor, also tried to win the help of Syphax, who invited the two antagonists to dine with him. It must have been a memorable dinner. Afterwards Hasdrubal reported to his government that Scipio "appears to me more to be admired for the qualities he displays on a personal interview with him than for his exploits in war. I have no doubt that Syphax and his kingdom are already at the disposal of the Romans, such is the knack this man has of gaining the esteem of others."

Hasdrubal was right. Syphax ratified the treaty by which he promised to help the Romans. Subsequently Scipio subjugated practically the whole of Spain by warfare, diplomacy, or a combination of both. Thus the Carthaginians were denied their principal base, arsenal, and recruiting ground in Europe. Only Gades held out, being an island fortress.

Each of Scipio's battles was a model of the military art. Yet in fairness it must be remembered that he had learned the basic principles of his craft from the man who had defeated his father and who still ranged, untamed and untamable, over southern Italy when Scipio returned to Rome to plan the next stage of his campaign.

On arriving before the city, he was met by the Senate at the temple of Bellona and gave them a formal address on his campaigns. But for the jealousy of certain elements within the Senate he would probably have been granted a "triumph" *i.e.*, he would have been permitted to march through the streets with his army, accompanied by all the traditional honors of a returning hero. But his reward came shortly afterwards, when at the usual election he was nominated as one of the two Consuls for the forthcoming season's campaigning. A larger number of voters gathered than at any time during the Punic War, and thousands swarmed to his house and to the Capitol to see the victor.

But his new office brought its drawbacks. Up to now he had been allowed a free hand in Spain, and could conceal his intentions from the enemy. Now, as Consul, he was governed by the rules of democratic procedure and had to describe his plan for the invasion of Africa to the full Senate, and obtain its approval. Secrecy was no longer possible as far as long-term strategy was concerned. Moreover, says Hart, "From now on he was to suffer, like Marlborough and Wellington some two thousand years later, the curb of political faction and jealousy, and finally, like Marlborough, end his days in embittered retirement."

His plan was bitterly attacked, especially by Fabius Cunctator. With an old man's jealousy of the young, he "damned with faint praise" Scipio's achievements in Spain and poured scorn on his proposal to draw Hannibal from Italy by attacking the Carthaginian homeland. "Why," he asked, in Livy's account, "do you not apply yourself to this, and carry the war in a straightforward manner to the place where Hannibal is, rather than pursue that roundabout course to which you expect that when you have crossed into Africa Hannibal will follow you thither?"

A tremor passed through the Senate when Fabius cleverly exploited the old fear. "What if, in your absence, Hannibal should march on Rome?" These were powerful arguments which swayed many of the older and more cautious Senators. Even more deadly was the criticism, voiced by this most admired and respected Roman commander of his time, that even if Hannibal were lured back to Africa, he would have the advantage of fighting in his homeland, near his principal base, with a full army, whereas now he commanded only a fragmentary force in a foreign land. "What sort of policy is that of yours," thundered Fabius, "to prefer fighting where your own forces will be diminished by one half, and the enemy's greatly augmented?"

When the old man sat down, frowning, and folded his toga around him, there was a murmur of agreement, and many suspicious and unfriendly eyes looked at the young, newly appointed Consul as he rose to deliver his reply.

His opening words, according to Polybius, were masterly:

"Even Quintus Fabius himself has observed . . . that in the opinion he gave a feeling of jealously might be suspected. And though I dare not charge myself with harbouring that feeling, yet, whether it is due to a defect in his phrasing, or to the fact, that suspicion has certainly not been removed. For he has so magnified his own honours and the fame of his exploits, to do away with the imputation of envy, that it would appear I am in danger of being rivalled by every obscure person, but not by himself, because he enjoys an eminence above everybody else. . . ."

Then he proceeded, with growing passion and conviction, to expound his reasons for believing that his plan must succeed. In this hour he was fighting, not with weapons, but with words, as did Sir Winston Churchill in 1940. Without the approval of the Senate, Scipio could do nothing.

"He who brings danger upon another has more spirit than he who repels it. Add to this, that the terror excited by the unexpected is increased thereby. . . . Provided no impediment is caused here, you will hear at once that I have landed, and that Africa is blazing with war; that Hannibal is preparing to depart from this country. . . . Many things which are not now apparent will develop; and it is the part of a general not to be wanting when opportunity arises, and to bend its events to his designs. I shall, Quintus Fabius, have the opponent you assign me, Hannibal, *but I shall rather draw him after me than be kept here by him.*"

Divided in its views, the Senate eventually reached a tame compromise. By law each Consul had to be allotted a province. Without sanctioning Scipio's plan to invade Africa in force, they gave to the Consul to whose lot Sicily fell permission to pass over to Africa "if he judged it to be to the State's advantage." By a curious coincidence Sicily became Scipio's province.

It was not much, but it was a beginning. He was not allowed to levy troops, so he obtained 7,000 volunteers. He was not allotted any existing warships, so, in just over six weeks, he

had built and launched twenty quinqueremes and ten quad-
riremes. In these he transported his small volunteer force to the
island, and began to train them. He divided them into the usual
cohorts and centuries, but left aside 300 men without assigning
them to any unit. These soldiers, watching their comrades
training in the usual legionary formation, must have wondered
why their commander had left them out. They did not have to
wait long to discover why.

Scipio informed the Sicilians that he intended to invade Africa, and that some of their noblest young citizens would be
given the honor of taking part in the enterprise. He gave orders
that 300 of these men should present themselves at his camp,
bringing their horses and arms. The rich parents of those so
nominated were only too anxious to buy them out, if this was
possible. Scipio told them that he had "heard rumours" that
some were averse to his service, and that as he was not anxious
to take unwilling soldiers, he would be ready to release them
from their obligation in return for their horses, arms and equipment. These the young Sicilians gladly surrendered, and also
agreed to train their substitutes—the 300 Romans whom the
commander had set aside. Thus Scipio obtained the nucleus of
his cavalry "at no expense to the State."

Although the setting is completely different, the incident is
slightly reminiscent of Falstaff's recruiting methods in Shakespeare's *Henry IV*. One wonders if the poet, who must have
known his Livy, remembered this story.

Scipio, having fought against Hannibal on several occasions,
recognized what every reader of this book must have noted:
that in practically every battle the Carthaginian's success had
been due, not only to his superb tactical skill, but to his formidable cavalry in which the Romans were weak. But being a
realist Scipio also recognized that it would be impossible, in a
short time, to break down the traditional Roman reliance on
the heavily armed foot soldier, the legionary, on whose dogged
valor they had depended for hundreds of years. Though he

might succeed in training a small force of Roman cavalry he could only hope to obtain a substantial body of experienced horsemen among the African allies of Carthage. Hence his wooing of the Syphax, the king of Massaeylia (modern Algeria), and of a young Numidian Prince, Masinissa, who had fought brilliantly against Scipio in Spain. In making diplomatic approaches to these two African leaders Scipio showed great subtlety, for their territories adjoined each other, and they were enemies. The young Consul may have reflected that if he could not persuade both to join him but one remained allied to Carthage, he could make use of the enmity of the one against the other to further his own cause.

It was probably to sound out the possibilities of an alliance with the Numidians that he sent his friend and colleague Laelius to Africa in the year 205 B.C. With a small force Laelius landed at Bône—a town which will be remembered by those who took part in the North African campaigns in the Second World War—and began his reconnaissance. In the meantime Scipio continued training his troops, and also succeeded in taking the town of Locri, in southern Italy, beating off an attempt by Hannibal to relieve it. As a morale raiser, this success was of great value, but it had political repercussions which nearly lost Scipio his command.

He left in command of Locri a man named Pleminius, who behaved so brutally towards the inhabitants that the two Roman tribunes who commanded the garrison protested. Pleminius responded by ordering them to be whipped. They called upon their troops to save them; a general fracas ensued, after which Pleminius was mutilated and left insensible. Scipio, recalled to Locri, gave judgment against the soldiers and restored Pleminius to his office. This decision—perhaps the most serious error of judgment in his career—led to such energetic protests that his enemies in the Senate seized upon them as a pretext to ruin Scipio. They were assisted by reports that the Consul was neglecting his military duties; even his dress was unsoldierly.

A quote in Hart's book says he "walked about the gymnasium in a cloak and slippers, and . . . gave his whole time to light books." Some of these slanders were carried back by the embittered Cato, who was praetor under Scipio and hated his Greek refinement and culture. Probably Scipio *was* unconventional in his dress and manners, like T. E. Lawrence, Orde Wingate, and others in more recent times.

But when the Senate sent a fact-finding commission to Sicily to investigate these charges they found nothing of which to complain. After entertaining them at a splendid meal, Scipio led them out to watch complex battle drill by his troops, and a mock naval battle in the harbor. They returned to Rome impressed, and the Senate voted that the Consul be given permission to take to Africa all the troops then serving in Sicily. There was a bitter irony in this, for, apart from his volunteers, the only regular troops in the island were the disgraced veterans of Cannae, who had been sent there as a punishment.

Characteristically, Scipio turned this to his advantage. He himself had fought at Cannae, and knew that the battle had been lost not through cowardice but by inefficient generalship. He talked to the veterans "man by man," encouraged them, inspired them with his own spirit, and replaced the unfit among them with his own volunteers. By the time he was ready to sail to Africa his army probably numbered about 16,000 foot and 1,600 horse, most of them experienced soldiers. It was still a very small force to pit against the combined might of Hasdrubal's Carthaginians and their African allies, but Scipio hoped and believed that Masinissa and possibly Syphx would eventually support him. He was right concerning Masinissa, but wrong—at first—about Syphax.

Hasdrubal countered Scipio's success with the Massaeyliot king by a diplomatic master stroke. Hasdrubal had a very lovely daughter, Sophonisba, with whom Syphax fell passionately in love. Hasdrubal gave her to him in marriage, and "took advantage of the Numidian while under the influence of the first transports of love, and, calling to his aid the caresses of his bride, prevailed upon him to send envoys into Sicily to Scipio, and by them to warn him 'not to cross over into Africa in reliance on his former promise.' "

For the first time in this long and bloody war, Aphrodite entered the conflict, and her power proved greater than that of many armies.

Captain Liddell Hart has described Scipio as "greater than Napoleon." Without much exaggeration one could describe Sophonisba as "greater than Cleopatra" with whom she had much in common, for this Numidian princess had as deep an effect on the fortunes of Hannibal and Scipio as any one of their battles. It is amusing to notice how her intrusion irritates the exclusively male historians who have told the story, for in a male-dominated world she had few rights, and we know of her actions only through male writers most of whom were hostile to her. Yet no writer who attempts to tell the story of Hannibal can ignore Sophonisba. She is there, right in the front of the picture, fighting for her country with the only weapons she possessed—her physical allurements. This romantic interlude seems at times more fantastic than the wildest excesses of a Hollywood "spectacular."

After the defeat of Hasdrubal on the Metaurus, Hannibal withdrew to southern Italy. Collecting as many troops as he could gather, he established himself in Bruttium, where he could keep in communication by sea with Carthage. There, for the time being, we must leave him, while we follow Scipio's invasion fleet across the Mediterranean to Africa. For, in spite of Syphax's defection from the Roman cause, the Consul decided to implement his original plan. In the spring of the year 204 B.C. he embarked from Lilybaeum (modern Marsala) with forty warships, 400 transports and under 20,000 men. The provisioning of the army had been carefully planned. The fleet carried water and rations for fifty-five days, of which fifteen days' supplies were cooked.

He landed at Cape Farina, a few miles from the Carthaginian town of Utica. This was just inside the western horn of the two "horns" enclosing the bay of Tunis, in the midst of which lay Carthage. The Carthaginians, who had long been expecting the blow, had manned watchtowers along the capes, and Utica was strongly fortified. Scipio moved against this city, and attemped to take it by an enveloping action, using both his fleet and army. The young Numidian prince, Masinissa, the brilliant cavalry captain who had met Scipio in Spain and promised to come over to his side, was true to his word. But after his return from Spain he had been driven out of his father's kingdom and, when he rode into Scipio's camp, it was at the head of only 200 horsemen. As so often happened in the ancient world, when personality counted so much in securing the loyalty of armies, his very presence and his known reputation among his Numidians were in themselves a powerful reinforcement of Roman strength.

Scipio welcomed him warmly, and then sent him, with a small cavalry detachment, to skirmish up to the walls of Utica, hoping to lure the Carthaginian commander, Hanno, out to battle. I cannot help comparing the Numidian cavalry with the crack fighter pilots of a modern air force; a *corps d'élite*, few in numbers, individualists to a man, yet temperamental and relying greatly on the inspiring leadership of their most admired commanders. Such a leader was Masinissa. When he led his young warriors at a furious charge to the outposts of Utica, and then, at his command, the formations "peeled off" in complex and bewildering formations, charging, retreating, and reappearing again from a different quarter, one is reminded irresistibly of a "dive-bombing." The deadly riders "without bridle or saddle," who had been one of the main strengths of Hannibal at Trebbia, Trasimene, and Cannae, were now fighting on the side of Scipio; in small strength as yet, but still formidable. Their javelins stung like wasps, and Hanno, irritated beyond measure, moved out to meet them. Then, just as at Trebbia, a force of enemy cavalry, which had been hidden by Scipio behind a ridge, descended at the gallop and encircled Hanno's cavalry, while Masinissa shouted to his men to re-form. Obeying in the instant, they wheeled and charged into the front of Hanno's cavalry.

The result was deadly. The first Carthaginian line went down almost in the instant, leaving 1,100 dead on the field. The rest were killed or captured in the pursuit. Scipio, having beaten Hanno back into Utica, ravaged the country around, carrying off all his supplies, just as Hannibal had done in Italy, but Utica, impregnable behind its walls, defied all attempts to storm it. There was not to be another Cartagena. One can only imagine the joy of Scipio as he saw his tactics succeeding. Greeting Masinissa as he rode into camp, perhaps he thought of that terrible moment at Trebbia, thirteen years ago, when he had rescued his father, severely wounded, from just such an attack.

But he was still greatly outnumbered, Hasdrubal had collected some 30,000 foot and 3,000 horse, and Syphax, his uxorious son-in-law, had joined him with 50,000 foot and 10,000 horse. Scipio, with barely 20,000 men, in enemy country, was confronted by an army of nearly 100,000. In fact he was in almost exactly the same situation which Hannibal had faced in Italy for the previous fourteen years. And, like Hannibal, he retreated for the winter to a secure base.

He retired to a small peninsula, connected by an isthmus to the mainland. His base lay on the eastern side of Utica, threatening that city's communications with Carthage. Thus, having secured his army against attack, he had time to prepare for the next year's campaign. He still needed the support of Syphax, and, in Livy's words, "hoping that his passion for his bride . . . might now have been satisfied," wrote asking Syphax if he might reconsider his decision. In this he was disappointed.

Syphax's reply may have been dictated by his father-in-law, but I wonder if it is too fanciful to see Sophonisba's own hand in it? The gist of it was a suggestion that the war might be ended if, in return for a Roman withdrawal from Africa, Hannibal left Italy. It seems to me the kind of humane proposal which an intelligent woman might offer, but this is probably a sentimental illusion. In any case it failed, for Scipio, far from considering retiring to Italy, was more determined than ever to prosecute the war, convinced that if he continued to threaten Carthage, the enemy government would be bound, in the end, to recall Hannibal to meet the threat.

Disguising his true intentions, he agreed to open negotiations with Syphax and Hasdrubal and sent envoys to discuss terms. But with these envoys he also sent, disguised as officers' servants, picked scouts and centurions to observe the layout of the camps, and particularly the method and times of stationing the guards. With every visit of his envoys a new body of disguised spies accompanied the deputation, so that as many as possible should familiarize themselves with the two camps of Syphax and Hasdrubal Giscon, which adjoined each other. Scipio's main concern was to reduce the disparity in numbers between his own army and those of the Carthaginians. The method he used, though justified by the ruthless logic of war, is none the less horrifying. Yet, in effect it was exactly the same method which the Allies used at Hiroshima and Nagasaki—destruction by fire.

Scipio had observed that the Carthaginian camps were built of highly inflammable material—huts made of interwoven reed mats. The huts were built in close lanes, with no provision made against a major conflagration, and the spies reported that Syphax's camp was more vulnerable to fire than that of Hasdrubal. By deliberately prolonging the negotiations Scipio obtained more and more information, until at last Hasdrubal became tired and decided to try the issue by battle, on open ground, where his cavalry would have the advantage. Had he

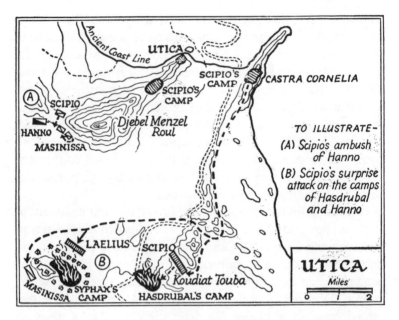

UTICA

TO ILLUSTRATE—

(A) Scipio's ambush of Hanno

(B) Scipio's surprise attack on the camps of Hasdrubal and Hanno

UTICA
Miles
0 1 2

succeeded in this plan it is doubtful if the Roman army would have survived, but before he could put it into force Scipio had struck. He began by mounting a feint attack on Utica. His ships, loaded with siege engines, were launched as if for an assault on the Carthaginian city. At the same time he sent 2,000 troops to occupy a neighboring hill. Thus, just as at Cartagena, he "fixed" the enemy's attention on the wrong objective. Again one sees the terrible shadow of Hannibal behind Scipio. These were just the tactics which he would have used, but this time they were directed, by his greatest enemy, against his own people.

Night came, and there was no attack. Then, from the camp of Syphax, great tongues of flame leaped into the night sky. Roman "commandos" creeping through the defenses, had fired the camp at several places.

The soldiers in Hasdrubal's camp, seeing the fire, thought at first that it was merely an accident, and half-armed and unprepared, rushed to the assistance of their companions. Then Scipio fell on them, while Masinissa and Laelius attacked Syphax's camp from another direction and other incendiaries set fire to the camp of Hasdrubal. Under a strong wind the flames spread, leaping the narrow lanes between the close-packed rows of huts, until the shepherds on the hills above the Bagradas River saw a glow in the sky comparable to that which overlay Coventry in 1941. Thousands were burned to death, and those who managed to escape from the wall of flames found Scipio's legions waiting outside. Hasdrubal gave up, and, fighting his way through the encircling Romans, escaped with only 2,000 infantry and 500 cavalry. According to Hart:

> The armies of Sennacherib had not suffered a swifter, more unexpected and more complete fate than those of Hasdrubal and Syphax. Livy states that 40,000 men were either slain or destroyed by the flames, and five thousand were captured. As a spectacle of disaster it surpasses any in history.

No historian tells us what Sophonisba was doing on this occasion. Presumably she was within the camp of Syphax, and, since she survived, her husband must have secured her escape as the flames came nearer. Perhaps she was—as the Romans represent her—a self-indulgent beauty, avid for power, and interested only in exercising that power to her own advantage. But what if she was not? Rightly or wrongly, I cannot help seeing the beautiful wife of Syphax, mounting her horse, urged on by her husband and his companions, but looking back to the sweeping crescent of flames, and, with tears in her eyes, lamenting—perhaps cursing—the insensate cruelty of men.

When the dawn came the Romans saw, where the Carthaginian camp had been, a blackened patch of earth, from which the smoke still rose, above the corpses of some 40,000 men.

Whatever Sophonisba may have felt, her revenge was both sweet and swift. The events following the burning of the Carthaginian camps came quickly upon each other, and at the end the Numidian princess found the reins of power in her own delicate hands. She had the satisfaction of defeating Scipio—albeit temporarily—when the armies of her husband and brother-in-law had proved powerless. At first Syphax and his Numidians decided to abandon the war, but Sophonisba, urging her husband not to desert her father, persuaded him to continue the struggle. Then new reinforcements arrived from Spain. So, when envoys from Hasdrubal arrived at the headquarters of Syphax, he told them that he would continue to co-operate with his wife's father. With the newly recruited troops, plus the armies in the field, the two commanders had between 30,000 and 35,000 men available within a month, but before the two armies could consolidate, Scipio struck again and destroyed them. Sending Masinissa and Laelius in pursuit of Syphax's army, he cleared the surrounding country, destroyed its strong points, and prepared to move on Carthage itself.

The climax of the war was approaching. So far all Scipio's plans had matured, and he was within sight of his final objective. Even when the Carthaginian government sent its fleet to break the siege of Utica, it failed. The Roman ships, being built higher out of the water than the enemy vessels, had the advantage, in that the sailors and marines could fire downwards, whereas their foes had to shoot upwards. The fleet was defeated, and at the same time ·Masinissa and Laelius reported that their pursuit of Syphax had been successful. Syphax himself, after trying desperately to rouse his men to counterattack, exposed himself to danger, was unhorsed and taken prisoner. At last Scipio had what he had wanted—access to Numidian manpower to augment his cavalry.

Now came Sophonisba's turn. Masinissa, triumphant after his recent victory, arrived before the town of Cirta, the capital of his defeated enemy, which opened its gates to him. Sophonisba prepared to meet the conqueror, after making her own feminine preparations. Masinissa was accompanied by Scipio's friend, Laelius, but it is doubtful if he was present when Sophonisba received the young Numidian in audience. For Masinissa was so completely overwhelmed by Sophonisba's beauty that he fell in love, and promptly went to bed with her.

The young cavalry captain, Scipio's most powerful ally, the man on whom he depended for the recruitment of the Numidian horsemen without whom he could not win the forthcoming battle with Hannibal, had been captured by the wife of his defeated enemy. Livy drily remarks that "as the Numidians are an excessively amorous race, he [Masinissa] became the slave of his captive."

When he had left Sophonisba's bed Masinissa was overcome by remorse. He admired and respected Scipio and had been loyal to him, but now he was enslaved by Sophonisba. Masinissa could see only one way out of his difficulty, and that was to marry her himself. When Laelius at last managed to get him on one side and remind him of his duties, the deed was done.[1] Laelius, Scipio's closest friend, and, one gathers, a typical unimaginative Roman, was for "dragging her from the marriage bed and sending her with the other captives to Utica." Then realizing that he was out of his depth he relented and agreed to leave the decision to Scipio.

In this he showed true judgment, for if there was anyone who was capable of understanding Masinissa's problem, it was Scipio himself. He understood—none better—the power of a beautiful woman, and I suspect that if Sophonisba's victim had been any other young cavalry commander, Scipio would have dismissed him with a slap on the shoulder and his own encouragement and good wishes. But this was Masinissa, the man on whom he had relied to provide the essential Numidian reinforcements without which he could hardly hope to win his battle with Hannibal.

[1] The fact that Sophonisba was already married to Syphax, presumably still alive, apparently proved no objection to this extraordinary maneuver.

Even when Syphax was brought to his camp, and the troops poured out to see the formidable enemy against whom they had fought for so long, Scipio still remained uneasy. He talked sympathetically to Syphax, who, encouraged by the Consul's manner, told him that he had been "mad" to make war on the Romans, and that it was all the fault of Sophonisba. She had, says Hart, "fascinated and blinded him to his undoing. Yet, ruined and fallen as he was, he declared that he gained some consolation from seeing her fatal lures transferred to his greatest enemy. These words caused Scipio great anxiety, for he appreciated both her influence and the menace to the Roman plans of Masinissa's hasty wedding. She had detached one passionate Numidian; she might well lead astray another."

Livy says he called the young man before him and talked to him quietly and without resentment. "I suppose, Masinissa," he said, "that it was because you saw in me some good qualities that you first came to me when in Spain for the purpose of forming a friendship with me, and that afterwards in Africa you committed yourself and all your hopes to my protection. But of all those virtues, which made me seem worthy of your regard, there is none of which I am so proud as temperance and control of my passions." We are told that such was the force and charm of this friendly "man to man" appeal that Masinissa broke into tears and retired to his tent.

After a long inward struggle, the unfortunate young man sent his servant to Sophonisba with a cup containing poison. His message to his bride was short, subtle, but meaningful. "Masinissa would gladly have fulfilled the first obligation which as a husband he owed to her, his wife; but as those who had the power had deprived him of the exercise of those rights, he now performed his second promise—that she should not come alive into the power of the Romans."

Sophonisba, faced with this characteristic piece of male sophistry, must have smiled cynically. Here was her adoring husband of yesterday offering her, as a wedding gift, the way of death. If she had any regrets they may have been that she had not met Scipio first. Scipio, for his part, may have been relieved at not having met her, for if he had the outcome of the war might possibly have been different. Before taking the cup she dictated a message to Masinissa which is a masterpiece of brevity and wit. It read, simply, "I accept this nuptial present; nor is it an unwelcome one, if my husband can render me no better service. Tell him however, that I should have died with greater satisfaction had I not married so near to my death." Then, after signing the letter, she calmly drank the poison and fell dead.

By those few pungent lines, Sophonisba, who was vilified by the Romans and deserted by her husband, has insured for herself a permanent place among the enchantresses of history.

To Scipio's credit it must be reported that, immediately on hearing of Sophonisba's death, he sent for the distraught Masinissa and, after trying for a time to solace him, gently reproached him for "trying to expiate one rash act by another, and making the affair more tragic than was necessary."

25

BATTLE OF GIANTS

AFTER the disastrous defeat of their armies the Carthaginian government sent envoys to Scipio and asked for a truce. With final victory within reach he was still prepared to make a peaceful accommodation, on suitable terms. These were (*a*) the restoration of all prisoners and deserters; (*b*) the withdrawal of the Carthaginian armies from Italy; (*c*) the withdrawal of Carthaginian forces from Gaul and all Mediterranean islands. Carthage was also to give up all but twenty ships. Though severe, these terms were not unreasonable. The Carthaginians accepted them and sent envoys to negotiate final terms of peace. The joy and relief in the capital was tempered somewhat by anxiety about Hannibal's intentions. The Roman commanders in southern Italy had been instructed to try to keep him there lest, by returning to Africa, he might upset Scipio's plans before he had achieved a decisive victory. But now Hannibal received the message which he had expected, ordering him to return with his armies. It was the year 202 B.C., sixteen years after he had crossed the Alps.

Technically Rome and Carthage were still at war, and it would have been in order for the Roman commanders to try

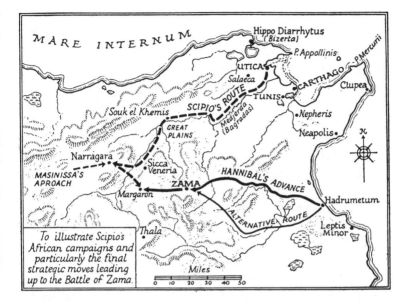

To illustrate Scipio's African campaigns and particularly the final strategic moves leading up to the Battle of Zama.

to hamper and molest his army during the embarkation. But though they advanced sufficiently near to keep him under distant observation they were careful not to come too close. From the Bruttian hills, they watched their great and unbeaten enemy as he marched his veterans down to the waiting ships. When he had entered Italy he was twenty-nine. Now he was forty-five. What were his feelings as he watched, from the deck of his ship, the Italian coast gradually disappear behind the northern horizon?

From youth to middle age Italy had been his home, and it is said that his sorrow at leaving his beloved Apulia was great. He had kept the oath which he had sworn at his father's side—to remain an enemy of Rome—but that enemy was still undefeated, and after his brother's death on the Metaurus he told his fellow officers, that he "foresaw the doom of Carthage." So it must have been with a heavy heart that he landed again in his homeland, at Leptis in the Gulf of Hammamat. Meanwhile, war had flared up again in Africa. The Carthaginians had broken the truce, for Hasdrubal Giscon had seized 200 transports which were taking Scipio stores and reinforcements from Sardinia and Sicily. It was a rash and stupid act, prompted more by greed for plunder than anything else, but the result was to play into the hands of the Carthaginian war party which did not wish for peace. With Hannibal back in Africa they hoped to turn the tide in their favor, and as the Carthaginian marched his army of some 24,000 men from Leptis to Hadrametum he knew that he must still fight, and that this time his opponent would be Scipio.

Immediately he sent word to a Numidian chief, Tychaeus, "who was thought to have the best cavalry in Africa," appealing to him to send reinforcements. Tychaeus arrived with 2,000 horsemen. Hannibal could also rely on a further 12,000 troops from Liguria under Mago (who had been recalled), and a considerable body of new African levies; Philip of Macedon, too, had sent 4,000 Macedonians. The Carthaginian would therefore have at his disposal some 45,000 men, of whom more than half were his veterans from Italy. Scipio, having lost most of his supplies and reinforcements, had a much smaller force, isolated in a hostile land. His most desperate need was for cavalry. Masinissa had gone first to Rome where he had been fêted, honored and given the title of King. He then returned to his own country, believing that the war was over. Scipio sent him a message, urging him to march immediately to his assistance with as many horsemen as he could gather, but the young man was still a considerable distance away from Scipio's base, and it was essential to the Roman's plan that he intercept Hannibal's force before it could reach Carthage.

Scipio, outnumbered and still waiting anxiously for Masinissa to arrive, behaved with his usual calm courage. Instead of placing himself across Hannibal's line of march towards Carthage, he moved *away* from that city, up the valley of the Bagradas River, threatening the fertile territory on which Carthage depended for its supplies. At the same time he was shortening the distance between himself and Masinissa. During this march he must have been on tenterhooks, waiting to see if his great opponent would do what he, Scipio, wished him to do. The Carthaginian government had, in fact, asked Hannibal to move towards Scipio, and had received a sharp answer, stating that Hannibal would decide his moves for himself. Nevertheless, after a few days he marched out of Hadrametum and moved west, towards Scipio. When the latter's scouts rode in to tell him that the Carthaginians were moving, not towards Carthage, but in the track of the Roman army, one can imagine Scipio's relief; for it was part of his plan to lure his enemy away from his principal base. Hannibal's reasons may have been that he believed he would beat Scipio anyway, and from his record one imagines that he had no great love of fighting from behind walls.

Within a few days Hannibal's army arrived near the town of Zama which, Polybius says, lay five days' journey to the west of Carthage. It is probably represented by Zama Regis, an old Numidian city lying ninety miles west of Hadrametum. It stood on the edge of a plain just west of the ridge which stretches from Cape Bon to Kasserine and Tebessa.

Following the usual procedure Hannibal sent a scouting party to reconnoiter the Roman camp. Some returned with the information that three of their comrades, who had gone too close to the ramparts, had been captured. This was one of the normal hazards of reconnaissance and did not surprise Hannibal. What did astonish him was the sight of the three missing spies riding into the camp a few hours later, unharmed but somewhat bewildered. Instead of making them prisoners, Scipio had sent them on a conducted tour of his camp, accompanied by officers who were instructed to show them everything they wished to see. After their inspection they were brought back to Scipio, who first inquired whether there was anything else they wished to inspect. On being told that they were quite satisfied, he gave them provisions and sent them back to the Carthaginian camp.

This audacious, almost insolent gesture achieved its intention, which was to assure Hannibal that Scipio was so confident of victory that he had no objection to his enemy knowing all about his troops, their number and dispositions. Hannibal was so impressed that he took a step which is almost without parallel in the history of warfare. He sent messengers to Scipio saying that he would be honored if the Roman general would meet him on neutral ground, for a talk. Scipio sent back a courteous reply, agreeing to a meeting, but first he shifted his headquarters to more suitable ground so that the meeting might be at a short distance from both camps. He established his headquarters near the city of Naraggara —probably Sidi Yousseff, on the modern Tunisian-Algerian boundary. The site was well chosen, on rising ground, and within a javelin's throw of water. Hannibal also moved forward and camped on nearby ground some four miles away; but he found that his own water supply was considerably farther than a javelin's throw, and his troops suffered some inconvenience.

Then followed one of the most extraordinary and moving episodes in this or any other war. Although the story has been told many times, one can hardly begin to describe it without a tingling of the spine. From each of the opposing camps a little party of horsemen rides out, under banners of truce. The parties halt when they near each other and only three men ride forward to meet. One is Hannibal, the second Scipio. The third man is the interpreter; we are not told from which side. One wonders if it could have been Silenos, and if it was he who recorded the conversation which both Polybius and Livy describe.

For a long time the two antagonists, one aged forty-five, the other ten years his junior, stand gazing at each other in silent admiration. Scipio sees before him the great general who has roamed, undefeated, through Italy for sixteen years; the man who has defeated the army of the elder Scipio at Trebbia, who has destroyed the armies of Flaminius at Trasimene, and those of Varro and Aemilius at Cannae. Hannibal sees the young commander who, alone among all the Roman generals, has succeeded consistently in winning victories over the Carthaginians by the use of methods akin to his own. Master has met pupil.

Hannibal was first to break the silence, and the conversation, reported by Polybius, began:

> "Would that neither the Romans had never coveted any possessions outside Italy; nor the Carthaginians any outside Africa; for both these were very fine empires, and empires of which it might be said on the whole that Nature herself had fixed their limits. But now that in the first place we went to war with each other for the possession of Sicily and next for that of Spain, now that, finally refusing to listen to the admonition of Fortune we have gone so far that your native soil was once in imminent danger and ours now is, what remains but to consider by what means we can avert the anger of the gods and compose our present contention? I myself am ready to do so as I learnt by actual experience how fickle Fortune is, and how by a slight turn of the scale either way she brings about changes of the greatest moment, as if she were sporting with little children."

So Hannibal began, and he continued on a more personal note:

> "But I fear that you, Publius, both because you are very young [flattery; Scipio was thirty-five], and because success has constantly attended you both in Spain and in Africa, and you have never up to now at least fallen into the counter-current of Fortune, will not be convinced by my words, however worthy of

credit they may be. Consider things by the light of one example, an example not drawn from ancient times, but from our own. I, then, am that Hannibal who after the battle of Cannae became master of almost the whole of Italy, who not long afterwards advanced even up to Rome, and encamping at forty stades [1] from the walls deliberated with myself how I should treat you and your native soil. And now here am I in Africa on the point of negotiating with you, a Roman, for the safety of myself and my country. Consider this, I beg you, and be not overproud, but take such counsel at this present juncture as a mere man can take, and that is ever to choose the most good and the least evil. What man of sense, I ask, would rush into such danger as that which confronts you now? If you conquer you will add but little to the fame of your country and your own, but if you suffer defeat you will utterly efface the memory of all that was grand and glorious in your past."

Hannibal then outlined his proposals, which, according to Polybius, were that:

". . . all the countries that were formerly a subject of dispute between us, that is Sicily, Sardinia and Spain, shall belong to Rome, and that Carthage shall never make war upon Rome on account of them. Likewise that the other islands lying between Italy and Africa shall belong to Rome. Such terms of peace would, I am convinced, be most secure for the Carthaginians and most honourable to you and to all the Romans."

In his reply Scipio first pointed out the flaws in Hannibal's proposals, reminding him that after the Roman victory over Hasdrubal and Syphax, the Carthaginians themselves had sued for peace, and accepted terms far less favorable than those for which Hannibal now asked. For, in addition to surrendering Spain, Sicily, and Sardinia, they were to return their prisoners without ransom, hand over most of their warships, and pay the Romans five thousand talents. Having accepted these terms, they had violated the peace, so that the war continued.

[1] About five miles.

"If, before the Romans had crossed to Africa you had retired from Italy and then proposed these terms, I think your expectations would not have been disappointed. But now that you have been forced reluctantly to leave Italy, and that we, having crossed to Africa, are in command of the open country, the situation is manifestly changed. . . . What remains to be done? Put yourself in my place and tell me. Shall we withdraw the most onerous of the conditions imposed? That would be to reward your countrymen for their treachery and teach them to continue to betray their benefactors. Or shall we grant their present request in the hope of obtaining their gratitude? But now after obtaining their request by earnest supplication, they at once treated us as enemies and foes. . . . Of what further use then is our interview? Either put yourselves and your country at our mercy or fight and conquer us."

After this conversation, which held out no hopes of reconciliation, the two generals parted from each other. On the following morning at daybreak they led out their armies and opened the battle, the Carthaginians fighting for their own safety and the Romans for the empire of the world.

Is there anyone who can remain unmoved in reading the narrative of such an encounter?

Scipio's confidence, during his interview with Hannibal, must have been strengthened by the knowledge that Masinissa, with 6,000 foot and 4,000 of his formidable Numidian cavalry, had ridden into his camp a few days before. On the day of battle he placed these horsemen, under Masinissa's command, on his right wing. The fleet commander Laelius, who, unlike most modern admirals, could evidently ride a horse, commanded the Italian cavalrymen on the left wing. In between these cavalry wings the heavy Roman infantry were arranged in the usual three lines, but deployed in most unorthodox manner. The normal usage was to station the maniples (subunits of 120 men) in checker formation, like the black (or red) squares on a checker board. In this way, says Hart, "the maniples of the second line were opposite to, and covering the intervals between the maniples of the first line." Scipio

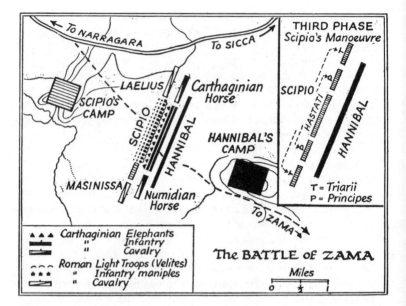

The BATTLE of ZAMA

placed them one behind the other, leaving clear lanes between each cohort, running right through the army from front to rear.

His main reason for this formation was to lessen the menace of Hannibal's war elephants, of which he had eighty, and which he placed in front of his army so that their charge would break the enemy ranks. The second reason for Scipio's unusual infantry deployment was to help the movement of his skirmishing troops who could sally out through the lanes, and then retire swiftly. Even their withdrawal was to be carefully controlled, for he gave orders that those who had time should fall back to the rear of the army, while those harried by pursuers should turn right or left between the infantry ranks. To quote Hart: "This wise provision economized life, ensured smooth functioning, and increased the offensive power."

Hannibal's battle plan was as follows. First, facing the Roman infantry, came the line of eighty elephants, the largest number he had ever used in a single battle. Behind them he placed his first line of infantry, consisting of Ligurian and Gallic mercenaries, with some Moorish and Balearic light troops. Drawn up behind them, but at a distance, stood the Carthaginian and African levies, probably greater in numbers than those in the front line. Finally, at a good 200 yards to the rear, he placed his "Old Guard," veterans of his Italian campaigns, under his personal command. The cavalry, as usual, occupied the wings, the Carthaginians being on the right, facing Laelius, and the Numidians on the left, facing Masinissa. Hannibal's total force was probably about 55,000 men. Scipio, even with the addition of Masinissa's 10,000, commanded at most about 36,000.

The battle opened with the charge of the elephants, but as the great animals pounded across the space separating the two armies there rose from the Roman line the jarring blast of hundreds of war trumpets, accompanied by such a tremendous shout that many of the beasts took fright, turned and crashed into their own lines with an impact which sent men flying in terror. Some of the elephants broke in among the Numidians, stampeding the horses, and as the cavalrymen strove to re-form for their charge, the Roman left wing stormed in among them, for Laelius, who commanded the Italian horse was quick to profit from the Carthaginian disaster.

Some of the elephants reached the Roman lines and did much damage to the *velites*, the light-armed troops who stood before the first rank of heavy infantry, the *hastati*. Breaking through this line, certain elephants drove into the Roman infantry, but the effect of their charge was minimized by Scipio's battle formation. For the animals naturally rushed down the open lanes which Scipio had left between the maniples, for just this purpose, while the *velites* who had survived the attack dashed between the steady, unmoving ranks of the legionaries, hurling their javelins at the elephants as they streamed past, and then pursuing them to the rear.

Other elephants, met by a shower of javelins from the Roman front line, turned about, and in spite of the efforts of their riders to control them, blundered into the Carthaginian cavalry's left wing. Before the enemy horsemen could recover, Masinissa charged them furiously at the head of his 4,000 Numidians. Thus, states Livy:

> On both sides the Punic battle-line had been stripped of its cavalry when the infantry clashed, now no longer matched either in their hopes or in their strength. In addition there were what seem small things to mention, but at the same time were highly important in the battle; a harmony in the shouting of the Romans, which consequently was greater in volume and more terrifying; on the other side discordant voices, as was natural from many nations with a confusion of tongues; for the Romans a battle of little movement, as they pressed on into the enemy by their own weight and that of their arms; on the other side repeated charges at high speed but with less power.

So far Hannibal's African and Carthaginian levies, who formed the second line, had not moved. As at Cannae, it was evidently his plan that the Romans should waste their strength in fighting the inferior front-line troops only to come upon fresh and unwearied soldiers.

And now the *hastati* came to grips with much tougher troops who formed Hannibal's second line. These men had been so determined to maintain their intact formation that when the wearied Gauls and Ligurians who formed the front line were forced back upon them they refused to open their ranks so that the Gauls, after first trying to break through, had to retire behind the flanks, and many fled the battlefield. This ruthless insistence on keeping the three lines separate was part of Hannibal's plan. Now he ordered the second line into action, and as they were fresh and vigorous they succeeded at

first in thrusting back the Roman first line. Seeing their comrades in difficulties, the *principes* and *triarii* of the Roman
second and third lines also began to waver, but they responded
to their officers' call and restored the situation in the nick of
time. The Roman infantry now outnumbered the second line
of Carthaginians, so that their line flowed around the flanks of
their enemies, hemming them in. Gradually, this second line
of Hannibal's troops was overcome, and those who survived
fled back to the place where the third line still waited the
order to attack.

Once again the Carthaginian fugitives were not permitted
to mix with, or pass through, the ranks of those who had yet
to enter the battle. When the remnants of the second line tried
to force their way back they were met by a row of spear
points and were forced to retreat towards the flanks. So began
the third and final phase of the battle, when, says Livy, "the
Romans had penetrated to their real antagonists, men equal
to them in the nature of their arms, in their experience of
war, and in the fame of their achievements." Scipio's infantry
were about to come to grips with Hannibal's "Old Guard,"
24,000 veterans from the Italian campaign, under the personal
command of their great leader.

It was at this moment that Scipio showed his greatest genius.
Faced with this moving wall of men, who now outnumbered
his own infantry force, and while his own men were only a
bowshot from the enemy, he sounded the recall. Such was the
discipline of his troops that, in the midst of the battle and
with their foes advancing on them, they immediately responded to the sound of the trumpets, and under the shouted
orders of their officers, rapidly altered their battle formation.

Scipio, seeing that the Carthaginian third line now overlapped his, and fearing to be outflanked, abandoned the conventional infantry formation of three lines, *hastati*, *principes*,
and *triarii*, one behind the other. Instead he formed them into
a solid but extended line, with no gaps between the maniples

(since these were no longer necessary) and marshaled in such a way, says Hart, that "the blow should be as concentrated as possible in time and as wide as possible in striking force."

Now, once again, Scipio's line overlapped that of the enemy, so that when Hannibal's 24,000 veterans closed with the Romans for the final death struggle Scipio's men were in a position to bring to bear their maximum missile power against the Carthaginians' entire front. It was, of course, a risky maneuver, for one would have thought that if the Carthaginians had succeeded in punching holes in Scipio's line they could have broken it up into separate units which could then have been encircled and destroyed. Indeed Polybius says that "the contest was for long doubtful, the men falling where they stood out of determination, until Masinissa and Laelius arrived providentially at the proper moment."

The key to the success of Scipio's plan was, of course, his cavalry, which, having driven the Carthaginian horse from the field, should return in time to deal the final blow at the enemy infantry. Probably, like Rupert at Naseby, Masinissa had carried the pursuit too far, and one imagines Scipio, in the midst of his struggling weary footsloggers, cursing that brave but impetuous young man and looking round desperately for the sight and sound of his cavalry and that of Laelius. In modern terms it was like a hard-pressed infantry battalion looking for air support.

Before long, the sound of hoofs and the war cries of the Numidian and Roman horsemen were heard above the tumult, as the returning commanders took the Carthaginians in the flank and rear. Then it was Cannae in reverse. The battle became a massacre, and though most of Hannibal's veterans fought grimly on, they were cut to pieces.

At the end of the day 20,000 lay dead on the field, and of the rest, nearly another 20,000 were captured in the pursuit which followed.

Hannibal, slipping off during the confusion with a few horse-men, came to Hadrametum, not quitting the field till he had tried every expedient both in battle and before the engagement; having, according to the admission of Scipio, acquired the fame of having handled his troops on that day with singular judgment.

With the defeat of Hannibal and the total collapse of Carthaginian power, the Battle of Zama brought to an end the Second Punic War, which had lasted nearly seventeen years.[1]

[1] I am indebted for some of the material of this chapter to Captain Liddell Hart's book *A Greater than Napoleon*, which contains the clearest account of the Battle of Zama that I have read. L.C.

26

THE END OF HANNIBAL

W<small>E</small> have followed Hannibal from New Carthage, through France, Italy, Africa, and back to Old Carthage. Although he lived for a further twenty years his career as a general—with which we are concerned in this book—was over, and he never again commanded large armies in the field. But his formidable mind was never at rest, and he remained, until the day of his death, a thorn in the side of the Romans.

Here there is space only to summarize the last phase of his life. Immediately after Zama he retired to Carthage and set himself a new task, that of statesman; in this, as in practically everything he undertook, he showed great distinction. No one knew better than Hannibal that, with her military power destroyed, probably forever, Carthage's best hope was first to negotiate as satisfactory terms as possible with the Romans, and then set about rebuilding the State on firmer foundations.

There is a characteristic anecdote which describes the meeting of the *Suffete* after Zama. Hannibal was present, not then as leader, but as a member of the council. He had to listen to long debates, in the course of which one Senator got up, and in a "fire-eating" speech, urged the *Suffete* not to accept the Roman peace terms but to continue the war. These terms were still acceptable, since Scipio had sufficient influence over the Roman Senate to prevent it imposing a harsh and vindictive settlement. After this senatorial firebrand had been orating for some time, there was a movement among the assembly, as Hannibal, rising impatiently from his seat, mounted the rostrum and pulled the man down from it.

The Senators, indignant at his violating the usages of the house, called on Hannibal to apologize, which, says Polybius, he did, but in words which must have cut deep:

> "You must pardon me if I have acted contrary to your usage, for you know that I left Carthage at the age of nine, and am now returned at the age of forty-five. I beg you not to consider whether I have transgressed parliamentary custom, but rather to ask yourselves whether or not I really feel for my country; for it is for this reason that I was guilty of the offence. It seems to me astounding and quite incomprehensible that a man who is a citizen of Carthage and is conscious of the designs that all we, individually and as a body, have entertained against Rome does not bless his stars that now he is at the mercy of the Romans he has obtained such lenient terms. If you had asked but a few days ago what you expected your country to suffer in the event of the victory of the Romans, you would not have been able to give utterance to your fears. . . . So now I beg you not even to discuss the matter, but to agree with one accord to the proposals, to sacrifice to the gods and to pray, all of you, that the Roman people may ratify the treaty.

And Polybius concludes: "As it seemed to all that his advice was wise and opportune, they voted to make the treaty on the above conditions, and the Senate at once despatched envoys with orders to agree to it."

Scipio, who admired and was admired by Hannibal, saw to it that the firebrands in his own government did not wreck the hope of future peace by imposing harsher conditions, while Hannibal, for his part, now had the power to see that those conditions were faithfully kept by his countrymen. On the return of his envoys from Rome peace was concluded and the terms fulfilled. Among these was the destruction of the Carthaginian battle fleet; five hundred warships were towed out to sea and there set on fire.

When Scipio returned to the capital he was accorded a "triumph" of great splendor. Like the victorious Roman generals of former times he rode through the decorated streets at the head of his conquering troops, and was, Livy tells us, surnamed Africanus, "the first general who was distinguished by a name derived from the country which he had conquered." The title may only have been a nickname given to him by the troops, but it stuck. He could almost certainly have been made perpetual Consul and dictator, as Caesar became over two hundred years later, but he refused the honor. "Such particulars as these, . . . would demonstrate an uncommon greatness of mind, in limiting his honours conformably with his position as a citizen."

For seven years, from 202 to 195 B.C., Hannibal strove to rebuild his country, and to heal as far as was in his power, the wounds caused by the disastrous war. He kept faith with the Romans, and while Scipio's influence over the Senate remained strong, they did not attempt to make any further move against their former enemies. But in striving to improve the finances and administration of his country, Hannibal made bitter enemies among his own countrymen. He discovered that certain high-placed officials were plundering the public funds, and when he exposed them, they allied themselves with the order of judges and tried to instigate the Romans against him. There were many in the Roman Senate who watched with suspicion and jealousy the commercial revival of Carthage under Hannibal's direction. Small-minded men such as the envious Cato could not rest while Hannibal lived, and was in power. He and his followers seized eagerly on the accusations made by the Carthaginian judges against Hannibal as a pretext to act against him. Hannibal, after only four years of political life, must have longed at times for the cleaner atmosphere of the battlefield.

But Livy tells us that Scipio intervened on behalf of his old enemy, and in a speech of great power, told the Senate that he thought it "highly unbecoming the dignity of the Roman people to make themselves a party to the animosities and charges against Hannibal; to interpose the public authority in the faction strife of the Carthaginians not deeming it sufficient to have conquered that commander in the field, but to become as it were his prosecutors in a judicial process."

Scipios' intervention only delayed the issue a few years longer. Cato, who had now become Consul, sent an embassy to arraign the Carthaginian and bring him back to Rome. Hannibal realizing that he would be betrayed by his own people, then escaped from Carthage and sailed for Tyre, "lamenting the misfortunes of his country oftener than his own."

This was in the year 195 B.C., and for the remaining thirteen years of his life Hannibal moved, a lonely exile, among the courts of the princes of western Asia who were still hostile to Rome. He went first to Antiochus, king of Seleucia, and tried to help him, but with little success. There are one or two stories about this period which throw a little light on Hannibal in his later years. De Beer's book says that on one occasion Antiochus invited him to attend a lecture given by an academician named Phormio, on "the duties of army commanders." After the lecture Antiochus asked his distinguished guest what he thought of it. "Well," replied Hannibal, rising from his seat and stretching his cramped legs, "I've had to listen to some old fools in my time, but this one beats them all."

On another occasion he met Scipio for the second and last time. The Roman was visiting the neighborhood and asked if Hannibal would meet him. Hannibal gladly complied, and once again the two former enemies exchanged courtesies and talked of old times. In *Alps and Elephants* part of their conversation is recorded by Acilius. Scipio asked Hannibal whom he thought the greatest captain of all time.

"Alexander the Great," replied Hannibal, "because with a small force he defeated armies whose numbers were beyond reckoning, and because he overran the remotest regions, merely to visit which was a thing above human aspirations."

"To whom would you give second place?" asked Scipio.

Hannibal reflected for a moment and then said: "Pyrrhus, for he first taught the method of encamping, and besides no one ever showed such exquisite judgement in choosing his ground and disposing his posts; while he also possessed the art of conciliating mankind to himself to such a degree that the natives of Italy wished him, though a foreign prince, to hold the sovereignty among them, rather than the Roman people. . . ."

Scipio, whose ego was probably becoming a little nettled by this time, asked Hannibal whom he esteemed the third greatest general.

"Myself, beyond doubt," replied the Carthaginian. Scipio laughed, and then asked,
"What would you have said if you had conquered me?"
"Then," came the reply, "I would have placed Hannibal not only before Alexander and Pyrrhus, but before all other commanders."
"This answer," comments Acilius, "turned with Punic dexterity, and conveying an unexpected kind of flattery, was highly grateful to Scipio, as it set him apart from the crowd of commanders, as one of incomparable eminence."

I suspect that Hannibal knew his Scipio, for despite the Roman's genius, his tolerance and moderation, there was still an element of egotism and self-containment which made him different from his great antagonist. Arnold compares the two with Achilles and Hector, and suggests that Scipio was like "the Achilles of Homer, the highest conception of the individual hero, relying on himself and sufficient to himself. But the same poet who conceived the character of Achilles has also drawn that of Hector; of the truly noble, because unselfish hero, who subdues his genius to make it minister to the good of others, who lives for his relations, his friends and his country. And as Scipio lived in himself and for himself, like Achilles, so the virtue of Hector is worthily represented in the life of his great rival, Hannibal, who, from his childhood to his latest hour, in war and in peace, through glory and through obloquy, amid victories and amid disappointments, ever remembered to what purpose his father had devoted him, and withdrew no thought or desire or deed from their pledged service to his country."

Arnold may seem to have been a little unfair to Scipio, whose services to his country were as great as those of Hannibal to his, yet I find the comparison a just one. Certainly Hannibal remained faithful, to the very end, to what he conceived to be his duty. Driven from his own land by Roman hate and the corruption of his own countrymen, he continued at great personal risk, trying to injure the Roman State by intriguing with its enemies, and offering his splendid gifts to those who were capable of using them. As long as he remained alive the Romans could not sleep in peace. Their agents followed him from country to country, hoping to persuade his hosts to betray him. Leaving the court of Antiochus, he went to Prusias, King of Bithynia, in Asia Minor, and there, eventually, he was betrayed. Trapped in his house, and seeing the agents of Rome guarding the exits, he realized that there was no longer any hope of escape. De Beer's book quotes his last words: "Let us now," he said, "put an end to the life which has caused the Romans so much anxiety." Then he took poison.

Rome's greatest enemy, the man who had crossed the Alps; the victor of Trebbia, Trasimene, Cannae, and countless lesser battles; the man who, for sixteen years, had held together an undefeated army in the midst of a hostile land, lay lifeless in the palace of a foreign king, far from the country to the service of which he had devoted his life. He was sixty-five.

Hannibal was dead. Yet for centuries afterwards, whenever the Roman State was threatened, or in a less heroic sphere, when Roman matrons wished to quiet their rebellious children, Arnold says, the cry would go up, *"Hannibal ad portas!"*— "Hannibal is at the gates!"

EPILOGUE

I MUST now make a confession which may surprise some readers. When I wrote the Introduction to this book I stated that, though Hannibal was a genius, that genius may have been evil. I had read a great deal about him, mostly adulatory, and was determined to take as detached a view as possible. I do not think I have glossed over his vices and failings, which were many. Yet now, having followed his journey, and lived, imaginatively, in his mind for a very long time, I have grown to admire the man. I also believe that if he were alive today, eight out of ten men would be ready to follow him, as did the Carthaginians.

He was a destroyer. So, in their various ways, were Washington, Lee, and Marshall, who can also claim to have been liberators. He hated Rome, and had every reason to do so. He sought to destroy her, which, from his viewpoint, was a just and not ignoble aim. He failed to do so, which from our point of view was fortunate, since the mercantile empire of the Carthaginians, had it won, could never have been the liberating and civilizing force that Rome eventually became. Rome, through which we have inherited most elements in our Western civilization, is in our blood and bones. To wish that Hannibal had won is like wishing that our mothers had not existed.

Yet we cannot blame Hannibal for not knowing this. He could not foresee the future. To him Rome was an evil enemy to be overcome at whatever cost, and he dedicated his life to that destructive task.

Scipio Africanus, who learned most of his military art from Hannibal, developed into a new and unfamiliar type of leader, the soldier-statesman whose grand strategy extended into regions beyond the battlefield. Hannibal was never more than a great soldier, a brilliant innovator in the art of war, who applied his powerful mind and personality to one end—that of winning battles. Possessing as he did an ironic sense of humor, he would certainly be amused to learn that his campaigns are still reverently studied in the military academies of the world. He might also be pleased to know that the lessons he taught have sometimes been applied, with success, to destroy greater evils than he could have imagined or understood. In this sense, so long as war remains an instrument of policy, he was a creator and not a destroyer.

> *"He was a man; take him for all in all,*
> *I shall not look upon his like again."*

FURTHER READINGS

Arnold, T., *The Second Punic War*, Macmillan, London, 1886.

De Beer, Sir Gavin Rylands, *Alps and Elephants*: Hannibal's March, Dutton, New York, 1959.

Freshfield, Douglas W., *Hannibal Once More*, E. Arnold, 1914.

Law, W. J., *The Alps of Hannibal*, Macmillan and Co., London, 1866.

Liddell Hart, Captain B. H., *A Greater Than Napoleon—Scipio Africanus*, William Blackwood and Sons, Edinburgh and London, 1926.

Titus Livius (Livy), *The History of Rome*, Translated by Spillan and Edmunds, G. Bell and Sons, Ltd., London, 1919.

Torr, Cecil, *Hannibal Crosses the Alps*, Cambridge University Press, 1924.

The Odyssey of Homer, translated by T. E. Lawrence, Oxford University Press.

The Histories of Polybius, translated by W. R. Paton, William Heinemann, London, 1922.

Strachan-Davidson, J. L., *Selections From Polybius*, Oxford, 1888.

INDEX

Other DA CAPO titles of interest